Charles Augustus Briggs

**The Messiah of the Gospels**

Charles Augustus Briggs

**The Messiah of the Gospels**

ISBN/EAN: 9783337284305

Printed in Europe, USA, Canada, Australia, Japan

Cover: Foto ©Lupo / pixelio.de

More available books at **www.hansebooks.com**

# THE MESSIAH

OF

THE GOSPELS

# DR. BRIGGS' WORKS

AMERICAN PRESBYTERIANISM. Its Origin and Early History, together with an Appendix of Letters and Documents, many of which have recently been discovered. Cr. 8vo, with maps. . . . . $3.00

MESSIANIC PROPHECY. The Prediction of the Fulfilment of Redemption through the Messiah. A critical study of the Messianic passages of the Old Testament in the order of their development. Cr. 8vo, . $2.50

BIBLICAL STUDY. Its Principles, Methods, and History of its Branches. Fourth edition. Cr. 8vo, . $2.50

WHITHER? A Theological Question for the Times. Third edition. Cr. 8vo. . . . . . $1.75

THE AUTHORITY OF HOLY SCRIPTURE. An Inaugural Address. Fourth edition. Cr. 8vo, paper, . 50 cts.

THE HIGHER CRITICISM OF THE HEXATEUCH. An additional part of the Defence of Professor Briggs before the Presbytery of New York, 1892. Cr. 8vo, . . . . . . . . $1.75

THE BIBLE, THE CHURCH, AND THE REASON. The Three Great Fountains of Divine Authority. Second edition. Cr. 8vo. . . . . . $1.75

THE DEFENCE OF PROFESSOR BRIGGS Cr. 8vo, paper. Net, . . . . . . 50 cts.

THE CASE AGAINST PROFESSOR BRIGGS. Part I. Cr. 8vo. paper, . . . . . 50 cts.

THE CASE AGAINST PROFESSOR BRIGGS Part II. Cr. 8vo, paper. Net, . . . . 50 cts.

THE CASE AGAINST PROFESSOR BRIGGS. Part III. Cr 8vo. paper, . . . . . 75 cts.

BIBLICAL HISTORY. A Lecture delivered at Union Theological Seminary. 12mo, paper, net, . 30 cts.

OF

# THE GOSPELS

BY

CHARLES AUGUSTUS BRIGGS, D.D.

EDWARD ROBINSON PROFESSOR OF BIBLICAL THEOLOGY IN THE
UNION THEOLOGICAL SEMINARY, NEW YORK

NEW YORK
CHARLES SCRIBNER'S SONS
1894

TO

# HENRY PRESERVED SMITH, D.D.

TRUE SCHOLAR

FAITHFUL FRIEND

AND

BRAVE COMPANION IN HOLY WARFARE

This Book

IS DEDICATED IN SYMPATHY AND LOVE

# PREFACE.

In the autumn of 1886 the volume entitled *Messianic Prophecy* was published as the first of a series of volumes upon the Messianic Ideal. As was stated in the Preface to that volume: "It treats of Prophecy in general, of Messianic Prophecy in particular, and then traces the development of the Messianic idea in the Old Testament, concluding with a summary of the ideal therein unfolded. It will remain for a second volume to show how far this ideal has been fulfilled by the first advent of the Messiah, and how far it remained unfulfilled and was taken up into New Testament Prophecy and carried on to a higher stage of development. A third volume should trace the history of the Messianic ideal in the Christian Church, and show its importance in the development of Christian doctrine."

It was my intention at that time to publish the second volume of the series a short time after the first. The material had already been gathered and it was put in the form of a volume in the summer of 1888. But the Revision movement in the Presbyterian Church in the U. S. A. made it a duty to take my share in that great ecclesiastical struggle. Some of the fruits of these labors appeared in the volumes, *Whither*, 1889; and *How Shall We Revise*, 1890. The Revision movement had as its sequel a long struggle against ecclesiastical domination and in behalf of the right of Biblical Criticism and of the fountains of authority in Religion. The fruits of my labors during this period will be found in several volumes: *The Authority of Holy Scripture*, 1891; *The Bible, the Church, and the Reason*, 1892; *The Higher Criticism of the Hexateuch*, 1893; *The Defence of Prof. Briggs before the Presbytery of New York*, 1893; *The Case against Dr. Briggs*, Parts I.–III., 1892–1893.

I now return with gladness to the more important and more profitable task which was undertaken prior to these ecclesiastical controversies. In the meanwhile my work on the Messianic ideal of the New Testament has not been neglected. I have gone over the field with many successive classes of theological students, and have so greatly increased my own knowledge of the subject that I am thankful that the publication of the work has been so long delayed. On the one hand I feel that my knowledge would be greatly enriched by still further delay. On the other hand I have a contribution to make to a better understanding of the subject, and it seems to me that the time has come for me to make it.

The work will appear in two volumes. These will be published separately, and they may be used apart, although the one is a sequel to the other and both of them sequels to the volume on Messianic Prophecy. The first of these volumes, which is now offered to the public, treats of the Messianic ideas of pre-Christian Judaism, and of the Messiah of the Gospels. The second volume, to be published early in 1895, will discuss the Messianic ideas of the Jews of the New Testament times and the Messiah of the Epistles and the Apocalypse.

No one can feel more deeply than the author how far short he falls of his own ideals and how many mysteries still envelop the person and work of our Lord and Saviour to him as to others; but he is assured that, guided by the teachings of Christ and His apostles, he has caught glimpses of the Christ of the throne and of the Second Advent, which he did not learn from his theological teachers or from the writings of his predecessors or contemporaries. He is convinced that the faith of the Church of the day is defective in its lack of apprehension of the reigning Christ and in its neglect of the Second Advent of our Lord.

The Catholic faith of Christ's Church is expressed in the earliest of the creeds, that which bears the name of the Apostles. The proportions of that faith have been destroyed in most of the modern systems of dogmatic theology, which exaggerate one third of its clauses and depreciate or neglect two-thirds of them. This creed is Christological. It gave me great pleasure, after I had completed my work, to find that every one of the clauses of the Catholic creed is included in the matters that must be discussed in the study of the Messiah of the New Testament.

The faith of the Apostolic Church was fixed upon the Messiah enthroned at the right hand of God, ruling over the Church, and soon to come in visible presence to reward the faithful and to condemn and punish the unfaithful and the wicked. This is the normal Christian attitude at all times, looking upward to the enthroned Christ and looking forward to His Parousia.

The Christian Church of Western Europe, under the influence of the Augustian theology, has been looking backward and downward instead of upward and forward. In the doctrine of God it has been grubbing in the eternal Decree. In the doctrine of man it has been dissecting the corpse of the first Adam and searching for the germs of the disease of original sin which slew him and all our race. Accordingly, religion has been sad, gloomy, and sour. In the doctrine of Christ it has been living in Passion week, following the stations of the cross, and bowing in penitence before the crucifix. This is a very inadequate and one-sided Christianity. This is not the Christian faith of the Apostles. It is not that form of Christian theology which is to transform the world. There is an eternal Decree, yes, but its essential content for us is its final aim, that we may be conformed to the image of God's Son that " He might be the firstborn among many brethren." There is original sin in the first Adam. It is a terrible reality. But it has been annulled and destroyed once for all and forever in the Second Adam. "For as through the one man's disobedience the many were made sinners, even so through the obedience of the One shall the many be made righteous."

We must be buried by baptism into the death of the crucified, but the burial for the Messiah and His people alike does not accomplish its purpose until God has quickened us together with Christ and raised us up with Him and made us to sit with Him in the heavenly places in Christ Jesus. As Bishop Westcott well says: "The crucifix with the dead Christ obscures our faith. Our thoughts rest not upon a dead, but upon a living Christ." And so the late Prof. Milligan says: "No doubt the crucifix is to thousands upon thousands a spiritual help, and the figure of our Lord upon the cross preaches to them of the love of God with a power which the words of men can rarely, if ever, equal. Yet the empty cross is to be preferred as being a symbol, not a representation; as symbolizing, moreover, the resurrection as well as the death of the Redeemer. He has borne the cross and passed from it forever." With these eminent representatives of the modern Anglican and Presbyterian communions I must express my entire agreement as the result of my study of the Christ of the Gospels and the Christ of the Apostles.

The cross stained with the blood drops of our Redeemer is the most sacred symbol of our holy religion. Let it crown all our churches! Let it lead all our processions! Let it be worn on the hearts of all Christian people! But it is precious not because it points downward to death and the grave, but because it ever points upward to the living Christ who was lifted on that cross in order to be lifted thereby higher to His heavenly throne, to reign there as the one Mediator between God and man, whose pierced hands and feet and side, the scars of that cross, are the eternal pledges of His victory over Law and Sin and Death, and of the justification, sanctification, and glorification which He has won for our race and which He is graciously bestowing upon His kingdom.

# CONTENTS.

## I.

THE MESSIANIC IDEA IN PRE-CHRISTIAN JUDAISM, p. 1.

(1) The Palestinian Messianic idea, p. 4; (2) The Advent of the Apocalypse of Enoch, p. 9; (3) The Seventy Shepherds, p. 12; (4) The Ten Ages, p. 14; (5) The Earliest Sibylline Oracle, p. 16; (6) The Son of Man of the Similitudes of Enoch, p. 23; (7) The Messiah of the Psalter of Solomon, p. 31; (8) The Hellenistic Messianic idea, p. 36; (9) The Messianic ideas of the Jewish sects, p. 38.

## II.

THE MESSIANIC IDEA OF THE FORERUNNERS OF JESUS, p. 41.

(10) The Songs of Annunciation, p. 43; (11) The Songs of the Mothers, p. 54; (12) The Songs of the Fathers, p. 56; (13) The Herald of the Messiah, p. 63.

## III.

THE MESSIAH OF MARK, p. 70.

(14) The Son of God, p. 75; (15) The Kingdom at hand p. 78; (16) The Authority of the Son of Man, p. 80; (17) The Parables of the Kingdom, p. 87; (18) Jesus recognized as Messiah, p. 92; (19) The Resurrection and the Second Advent, p. 94; (20) The Transfiguration, p. 100; (21) The Kingdom of the Childlike, p. 101; (22) The Son of Man is a Ransom, p. 107; (23) The Messiah claims His Own, p. 112; (24) The Rejected Corner-Stone, p. 114; (25) The Lord of David, p. 118; (26) Ere another Communion Meal, p. 120; (27) The Rejected Shepherd, p. 125; (28) The Rejected Messiah, p. 126; (29) The Messiah's Death and Resurrection, p. 128.

## IV.

### THE APOCALYPSE OF JESUS, p. 132.

(30) The Prelude, p. 136; The Inquiry, p. 137; The Negative Answer as to the Time, p. 140; The Positive Answer as to the Time, p. 143; The Sign of the Destruction of Jerusalem and the Temple, p. 147; The Sign of the Second Advent, p. 151; The Relation of the Signs to the Advent, p. 156; Exhortation to Watch, p. 163.

## V.

### THE MESSIAH OF MATTHEW, p. 166.

(31) Jesus superior to Temptation, p. 166; (32) The Righteousness of the Kingdom, p. 171; (33) The Messiah's Credentials, p. 176; (34) The Kingdom which had come upon them, p. 179; (35) The Kingdom Nigh, p. 181; (36) The Sign of the Prophet Jonah, p. 186; (37) The Rock Peter, p. 189; (38) The disciple like the Master, p. 195; (39) The Kingdom the Supreme Quest, p. 202; (40) The Judgment of the Kingdom, p. 206; (41) The Obstructions to the Kingdom, p. 211; (42) The Head of the Corner, p. 215; (43) Watching, p. 218; (44) The Royal Judgment, p. 221; (45) The Rewards of the Kingdom, p. 227; (46) The Great Commission, p. 228.

## VI.

### THE MESSIAH OF LUKE, p. 233.

(47) The Son of God, p. 233; (48) The Rejected Prophet, p. 236; (49) The Guilt of rejecting the Gospel, p. 238; (50) The Invisible Kingdom, p. 244; (51) The Lesser Apocalypse of Jesus, p. 246; (52) The Shining forth of the Kingdom, p. 249; (53) The Woes of Jerusalem, p. 251; (54) The Risen Messiah, p. 252; (55) The Power from on High, p. 254.

## VII.

### The Messiah of John, p. 257.

(56) The Messiah in Glory, p. 257; (57) The Sign of the New Temple, p. 259; (58) The Kingdom of the Heaven-born, p. 261; (59) The Exalted Messiah, p. 266; (60) Universal Worship, p. 271; (61) The Father's own Son, p. 273; (62) The Bread from Heaven, p. 277; (63) Rivers of Living Water, p. 281; (64) The Light of the World, p. 282; (65) The Good Shepherd, p. 284; (66) The Seed and the Fruit, p. 287; (67) The Paraclete, p. 288; (68) The Kingdom of the Truth, p. 304; (69) Lord and God, p. 306; (70) The Martyrdom of Simon, p. 307.

## VIII.

### The Messiah of the Gospels, p. 309.

The Day of Yahweh, p. 310; The Advent of Yahweh, p. 313; The Father and the Shepherd, p. 314; The Promised Land, p. 315; The Messianic King, p. 316; The Kingdom of God, p. 324; The Holy Priesthood, p. 328; The Ideal Man, p. 328, Victory over Evil, p. 329; The Faithful Prophet, p. 329; The New Covenant, p. 332; The Second Advent, p. 333.

# THE MESSIAH OF THE GOSPELS.

## CHAPTER I.

### THE MESSIANIC IDEA IN PRE-CHRISTIAN JUDAISM.

THE Jewish people did not cease to produce a rich and varied religious literature, consisting of history, poetry, wisdom, and prophecy, during their subjection to the Greek and Roman yoke. The various types of character and schools of thought, which are represented in the sacred writings of the Jewish canon of the Old Testament, did not cease with the prophet Malachi in the Persian period, as the uncritical traditional opinion of former times supposed. These types and schools perpetuated themselves in numerous writings deep down into the Greek period, and even into the Roman period and the times of the New Testament. After the fixing of the canon of the Pentateuch by the priestly lawyers and narrators, who were especially active during the exile and the early years of the Restoration, the priestly school produced the memorials of Ezra and Nehemiah in the Persian period, and the work of the chronicler in the Greek period. The priestly tendency passed over into the schools of the scribes and renewed its life in oral traditional instruction, which found little expression in literature until the second century of the Christian era. The prophetic tendency, after the fixing of the canon of the former and latter prophets, was active in pseudepigrapha and in historical didactic stories such as the books of Daniel, Esther, and Ruth, which found their way into the third canon; and in a great number of other pseudepigrapha and didactic stories, some of which were taken up into the apocryphal books of the Hellenistic canon, a still larger number remaining in an uncertain condition outside the collection of sacred books of the Hebrew and Hellenistic Scriptures, but making their way, in part, into the Ethiopic and other ancient versions of the Old Testament Scriptures, and, in part, into canonical recognition in the private opinion of certain early Christian writers.

The writings of the third Hebrew canon also represent the lyric type of the Psalter and Lamentations, and the type of Wisdom in the books of Proverbs, Job, Song of Songs, and Ecclesiastes. Both of these types had a long literary development. The Psalter embraces many psalms from the Greek period, and a considerable number of Maccabean psalms. The Wisdom Literature includes Ecclesiastes, which belongs to the Greek period. These were taken up into the third canon. But other writings of the same types were subsequently composed, some of which appear in the Apocrypha, others among the Pseudepigrapha. The lines between the canonical and the extra-canonical writings were drawn by the pious judgment of those who fixed the several successive canons. The judgment of later ages has in the main confirmed these lines, although there are some writings with regard to which opinion has fluctuated.

In general it may be said that the extra-canonical writings do not exhibit the pure Biblical types. The writers, unrestrained by divine inspiration, were deflected from the normal lines of Biblical development by various influences bearing upon them, either from internal weaknesses and defects of Jewish disposition and character, or from the religious ideas of the Persians or the Greeks, which became the historical environment of their thinking and of their life.

Hellenistic culture was spread over the Orient by the conquests of Alexander and propagated in the kingdoms of his successors by Greek officials and colonists. This culture attracted not a few of the Jews in Syria, Palestine, and especially in Egypt, by its wealth of beauty and richness of thought. The two centuries divided by the advent of the Messiah are those in which this type of thought became powerful. It idealized the Messianic promise, and resolved the person of the Messiah and His kingdom into the mystic and hazy hope of a better and more ethical future.

Persian religious ideas seem to have had little influence during the period of the Persian domination; but in the Greek period these made their influence felt in a direction contrary to that of the Greek culture, especially among the Jews remaining on the east of the Euphrates and in its broad valley. The prophetic times were reduced to definite numbers, and the person of the Messiah was resolved into a series of human saviours. These ideas came into Palestine in connection with the Maccabean revolution, and subsequently in the rise and predominance of the zealots among the Jews.

The internal weakness of Jewish character disclosed itself in the tendency to overlook the spiritual elements of the Messianic idea and to hope for the restoration of the kingdom to Israel, with all the worldly prosperity that seemed involved therein. The Messiah, the Son of David, who is not so prominent in the last period of the Messianic promise of the Old Testament as He was during the existence of the Hebrew monarchy, was crowded into the background or else forgotten, and the common desire of the nation, especially in times undisturbed by revolutionary efforts on the one hand or of persecution on the other, was for the judicial interposition of God Himself.

The Biblical Messianic idea was not altogether forgotten. It was retained, and found expression in several writings which adhered closely to the Biblical models. But these were overwhelmed by the mass of literature and the weight of opinion, which were constantly leading the nation away from the pure Messianic ideals of the Old Testament.

## THE PALESTINIAN MESSIANIC IDEA.

§ 1. *The stricter Palestinian Judaism fixed its hopes upon the triumph of Israel through divine intervention and judgment. Elijah was to return and restore the tribes of Israel. The kingdom of David was to be revived. Jerusalem was to be rebuilt of precious stones and become the everlasting abode of God and His people. All nations would become tributary. There would be an everlasting covenant.*

One of the latest writings of the Old Testament was doubtless the book of Ecclesiastes, a product of the type of Hebrew wisdom, written by an unknown author of the Greek epoch. The first writing of the apocryphal literature was of the same type. It is called the book of Ecclesiasticus, or the Wisdom of

Sirach.¹ There is no Messianic prophecy in the book of Ecclesiastes. We could hardly expect any in Ecclesiasticus. "It represents an orthodox but moderate and cold Judaism, before there were either Pharisees or Sadducees."²

There are, however, in the section on the ancient worthies, several passages referring to the ancient covenants with their Messianic ideals. Those mentioned are the covenants with Noah,³ Abraham,⁴ Aaron,⁵ Phinehas,⁶ David.⁷ And there is an important passage which seems to set forth the author's own Messianic ideal. In a long eulogy of Elijah he refers to the prediction of Malachi respecting Elijah, which he paraphrases:

> Who wast written of in reproofs for set times,
> To pacify wrath before rage
> To turn the heart of father to son,
> And to restore the tribes of Jacob.
> Blessed is he that hath seen thee and died.
> Yet he will not die, he will fully live.⁸
>
> (xlvii. 10-11.)

The Syriac paraphrases the first line "who is destined to come before the day of the Lord cometh," and gives the correct interpretation. Elijah was to come before

---

¹ The book was composed in Hebrew and translated into Greek by the grandson of the author. There is also a Syriac version from a Hebrew original, and many other versions have been translated from these. The translations only have been preserved, but these help to restore the Hebrew original. Authorities differ as to the time of composition of the book. It is assigned to 180 B.C. by De Wette, Ewald, Dillmann, Drummond, and Cheyne. But Scholtz, Vaihinger, and Keil place it as early as 260 B.C. Edersheim conjectures that the original work was written about 235 B.C., Schürer puts it between 190 and 170 B.C.

² Edersheim, *Ecclesiasticus* in *Apocrypha*, ii., p. 2. London, 1888.

³ xliv. 18.    ⁴ xliv. 21-23.    ⁵ xlv. 7.    ⁶ xlv. 24.    ⁷ xlv. 25; xlvii. 11.

⁸ I agree with Edersheim in preference for the Syriac text of lines 5 and 6, which is more consistent than the Greek, and which gives better rhythm and fine antithesis.

the day of the Lord, the judgment day. He was taken up in a chariot and whirlwind of fire to heaven. He will return to accomplish his predicted mission, and that man will be happy who has the privilege of seeing him before he dies. He will enjoy the fulness of life.

The first book of Maccabees [1] knows nothing more of the Messianic idea than the ancient promises of the everlasting priesthood of Phinehas and the everlasting kingdom of David.[2] The story of Judith [3] brings into prominence the day of judgment. In her song of thanksgiving Judith concludes with these words:

> Woe to the nations that rise up against my kindred!
> The Lord Almighty will take vengeance on them in the day of judgment,
> Putting fire and worms into their flesh
> And they will feel them and weep forever.[4]

It is evident that the author has in mind the judgment scene of the great prophet of the exile,[5] the rotting, burning carcasses of the wicked outside the holy city in the valley of Hinnom.[6]

The second book of Maccabees [7] has no trace of the Messianic idea except in the expectation of the fulfilment

---

[1] The first book of Maccabees was written in Hebrew and translated into Greek. It is assigned by Ewald to 105 B.C., by Grimm to 105–64 B.C., by Westcott to 120–100 B.C., by Rawlinson to 116–106 B.C.

[2] ii. 54, 57.

[3] The book of Judith was written by a Palestinian Jew in Hebrew and was translated into Greek. The translation only has been preserved. The date is uncertain. It is assigned to 79–70 B.C. by Ball, to 131–129 B.C. by Ewald.

[4] xvi. 17.   [5] Isaiah lxvi. 24.

[6] Ball renders the last line on the partial authority of Vulgate and Syriac, "burn in evil forever."

[7] This is an epitome of a larger work written in Greek by Jason of Cyrene, not long after 160 B.C. This work was also written in Greek not much later than the original. It is assigned by critics to the latter part of the second century or the first half of the first century B.C.

of the promise: "He will shortly have mercy upon us, and gather us together out of every land under heaven into the holy place."[1]

Tobit,[2] in his prayer, praises the Lord in His promises respecting the glorious future of Jerusalem:

> O Jerusalem! city of the Holy One,[3]
> He will scourge thee for thy children's works,
> And will have mercy again on the sons of the just.
> Praise the Lord aright,[4]
> And bless the king of the ages,
> In order that his tabernacle may be built in thee again with joy,
> And to make joyful the captives in thee,
> And to love the miserable in thee,
> Unto all generations of the age.
> Many nations from afar will come
> Unto the name of the Lord God,
> Having gifts in their hands,
> Even gifts to the king of heaven.
> Generations of generations will give thee great joy.
> Cursed will be all who hate thee;
> Blessed will be all who love thee (for ever).
> Rejoice and be glad for the sons of the just,
> For they will be gathered together and bless the Lord of the just.
> O blessed are those who love thee,
> They will rejoice in thy peace.
> Blessed are they who have been sorrowful for all thy scourges;

---

[1] ii. 18.

[2] The book of Tobit was written by a Palestinian Jew in Hebrew. The original has been lost and only translations are preserved. Great differences exist among critics as to its time of composition. Graetz, Neubauer, and Rosenthal ascribe it to the time of Hadrian. It is assigned by Ewald to the fourth century B.C., by Fuller to the second century B.C., by Vaihinger to the first century B.C. It may be appropriately used in this place so far as the Messianic idea is concerned.

[3] The LXX. πόλις ἁγίου sustained by the Vulgate *civitas Dei* is better than the "holy city" of A. V. after the Itala.

[4] ἀγαθῶς of the LXX. is sustained by the Vulgate *in bonis tuis*, and the Itala *in bono*, and is preferable to the variant ὅτι ἀγαθός.

> For they will rejoice in thee when they have seen all thy glory,
> And my soul will be glad forever.[1]
> Let it bless God the great king.
> For Jerusalem will be built (up) with sapphires and emeralds,
> And thy walls with precious stones,
> And thy towers and battlements with pure gold,
> And the streets of Jerusalem with beryl and carbuncle,
> And with stone of Ophir they will be paved;
> And all her streets will say Alleluia,
> And will praise, saying, Blessed be God,
> Who hath exalted her for all ages. (xiii. 9–18.)

This prayer of Tobit combines elements from the Old Testament prophets, especially from the great prophet of the exile.[2]

Tobit on the bed of death encourages his son with the Messianic promise:

> And again God will have mercy upon them,
> And bring them again into the land;
> And they will build the house, not as the former,
> Until the times of the ages be fulfilled;
> And afterward they will return from their captivities,
> And will build Jerusalem gloriously;
> And the house of God in it will be built gloriously,
> As the prophets have spoken thereof;
> And all nations will turn
> To truly fear the Lord God,
> And they will bury their idols;
> And all nations will bless the Lord,
> And his people will confess God;
> And the Lord will exalt his people,
> And all who love the Lord God
> Will rejoice in truth and righteousness,
> Shewing mercy to their brethren. (xiv. 5–7.)

This passage does not go beyond the predictions of

---

[1] ἡ ψυχή μου belongs with this line rather than the following, and the singular εὐφρανθήσεται of several codices is preferable.

[2] Isaiah liv. 11–12; lx. 1–3.

the prophets as to the restoration of Israel and Jerusalem. It distinguishes, however, between a partial return and an inferior temple, and a complete return and a glorious temple such as the prophets have predicted. The author clearly saw that the temple of Zerubbabel and the return in the times of the Persians did not correspond with the ideals of the prophets.

THE ADVENT OF THE APOCALYPSE OF ENOCH.

§ 2. *God comes to Mount Sinai with myriads of holy ones to hold judgment. The earth will be transformed, the wicked destroyed, the righteous blessed. The righteous will eat and drink and beget each a thousand children. The earth will become exceedingly fruitful and will be free from misery.*

The book of Enoch was written originally in Hebrew. It has been preserved in part in a Greek revision, but chiefly in an Ethiopic version, which was first given to the modern world by Laurence. It has an original nucleus about which several writings have clustered, the remnants of a larger literature assigned to Enoch. The two chief parts are the Similitudes, ch. xxxvii.–lxxi., and the Apocalypse, ch. i.–xxxvi., lxxii.–civ., by different authors. Ewald and Dillmann give the priority to the Similitudes, placing them in the second century B.C., and assigning the Apocalypse to the latter part of the same century, or the earlier part of the first century B.C. But Langen, Schürer, and most critics assign the Similitudes to the close of the first century B.C., and regard the Apocalypse as older.[1]

---

[1] Vernes, however, places them in the Christian era, and thinks the Apocalypse belongs to the time of John Hyrcanus, 110 B.C. Schodde assigns the Apocalypse to a time prior to 160 B.C., and the Similitudes to the reign of Herod.

Charles[1] analyzes as follows: 1. Chaps. i.–xxxvi. written prior to 170 B.C., on the basis of Is. lxv.–lxvi., the oldest section. 2. Chaps. lxxxiii.–xc. written between 166–161 B.C., mainly from the same standpoint as Daniel. 3. Chaps. xci.–civ. written between 134–94 B.C., or possibly, 104–94 B.C. 4. The Similitudes, chaps. xxxvii.–lxx., written between 94–79 or 70–64 B.C. 5. The book of Celestial Physics, chaps. lxxii.–lxxviii., lxxxii., lxxix., date unknown. 6. Noachian and other interpolations, before the Christian era, chiefly from an older Noachian apocalypse.[2] We cannot go into the details of the criticism. It is sufficient for our purpose to distinguish the parts containing the Messianic material. It seems to be evident that the Similitudes were earlier than the Psalter of Solomon, and that they were later than the other sections of the book.

The Apocalypse opens with a judgment scene which is based on the theophany described in the Blessing of Moses.[3]

Concerning the elect I spake, and uttered a parable concerning them. The Holy and Great One, the God of the world, will come from His abode. And from there He will step on Mount Sinai and appear with His hosts, and appear in the strength of His power from heaven. And all will fear and the watchers will tremble, and great fear and terror will seize them unto the ends of the earth. And the lofty mountains will be shaken and the high hills will sink down, and will melt like wax before the flame. And the earth will sink down and everything that is on the earth will be destroyed, and there will be a judgment upon everything, and upon all the righteous. But to the righteous He will give peace and will protect the elect, and mercy will abide

---

[1] *Book of Enoch*, p. 26 seq. 1893.
[2] vi. 3–8; viii 1–3; ix. 7; x. 1–3,11; xvii.–xx.; xxxix. 1, 2a; xli. 3–8; xliii.–xliv.; liv. 7–lv. 2; lvi. 5–lvii. 3a; l., lix.–lx.; lxv.–lxix. 25; lxxi.; lxxx.–lxxxi.; xc. 15; xci. 11; xciii. 11–14; xcvi. 2; cv.–cvii.
[3] Deut. xxxiii. 2.

over them, and they will all belong to God, and will be prosperous and blessed, and the light of God will shine upon them. And behold, He comes with myriads of His holy ones to hold judgment upon them, and He will destroy the ungodly, and will call all flesh to account for everything the sinners and ungodly have done and ungodly committed against Him.¹ (i. 3-9.)

The judgment is a theophany of God which throws all nature into convulsions, and mankind and angels into terror. Mount Sinai is the place of judgment. The earth will be transformed at the advent. All will be judged, the righteous will be rewarded, and the wicked will be destroyed.

The Apocalypse also gives an account of the judgment of the angels who seduced the daughters of men.² They are bound under the earth for seventy generations until the day of their final judgment, the last judgment for all eternity. In those days they will be led away into the fiery abyss. In misery and prison they will be shut up for all eternity.³

And then will all the righteous escape and remain in life until they beget a thousand children, and all the days of their youth and their sabbath will they accomplish in peace. And in those days the entire earth will be cultivated in righteousness and will all be planted with trees, and will be full of blessings. And all the trees of pleasure will be planted on it, and vines will be planted on it. The vine planted on it will bear fruit in abundance, and from all the seeds sown thereon, one measure will give ten thousand, and one measure of olives will give ten presses of oil.⁴ And cleanse thou the earth from all oppression, and from all unrighteousness, and from all sin, and from all godlessness, and from all uncleanness which is wrought upon the earth: destroy them from off the earth. And all the children of men will become righteous, and all nations will offer me adoration and praise, and all will worship me. And the earth will be cleansed

---

¹ Quoted Jude 14-15.  
² Gen. vi. 1-4.  
³ Enoch x. 12, 13; cf. Is. xxiv. 21, 22.  
⁴ cf. Is. lxv. 20-25.

from all corruption and from all sin and from all punishment and all misery,[1] and I will never again send a deluge upon it from generation to generation for ever.  (x. 17-22.)

The author connects the judgment of the deluge with the ultimate judgment after the manner of the ancient prophets.  Charles thinks that the reference to the deluge comes from a corrupt MS., but he does not present sufficient evidence for his opinion.  The doctrine of future blessedness is based on the representation of Isaiah and the great prophet of the exile, but is less refined and less spiritual in conception.

This is all that we have of the Messianic idea in this earliest section of the Apocalypse, and it is essentially true to the Old Testament idea.  A later section of the Apocalypse is richer in material.

### THE SEVENTY SHEPHERDS.

§ 3. *God will set up His throne in Jerusalem and judge evil angels and wicked men, casting them successively into the abyss of fire.  The Messiah appears at the head of His people.  They are white sheep; he a white bull.  The old temple is removed and a new and more glorious one put in its place.  The sheep are transformed into cattle and the Messiah into a gigantic yore ox.  Israel will be honored and obeyed by all nations.*

Seventy shepherds have charge of the flock of Israel from the destruction of Jerusalem until the judgment, when they are cast into the abyss of fire.  These are subdivided into $12 + 23 + 23 + 12$,[2] after the model of the seventy weeks of Daniel $7 + 62 + 1$.[3]  They are regarded by Ewald and others as representing heathen monarchs who held Israel under their dominion.  But Hoffman,

---

[1] Is. xi. 6-9.   [2] Chap. lxxxix. 59 *seq.*   [3] Dan. ix. 25-27.

Schürer, Charles, and others rightly hold that they are angel princes, after the method of the angel princes of Daniel[1] and the Septuagint version of the Song of Moses,[2] because the heathen monarchs are represented as beasts in the context. The judgment is described as follows.

A throne was set up in the lovely land and the Lord of the sheep sat down thereon, and all the sealed books were opened before the Lord of the sheep. The judgment was first upon the stars [the evil angels]: they are found guilty and are sent unto the place of punishment, and are cast into a deep place full of flaming fire and pillars of fire. Then the seventy shepherds (the evil angel princes) are judged and found guilty, and also cast into that fiery abyss. Then a similar deep place in the middle of the earth was opened full of fire, and the blinded sheep (wicked men) were brought together and all judged and found guilty and cast into that fiery abyss and burned.[3] This abyss was at the right of the house (the temple), just as in the great prophet of the exile Gehenna is the place of refuse outside the city.[4]

And I saw the sheep burning and their bones burning. And I stood up in order to see until he wrapt up that old house, and removed all its pillars ; and all its beams and decorations were at once rolled up with it, and it was taken away and put in a place in the south of the land. And I saw the lord of the sheep until he brought a new house greater and higher than that first one, and put it in the place of the first that had been rolled up. All its pillars were new, and its decorations were new and larger than those of the first house which he had taken away, and the lord of the sheep was therein. And I saw all the sheep that remained over, and all the beasts of the earth, and all the birds of heaven, how they fell down and sought the favour of those sheep and supplicated them and obeyed them in everything. (xc. 27-30.)

---

[1] Dan. xii. 1.  [2] Deut. xxxii. 8.  [3] xc. 20-26.  [4] Is. lxvi. 24.

Those sheep were all white and their wool large and pure. The Messiah now appears.[1] He was born a white bull with great horns, and all the beasts of the field and all the birds of heaven fear and supplicate him at all times. All the sheep are at last transformed into white oxen, and the first of them becomes a great animal, probably a gigantic bull[2] having large black horns upon his head, and the lord of the sheep rejoices over them. The Messiah has little place in this prediction and little to do. The Messianic idea is more external and carnal than in the Similitudes. This is still more the case in the sections relating to the corruption of the earth through the intercourse of fallen angels with the daughters of mankind now to be considered.[3]

### THE TEN AGES.

§ 4. *The duration of the world is divided into ten periods of sevens, the last three of which are times of advancing judgment. In the first of these the wicked are given into the hands of the righteous, in the second there is a righteous judgment of the entire world and the banishment of evil from the earth. In the tenth week the evil angels are judged with the judgment for eternity; the old heavens vanish and new heavens appear with luminaries shining with sevenfold brilliancy. Then will follow innumerable periods of righteousness.*

The book of Enoch contains a little apocalypse, xci.–xciv., that has been interpolated by a later writer or editor in the original apocalypse. The editor has de-

---

[1] Chap. xc. 32 *seq.*

[2] The Greek ῥῆμα is certainly alien to the context. It would introduce a heterogeneous and later conception. It is probably a translation of the Hebrew ראם the gigantic bull of the Old Testament, the yore ox.

[3] Charles puts this with the earlier apocalypse.

tached xci. 12–17 from its proper place after xciii. and attached it to xci. 1–11. The author of this apocalypse, assigned by Charles to 104–95 B.C., differs from the earlier authors in his more comprehensive view of human history and its close in a series of judgments. He divides the duration of the world into ten weeks of seven generations each, seven of these weeks belonging to the past and three to the future. These three weeks of judgment are thus described:

And afterwards will be another week, the eighth, that of righteousness, and there will be given a sword in order that with it judgment and justice may be executed on those who act violently, and sinners will be given over into the hands of the righteous. And at its close they will acquire houses by their righteousness, and the house of the great king will be built in glory forever and ever. And afterwards in the ninth week will be revealed the righteous judgment of the entire world, and all the works of the ungodly will vanish away from the entire earth, and the world will be written down for destruction, and all men will seek the way of righteousness. And after this, in the tenth week, in the seventh part, there will be the great judgment for eternity, which will be held over the watchers. And the former heaven will vanish and pass away and a new heaven will appear, and all the powers of heaven will shine forever with sevenfold brilliancy. And afterwards there will be many weeks without number forever in goodness and righteousness, and sin will be no more named forever. (xci. 12–17.)

We notice in this author the absence of the Messiah. He makes the distinction of three judgments, the first of wicked men, the second of the entire world, and the third of angels. The seventy sacred times are viewed as embracing the whole course of the world. This differs from the sacred times of Daniel and the earlier Enoch,[1] and is more in accord with Persian religious ideas.

---
[1] lxxxix. 59 *seq.*

The Persians divided the course of the world into twelve thousand years, arranged in four periods of three thousand years each. The first three millenniums were given to the creation, so that but nine thousand years belong to the course of the world proper. After the expiration of the nine thousand years evil would be entirely conquered. Three thousand of these belonged to the golden time, three thousand to the great struggle with evil, lasting until the time of Zoroaster and his revelation. Three thousand years, or the last quarter, is the time of redemption. The final redeemer, Sosiosh, at the close of the nine thousand years has two predecessors, one the prophet Hushedar coming in the seventh millennium, the other the prophet Hushedarmah coming in the eighth millennium to destroy idolatry and reform the world, so that Sosiosh may at last come for the universal resurrection and judgment.[1]

Our author's conception of the last three times is very much like these last three times of the Persians, except that the redemptive persons are not brought in.

### THE EARLIEST SIBYLLINE ORACLE.

§ 5. *The kings of the nations will come up with great masses against Jerusalem, but a judgment from God, with fiery swords and great torches falling from heaven and great earthquakes, will come upon them and destroy them. Afterwards there will be everlasting peace and felicity. The earth will become very fruitful and enmity between men and animals will cease.*

The Sibylline oracles are a collection of oracles of different periods; but it is agreed that the body of the

---

[1] Hulschmann, *Die Parsische Lehre von Jenzeits J. Prot. Theo.*, 1879, II. H. Spiegel *Parsimus* in Herzog, *Real Ency. II. Aufl.*

third book is the earliest of all. It gives an apocalypse of the second century B.C.[1]

The passage first to be considered is doubtful as to its Messianic bearings:

> Therefore seven decades shall thy fruitful land
> And the wonders of the temple be a waste.
> And yet for thee a goodly end remains,
> And highest glory from the immortal God.
> But wait thou, and confide in God's pure laws,
> When to the light he lifts thy wearied knee.
> And then will God send out of heaven a king
> To judge each man in blood and light of fire.
> There is a royal tribe, whose progeny
> Shall be unfailing, and in course of time
> Will it rule, and God's temple build anew.
> And all the kings of Persia will assist
> With gold and brass and well-wrought iron, and God
> Himself will give by night the holy dream,
> And then the temple shall be as of old.[2] (331–345).

This passage is referred by Hilgenfeld, Vernes, Schürer, and Terry to Cyrus, on account of the mention of the temple and the Persian kings; but it is difficult to see the propriety of representing Cyrus as a king from heaven and as executing judgment by fire. This repre-

---

[1] It is admitted that this third book belongs to the second century B.C. Hilgenfeld, Schürer, Vernes, assign it to 140 B.C.; Bleek and Friedlieb give it the earlier date of 170–160 B.C.; Ewald 124 B.C.; Alexandre finds the date 168 for the section iii. 97–294, 489–817, but assigns the middle section 295–488 to a Christian author. The middle section is a collection of miscellaneous oracles, but Schürer sees no reason for a different author. There is no Messianic passage in them, and therefore we have no occasion to discuss this question. The oracle was composed by an Alexandrine Jew, who puts the prediction in the mouth of the Erythræan sibyl. See Alexandre, *Oracula Sibyllina*, Paris, 1841; Friedlieb, *Oracula Sibyllina*, Leipsic, 1852; Terry, *The Sibylline Oracles*, N. Y., 1890.

[2] The translation of Terry is so good that I prefer to use it, especially as it gives the English reader some conception of the poetry of the original. The lines of Terry differ so slightly from the original that it seems unnecessary to give both. As I use Terry's lines I shall use also his numbers.

sentation is only in part justified by the exilic Isaiah.[1] The seventy times may be referred to the sacred weeks of Daniel,[2] or to the years of Jeremiah.[3] The king from heaven, if not Cyrus and if Messianic,[4] would be the Son of Man from heaven of Daniel.[5]

Woes are pronounced upon all nations in turn after the manner of the great prophets. The woes come upon Babylon, Egypt, Gog and Magog of the older prophecy; and also upon various cities of Asia Minor, Greece, and Italy, even Troy; and upon Homer, "the writer of lies," who is accused of appropriating the verses of the sibyl.

A great passionate king like an eagle, doubtless Antiochus Epiphanes, will come out of Asia, lay waste the holy land, overthrow Egypt, and even cross the sea. All the works of men's hands will fall by the flame of fire.

> And then great joy will God bestow on men.
> For land and trees, and countless flocks of sheep
> Will yield mankind the genuine fruit of wine,
> And of sweet honey, and white milk, and wheat,
> Which is for men the very best of all. (738–743.)

The future blessedness subsequent to judgment is connected with Antiochus very much as in Daniel.[6]

Then will God send a king from the sun, who will make the entire earth still from wicked war, will slay some and make a true covenant with others.

> But again the people
> Of the great God with wealth will be weighed down,
> With gold and silver and purple ornament,
> And of good things will earth and sea be full. (782–784.)

This king from the sunrise resembles the king from

---

[1] Is. xliv. 28; xlv. 1–4.   [2] Dan. ix. 24–27.   [3] Jer. xxv. 9–12.
[4] The Messianic reference attracted me for many years. But it now seems to me that the context favors reference to Cyrus.
[5] Dan. vii. 13.   [6] Dan. ix. 26, 27; xii. 11–13.

heaven already considered, and seems to be Cyrus likewise.[1] The prosperity here is similar to the prosperity described there.

This is followed by a description of the kings of the nations coming up with great masses against the temple of God and the holy land, when a judgment from the great God comes upon them and they are destroyed.

> And fiery swords
> Shall fall from heaven on earth, and mighty lights
> Shall come down flaming in the midst of men.
> And mother earth shall be tossed in those days
> By an immortal hand, and fish of the sea,
> And all earth's beasts, and countless flocks of birds,
> And all the souls of men, and all the sea
> Shall shudder at the face of the Immortal,
> And there shall be dismay. High mountain peaks
> And huge hills He will rend, and Erebus
> The dark and dismal will appear to all;
> And misty gorges in the lofty hill
> Shall be full of the dead; the rocks shall stream
> With blood, and every torrent fill the plain.
> And well-built walls shall all fall to the earth
> By hostile men, for they knew not the law,
> Neither God's judgment, but with senseless soul,
> All rushing to the temple, lifted spears.
> God judges all by war, and sword, and fire,
> And overwhelming flood; and there shall be
> Brimstone from heaven, and stones and grievous hail;[2]
> And death shall come upon the quadrupeds.
> Then shall men come to know the immortal God
> Who judges these things. Lamentation too,
> And uproar shall come on the boundless earth,
> Because men perish, and in speechless woe
> Shall all be bathed in blood, and earth herself
> Shall drink the blood of them that are destroyed,
> And the wild beasts will glut themselves with flesh.
>
> (800–828.)

---

[1] Lines 331–345.  [2] Ezek. xxxviii. 22.

Again the children of the mighty God
Shall all about the temple live in peace,
Delighting in those things which He shall give
Who is Creator, righteous Judge, and King.
For He alone, and standing wondrous near,
Can shelter as a wall of flaming fire [1]
From all around. And there shall be no wars
In cities or in country; not the hand
Of cruel war,[2] but rather there shall be
With them the immortal Champion Himself,
And the hand of the Holy One. And then the isles
And cities all shall speak, and tell how much
The Immortal loves those men, for He with them
Shares in all conflict and delivers them.
And heaven, and sun divinely formed, and moon,
And mother earth shall tremble in those days.
And a sweet word shall they lead forth in hymns:
"Come, falling on the earth let us all pray
To the immortal King, great God, most high.
Let us send to the temple, since sole Lord
He is, and let us all observe the law
Of God most high, who above all on earth
Is the most Righteous One. For we have strayed
Far from the path of the Immortal One,
And have done reverence with a senseless soul
To works of human hands, to images
Carved out of wood, and of departed men."
These things souls of the faithful cry aloud:
"Come, let us with God's people, falling down
Upon our faces, gladden in our homes
With hymns God the Creator, and procure
The weapons of our foes in every land
For seven lengths of the revolving years— [3]
Even shields and helmets and all sorts of arms,
And a great store of bows and harmful arrows,
For forest wood shall not be cut for fire" (834-869).

For earth, all-mother, shall to mortals yield
The best fruit, boundless store of wheat,

---
[1] Zec. ii. 5.    [2] Mic. iv. 3.    [3] Ezek. xxxix. 9, 10.

And wine and oil. And from the heaven a drink,
Delightful of sweet honey there shall be,
And trees, and fruits of trees, and fatted sheep,
And oxen, and young lambs, and kids of goats.
And forth shall burst sweet fountains of white milk,
And of good things the cities shall be full,
And fat the fields, and there shall not be sword
Nor uproar on the earth, nor shall the earth
Groan heavily and tremble any more.
Nor war nor drought shall longer be on earth,
Nor famine, nor the fruit-destroying hail,
But great peace shall be upon all the earth.[1]
King will be friend to king until the end
Of time, and a new law on all the earth
Will the Immortal in the starry heaven
Perfect for men, touching whatever things
Have been by miserable mortals done.
For He alone is God, no other is.
And He will burn with fire man's grievous power.
(885–905).

And then will He a kingdom for all time
Raise up for all men, and a holy law
Give to the pious to whom He has pledged
To open up the land, and the wide world,
And portals of the blessed, and all joys,
And mind immortal, and eternal bliss.
And out of every land unto the house
Of the great God will they bring frankincense[2]
And gifts, and there shall be no other house
To be inquired of by men yet to be;
But whom God gave to honor faithful men,
Him mortals shall call Son of the great God.
And all paths of the field and rough hills,
And lofty mountains, and the sea's wild waves,
Shall in those days be easy to pass over,
For all peace of the good shall come on earth.
And the sword shall God's prophets take away,
For they shall be the judges of mankind,

---

[1] Ps. xlvi. 9.   [2] Ps. lxviii. 29; Is. lxvi. 20; Zeph. iii. 9-10,

And righteous kings; for of the mighty God
This is the judgment and the sovereignty.
  Be of good cheer, O maiden, and exult,[1]
For the Eternal, who made heaven and earth,
Has given thee joy, and He will dwell in thee,
And for thee shall be an immortal light.[2]
And wolves and lambs promiscuously shall eat
Grass in the mountains, and among the kids
Shall leopards graze, and wandering bears shall lodge
Among the calves, and the carnivorous lion
Shall eat straw in the manger like the ox,
And little children lead them with a band.
For tame will be on earth the beasts He made,
And with young babes will dragons fall asleep,
And no harm, for God's hand will be on them.[3]
  Now tell I thee a sign exceeding clear,
That thou mayst know when of all things on earth
The end shall be. When in the starry heaven
Swords shall be seen by night toward west or east,
Straightway shall there be a dark cloud of dust,
Borne downward from the heaven o'er all the earth,
And the sun's brightness in the midst of heaven
Shall be eclipsed, and the moon's beams appear
And come again on earth, and there shall be
The sign of blood-drops issuing from the stones,
And ye shall see a war of foot and horse
In a cloud, like a hunting of wild beasts,
Like a dark mist. This is the end of war
Which God who dwells in heaven shall bring to pass.
But all must sacrifice to the great King.   (912–959.)

These representations are based upon many different prophetic passages of the Old Testament; but they are combined and developed in a manner foreign to the conceptions of genuine Biblical prophecy. The ethical and spiritual elements, which in the canonical prophets ever predominate, here retire into the background and are

---

[1] Zech. ii. 10.      [2] Is. lx. 1, 2, 19, 20.      [3] Is. xi. 6–9; lxv. 25.

overshadowed by the sensuous and carnal elements which are richly unfolded in the foreground of the poet's imagination and fancy. There is no clear reference to a Messianic king or prophet to introduce this golden age of sensuous pleasure. God Himself is the judge and the king, who destroys all enemies and rewards His people with felicity. The author was an Alexandrian Jew who wrote his poem in Hellenistic Greek, but he is not a Hellenist in his type of thought. He is a Palestinian Jew who is hostile to all that is Greek, and who looks forward with delight and ardent longing for the triumph of the Jew over the world.

THE SON OF MAN OF THE SIMILITUDES OF ENOCH.

§ 6. *The Similitudes of the Book of Enoch present the Messiah as the Elect, the Son of Man, full of grace as a holy angel, the righteous possessor of the treasures of wisdom. He was named before the sun and stars were made, and was concealed before God ere the world was created, and he will abide before Him forever. He will sit enthroned at His side in judgment. The dead will rise to be judged, and he will select the righteous to be saved and to dwell upon the earth with joy; but the wicked will be forced from his presence into shame and darkness, and will be committed to the angels of punishment.*

The Similitudes of the Book of Enoch differ from the other parts of the Book of Enoch in the prominence given to the person of the Son of Man and in the comparative purity of the Messianic idea. We shall first consider chap. xlv. 3–6.

On that day Mine Elect One will sit on the throne of glory and make selection among their deeds and their mansions will be innumerable, and their souls will grow strong within them when they see Mine Elect One and those who call upon my glorious name. And on that day will I cause Mine Elect One to dwell among them and I will transform the heaven and make it an everlasting blessing and light. And I will transform the earth and make it a blessing, and cause mine elect ones to dwell on it. But the sinners and evil doers will not tread it. For I have seen and satisfied my righteous ones with peace, and have caused them to dwell before me; but for sinners there awaits a judgment with me that I may destroy them from the face of the earth.

This passage brings to mind the prediction of the great prophet of the exile.[1] The Elect One sits on the judgment throne in the day of judgment. The heavens and the earth are transformed and give place to new heavens and a new earth of blessedness and light, the everlasting abode of the righteous. The wicked are driven from the face of this new earth upon which there will be no more sin. The Elect One is the first and the chief of all the elect from among men. He is the judge and the king by divine choice and selection, the Elect Head of an elect kingdom of the redeemed. The term elect, chosen, is applied to the servant of Yahweh, the one anointed with the divine Spirit, the covenant of the people and the light of the Gentiles, the gentle redeemer, of the great prophet of the exile.[2] The author of the Similitudes probably derived the term Elect One from that passage, as he shows great familiarity with and preference for this prophet.

The next passage is an unfolding of the judgment scene of the Apocalypse of Daniel.

And there I saw one who had a Head of Days, and his head was white as wool, and with Him another whose face was as the appearance of a man, and his face was full of grace like one of the holy angels. And I asked the angel who went with me and showed me all the hidden things, concerning that Son of Man,

---

[1] Is. lxv.–vi.      [2] Is. xlii. 1 *seq.*

who he was, and whence he was, and why he went with the Head of Days? And he answered and said unto me: This is the Son of Man who has righteousness, with whom righteousness dwells, and who reveals all the treasures of that which is hidden; for the Lord of Spirits has chosen him, and his lot hath surpassed all things before the Lord of Spirits in rectitude forever. And this Son of Man whom thou hast seen will arouse the kings and mighty ones from their beds and the powerful from their thrones, and will loose the bands of the powerful and crush the teeth of sinners. And he will cast the kings out from their thrones and kingdoms, because they exalt him not and praise him not, and do not thankfully acknowledge whence the kingdom was given them. And the face of the powerful will be cast away and shame will cover them; darkness will be their dwelling and worms their couch, and they will have no hope of rising from their couches because they did not exalt the name of the Lord of Spirits. (xlvi. 1–6.)

The Head of Days is the Ancient of Days of Daniel and is the God of judgment. The Son of Man is the Son of Man of Daniel.[1] This name is here given to a righteous man and not to Israel. The terms of the punishment are derived from the great prophet of the exile as well as from Daniel, for shame[2] and darkness and worms[3] are used, and not the river of fire. The use of the Elect One, the Servant of Yahweh of the exilic Isaiah, and of the Son of Man of Daniel and their reference to the same Messianic person enthroned with the Head of Days for judgment, involves a combination of these two Messianic ideals. This combination was not made in the Old Testament. It is a genuine combination first made by these Similitudes of Enoch and afterwards recognized in the New Testament. It may be that this combination influenced Jesus in His use of the Son of Man for Himself.[4]

---

[1] Dan. vii. 13.   [2] Dan. xii. 2.   [3] Is. lxvi. 24.
[4] See Charles, *Book of Enoch*, pp. 312 *seq*.

The next passage follows Daniel more closely:

And in those days I saw the Head of Days, as He seated Himself on the throne of His glory, and the books of the living were opened before Him,[1] and His entire host above in heaven and round about Him, stood before Him. And the hearts of the holy ones were full of joy that the number of righteousness was fulfilled, and the prayer of the righteous was heard and the blood of the righteous demanded before the Lord of Spirits. And in that place I saw an inexhaustible fountain of righteousness, round about it many fountains of wisdom, and all the thirsty drank of them[2] and were filled with wisdom, and had their dwellings among the righteous and holy and elect. And at that hour that Son of Man was named in the presence of the Lord of Spirits and his name before the Head of Days. And ere the sun and signs were created, ere the stars of heaven were made, was his name named before the Lord of Spirits. He will be a staff to the righteous that they may lean on him and not fall, and he will be the light of the peoples and the hope of those who are troubled in their hearts.[3] There will fall down and worship before him all who dwell on earth, and will praise and glorify and sing to the name of the Lord of Spirits. And for this was he elected and concealed before Him ere the world was created, and unto eternity will he be before Him. (xlvii. 3—xlviii. 6.)

In this passage the author dwells on the judgment throne, the books of judgment and the person of the Son of Man. The doctrine of the naming of the concealed Son of Man before the creation is new to the Messianic idea, but it is based on a combination of the Son of Man coming from heaven of Daniel,[4] and the ruler from Bethlehem whose going forth was from ancient times of Micah.[5]

The naming of the Son of Man before the heavenly hosts is an unfolding of the doctrine of his election, and does not imply any more than an ideal pre-existence in

---

[1] Dan. vii. 9–10; xii. 1.   [2] Is. lv. 1.   [3] Is. xlii. 6; xlix. 6.
[4] Dan. vii. 13.   [5] Mic. v. 2.

the plan or the decree of God. This would be only a strengthened statement of the doctrine of Micah. But the concealment of the Son of Man is stronger than this. It implies some sort of pre-existence of the Son of Man with God and the angels before the creation of the world. The conception of Daniel that the Son of Man comes from heaven on the clouds implies his pre-existence in heaven prior to his advent. But that is entirely consistent with a prior earthly life. This conception, however, is capable of a development, either in the direction of the New Testament, implying a previous earthly life, death, resurrection and ascension, or of the extra-Biblical Judaism, implying a pre-existence of the Messiah in heaven before his advent to judgment.

The author of the Similitudes adheres to the standpoint of extra-Biblical Judaism, and carries back that pre-existence to the time before the creation of the world. This is an important advance in the Messianic idea beyond the Old Testament. It is the highest stage reached before the advent of the Messiah. But it is not yet a Christian conception, and it might easily become anti-Christian. There is no trace of the doctrine of the divinity of the Messiah, or of his exaltation to an equality of rank with God or of a prior advent.[1]

The next passage that we shall consider is an unfolding of the scene of the resurrection of Daniel.[2]

In those days will the earth give back that intrusted to it, and Sheol will give back that intrusted to it which it has received, and Abaddon will give back what it owes.[3] And he will select

---

[1] See Dillmann in *l. c.* p. xxiv., and Charles, p. 134.　　[2] Dan. xii.
[3] Haguel is here the equivalent of the Hebrew אֲבַדּוֹן and the Greek ἀπώλεια the prison of the lost in the Middle State. The Book of Enoch agrees with the Eschatology of the New Testament and the Jewish Literature of that time, that the wicked are not consigned to the fires of Gehenna until the day of judgment. For the use of אֲבַדּוֹן with שְׁאוֹל see Job xxvi. 6; xxviii. 22; Prov. xv. 11.

the righteous and holy among them, for the day has come that they should be saved. And the Elect One will in those days sit on his throne and all the mysteries of wisdom will flow forth from the thoughts of his mouth; for the Lord of Spirits has given it to him and glorified him. And in those days will the mountains leap like rams and the hills skip like lambs[1] satisfied with milk, and they all will become angels in heaven. Their faces will shine with joy, because in those days the Elect One has appeared, and the earth will rejoice and the righteous will dwell on it, and the elect ones will go to and fro upon it. (li.)

This passage extends the general resurrection of Daniel to a universal resurrection. It then considers the rewards of the righteous. The fate of the wicked is described in chap. lxii. The three places, earth, Sheol, and Abaddon, hold all those who are to rise to the judgment, both the righteous and the wicked. The author conceives of the earth as the place of the bodies of men, Sheol as the abode of the elect, and Abaddon as the prison of the lost. The elect rise from the dead, come forth from Sheol and receive their bodies from the earth in order to dwell on the earth, which has been transformed for them and which rejoices with them.

And the Lord of Spirits seated him on the throne of His glory, and the spirit of righteousness was poured out over him, and the word of his mouth slew all sinners, and all the unrighteous before his face were destroyed.[2] And there will stand up in that day all the kings and the mighty, and the exalted, and those who hold the earth, and they will see and recognize him how he sits on the throne of his glory, and righteousness is judged before him, and no lying word is spoken before him. Then will pain come upon them as on a woman in travail, who finds it grievous to bring forth when her son enters the mouth of the womb and she has pain in bringing forth. And one portion of them will look on the other, and they will be terrified, and their countenance will fall, and pain will seize them when they see that Son

---

[1] Ps. cxiv. 4–6.  [2] Is. xi. 4.

of Man sitting on the throne of his glory.[1] And the kings, the mighty ones and all who are lords of the earth will honor and bless and exalt him who was concealed, who rules over all. For the Son of Man was concealed before Him and the Most High preserved him before His power, and revealed him to the elect. And the congregation of the holy and elect will be planted and all the elect will stand before him in that day. And all the kings and the mighty, and the exalted and rulers of the earth will fall on their faces before him and supplicate him, and set their hopes on that Son of Man, and pray to him and implore mercy from him. Nevertheless, that Lord of Spirits will now force them to hastily depart from His face, and their faces will be filled with shame, and darkness will be heaped thereon. And the angels of punishment will receive them to take vengeance on them, because they abused His children and His elect. And they will be a spectacle for the righteous and for His elect. These will rejoice over them because the wrath of the Lord of Spirits rests upon them, and the sword of the Lord of Spirits is drunk with their blood; and the righteous and elect will be saved in that day, and will henceforth never more see the face of the sinners and the unrighteous. And the Lord of Spirits will dwell over them, and they will dwell with that Son of Man, and eat and lie down and rise up to all eternity. And the righteous and elect will have risen up from the ground, and cease having downcast looks, and will be clothed with the garments of glory; and these will be your garments, garments of life with the Lord of Spirits, and your garments will never grow old,[2] and your glory will never decrease before the Lord of Spirits. (lxii. 2–16.)

The Son of Man, in one passage, according to most MSS. gives place to the Son of the Woman. This seems to be nothing more than an unconscious substitution of a Christian copyist. But if the reading should be correct, in the context it can only be a synonym of Son of

---

[1] Charles seems to be right in preferring the reading of an earlier MS. to the great number of later MSS. followed by Dillmann and other writers. His explanation of the unconscious change to *Son of the Woman*, by Christian scribes, is reasonable. See his valuable notes, *Book of Enoch*, pp. 128, 164.

[2] Deut. viii. 4.

Man. The Messiah was not conceived as God or as angel, but as man, as woman-born. It is not likely that the author is thinking of the mother of Emmanuel.[1] It is impossible that he should have given that passage the interpretation of the evangelist Matthew.[2] It is possible that the writer had in mind the mother of the ruler from Bethlehem,[3] because he had this passage in mind in his reference to the pre-existence of the Messiah. But that passage gives us nothing more than a ruler woman-born. There is nothing in the text or context to imply the virgin birth of this Son of Man. The joy of the redeemed at the wrath of the Messiah against the wicked is certainly not a Christian doctrine. It can hardly be found in the Old Testament. But even our writer does not dwell upon these woes; he leaves them, after a moment, to set forth again the blessedness of the redeemed.

The Messianic idea of these Similitudes is remarkably pure and of the genuine Biblical type. It is based chiefly on the Apocalypse of Daniel and on the great prophet of the exile, with occasional references to Isaiah and Micah. God is the judge, but the Son of Man takes part in the judgment. The resurrection seems to be universal, and in this respect there is an advance upon Daniel. The rewards and punishments are in accordance with character and endure forever. The most important feature for our consideration is the new element introduced into the Messianic idea in the doctrine of the concealment of the Son of Man before his manifestation, and of his naming before the creation of the sun and the stars, teaching the pre-existence of the Son of Man before his manifestation. This is a closer approximation to the doctrine of the New Testament than anything

---

[1] Is. vii. 14.     [2] Matth. i. 22–25.     [3] Micah v. 2, 3.

we have seen in the Old Testament. This has led some scholars to think of Christian influence. But the doctrine is really intermediate between the Old Testament and the New Testament. It is only a legitimate unfolding of the ideal pre-existence of the ruler from Bethlehem given in Micah. There reference was made to the ancient promises. Here reference is made further back to the design of God. He was elected and named. The author advances another step on the basis of Daniel. The Son of Man came from heaven. He was concealed there until the time for his manifestation. The author thinks of this pre-existence and concealment as prior to the creation of the world. The manifestation of this concealed Son of Man is not for redemption, as a Christian would have conceived, but for the judgment of the world at the universal resurrection, as Daniel predicts; and so the point of view of the old covenant is not abandoned.

### THE MESSIAH OF THE PSALTER OF SOLOMON.

§ 7. *God will visit His people in glory, and gather Israel from all lands. Jerusalem will become glorious and holy. The Messiah, the son of David, is the hope of Israel. He will be lord and king, sinless and free from sickness, and endowed with wisdom, prudence, power, and righteousness. He will judge and will purify Jerusalem, and all nations will come to see His glory.*

The Psalter of Solomon[1] has a more spiritual concep-

---

[1] The Psalter of Solomon is assigned by Ewald and Weiffenbach to the 2d century B.C., and by Langen, Hausrath, Vernes, and Schürer to the time of Pompey (63-48 B.C.), by Ryle to 70-40 B.C. These eighteen Psalms, originally written in Hebrew, have been preserved only in the Greek version. See article by B. Pick on the *Psalter of Solomon*, in *Presbyterian Review*, 1883, pp. 775 seq.; H. E. Ryle, *The Psalms of Solomon*, 1891.

tion of the Messianic idea than the writings thus far considered. It moves in the lines of the ancient psalms and prophets. We have first to consider especially Ps. xi.

Blow ye the trumpet in Sion, the holy trumpet of Jubilee.[1]
Proclaim ye in Jerusalem with the voice of him that bringeth
    good tidings;[2]
That God hath had mercy upon Israel in his visitation of them.
Stand up on high, O Jerusalem, and behold thy children
Gathered from the East and the West together by the Lord.
From the North they come in the gladness of their God,
From distant isles, God gathered them,
High mountains He made low unto a plain to them.
The hills fled before their entering in,
The woods gave them shade as they passed by,
Every tree of sweet savour God made to spring up for them
That Israel might pass by in the visitation of the glory of their
    God.[3]
Put on, O Jerusalem, the garments of thy glory,
Prepare the robe of thy holiness,[4]
For God hath spoken good to Israel forever and ever.
May the Lord do what He has spoken concerning Israel and in
    Jerusalem,
May the Lord raise up Israel in the name of His glory.
The Lord's mercy be upon Israel forever and ever.

This beautiful piece of poetry is on the divine side of the Messianic idea, and is after the style of the great prophet of the exile. It shows no advance in conception and no departure from the Biblical ideals.

The Messiah, the son of David, is predicted in Ps. xvii. The Psalmist represents that God is the eternal king of Israel. The Lord is reminded of the promise to David respecting the everlasting dominion of his seed, in the style of the older Psalter.[5]

---

[1] Cf. Joel ii. 1.    [2] Cf. Is. xl. 9.    [3] Cf. Is. xl. 5.    [4] Cf. Is. lii. 1.
[5] Pss. lxxxix. 19 *seq*.; cxxxii. 11–18.

Behold, O Lord, and raise up for them their king,
A son of David for the time which thou knowest, O God,
To reign over Israel thy servant;
And gird him with strength to crush unjust rulers.
Purge Jerusalem from nations who are trampling her in ruin.
In wisdom, in righteousness, cast out sinners from the inheritance.
Grind to powder the pride of sinners as a potter's vessel,[1]
With a rod of iron break in pieces all their substance
Destroy lawless nations with the word of his mouth;[2]
So that at his threatening nations may flee from his face,
And convict sinners with the word of their heart.
And he will assemble a holy people whom he will lead in righteousness,
And will judge the tribes of a people sanctified by the Lord his God,
And he will not suffer unrighteousness to dwell in the midst of them.
And no man will dwell among them who knows evil.
For he will know them that they are all sons of their God,
And he will portion them out in their tribes upon the land.
And stranger and foreigner will not dwell with them any more.
He will judge peoples and nations in the wisdom of his righteousness.
And he will bring peoples of nations to serve him under his yoke;
And he will glorify the Lord in a place to be seen of all the earth,
And he will purify Jerusalem in sanctification as also it was from the beginning,
That nations may come from the end of the earth to see his glory,
Bearing as gifts her wearied sons,[3]
And to see the glory of the Lord with which God glorified her.[4]
And he himself a just king taught of God will be over them;
And there will be no unrighteousness in his days in the midst of them,

---

[1] Cf. Ps. ii. 9.   [2] Cf. Is. xi. 4.   [3] Cf. Is. lxvi. 18-20.   [4] Cf. Is. 60.

For all will be saints and their king the Lord Messiah,[1]
For he will not trust in horse, and chariot and bow,
Neither will he multiply for himself silver and gold for war,
And from his army[2] he will not gather hopes for the day of war.
The Lord, himself, his king is the hope of him that is strong in the hope of God.
And he will set all the nations before him in fear;
For he will smite the earth with the word of his mouth forever.[3]
He will bless the people of the Lord in wisdom with gladness,
And he himself will be pure from sin to rule over a great people,
To correct rulers and to remove sinners by strength of word.
And he will not be weak in his days because of his God;
For God made him capable by the Holy Spirit,[4]
And wise in counsel of prudence with strength and righteousness.
And the blessing of the Lord is with him in strength,
And he will not be weak, his hope is in the Lord.
And who can do anything against him?
He will be mighty in his doings and strong in the fear of God,
Feeding the flock of the Lord[5] in faith and righteousness;
And he will not suffer any to be weak among them in their pasture.
In holiness he will lead them all,
And there will be not among them haughtiness to exercise oppression among them.
This is the beauty of the king of Israel, which God knew,
To raise him over Israel, to train him.
His words are refined above the most precious gold.

---

[1] χριστὸς κύριος is probably on the basis of אדני of Ps. cx. 1 (κυρίῳ τῷ κυρίῳ μου lxx.); so apparently Ryle, who gives an admirable discussion of the several explanations. Schürer follows Ewald, Hilgenfeld, Wellhausen, W. Robertson Smith and others in regarding it as a mistranslation of משיח יהוה and renders *The Lord's Anointed*. There is no justification for the theory that it is a Christian interpolation. See Luke ii. 11 and p. 52.

[2] The MSS. have πολλοῖς which seems to give no good sense. Hilgenfeld and Fritzsche conjecture ὅπλοις; Ryle, πλοίοις.

[3] Cf. Is. xi. 4.

[4] Cf. Is. xi. 2; lxiii. 10.

[5] Cf. Mic. v. 4; Ezek. xxxiv. 23 *seq.*

In the assemblies he will judge peoples, the tribes of the sancti-
fied.
His words are as words of holy ones in the midst of sanctified
peoples.
Blessed are they who shall be born in those days,
To see the good things of Israel which God will accomplish in
the assembly of the tribes.
May God hasten his mercy toward Israel!
Deliver us from the defilement of profane foes!
The Lord Himself is our king for ever and ever.
(xvii. 23–51).

Psalm xviii. also briefly utters the Messianic petition:

May God purify Israel for the day of mercy in blessing,
For the day of election in the bringing up of His anointed.
Blessed are they who shall be born in those days,
To see the good things of the Lord which he will do for the
generation to come. (xviii. 6–7).

These psalms present the pure and genuine faith of Israel, mingling the Biblical elements without the intrusion of foreign ingredients, and entirely in the spirit of the ancient psalter and the prophets.[1]

---

[1] Ryle, *Psalms of Solomon*, pp. lvi, lvii, says that "the picture of the Messiah in our xviith Psalm marks the most notable advance in the conception of the Messianic expectation. Here for the first time in *Palestinian* literature, the idea of a *personal* Messiah is unequivocally stated." "In this representation of the human Messiah, perfect in holiness and taught of God, free from sin and wielding only the weapons of spiritual power, we find ourselves brought more nearly than in any other extant pre-Christian writing to the idealization of the 'Christ,' who was born into the world not half a century later than the time at which these psalms were written." This advance seems to me to be imaginary. Ryle apparently does not do justice to the Messianic ideals of the Old Testament. This psalm of Solomon combines a number of different conceptions of several prophets and psalmists: Pss. ii. 9; lxxxix. 19 *seq.*; cx. 1; cxxxii. 11–18; Is. xi. 2–4; lx.; lxvi. 18–20; Ezek. xxxiv. 23 *seq.*; Mic. v. 4; but so far as I can see it does not develop them; it makes no advance on them by the combinations; it does not give a single new feature to the Messianic king. The personal Messiah is as unequivocally stated in several of these passages upon which this Ps. xvii. is built, as in this psalm itself. It is just as easy to idealize the king of Ps. xvii. into a dynasty as it is to do so in these passages of the older psalmists and prophets. See Briggs' *Mess. Proph.*, pp. 42–46, 55, 59–61, 73, 110, 492 *seq.*

## THE HELLENISTIC MESSIANIC IDEA.

§ 8. *The Hellenistic spirit idealized the Messianic promise into the hope of better and holier times to be accomplished by God, in which righteousness will triumph, wickedness be destroyed, and the righteous receive their reward.*

The chief writing of the Hellenistic group is the Book of Wisdom.[1] We should not expect the Messianic idea in a writing of this class any more than in the Book of Proverbs after which it was modelled. However, there are two passages.

For God created man to be immortal,
And made him to be an image of his own eternity.
Nevertheless through envy of the devil came death into the world:
And they that are of his side do find it.
But the souls of the righteous are in the hand of God,
And there shall no torment touch them.
In the sight of the unwise they seemed to die:
And their departure is taken for misery,
And their going from us to be utter destruction;
But they are in peace.
For though they be punished in the sight of men,
Yet is their hope full of immortality.
And having been a little chastised, they shall be greatly rewarded:
For God proved them, and found them worthy for himself.
As gold in the furnace hath he tried them,
And received them as a burnt offering.

---

[1] The Book of Wisdom is a pseudepigraph bearing the name of Solomon; the name of Solomon being used because he was regarded as the great master of Hebrew wisdom. Solomon and wisdom had become synonymous terms, just as was the case with David and Psalms, and Moses and Laws. It was composed in the Greek language by an unknown author at an unknown date. It is usually assigned to the 2d century B.C.: (so, Deane and Bissell). But Grätz, Kuenen, Plumptre, and Farrar assign it to 38-40 A.D. Schürer puts it between Sirach and Philo.

And in the time of their visitation they shall shine,
And run to and fro like sparks among the stubble.
They shall judge the nations, and have dominion over the people,
And their Lord shall reign for ever.
They that put their trust in him shall understand the truth:
And such as be faithful in love shall abide with him:
For grace and mercy are to his saints, and he hath care for his elect.
But the ungodly shall be punished according to their own imaginations,
Which have neglected the righteous and forsaken the Lord.
(ii. 23—iii. 10).

For the hope of the ungodly is like dust that is blown away with the wind,
Like a thin froth that is driven away with the storm;
Like as the smoke which is dispersed here and there with a tempest,
And passeth away as the remembrance of a guest that tarrieth but a day—
But the righteous live for evermore;
Their reward also is with the Lord, and the care of them is with the Most High.
Therefore shall they receive a glorious kingdom,
And a beautiful crown from the Lord's hand:
For with his right hand shall he cover them,
And with his arm shall he protect them (v. 14–16)

These passages bring out the Greek conception of the immortality of the soul and attach to it the Hebrew conception of the blessedness of the righteous dead. They are in the hand of God, where no torment can touch them. They only seemed to die; they have a hope full of immortality; they live forevermore. They will be greatly rewarded, they will abide with the Lord forever. They will receive a glorious kingdom and a beautiful crown, and will judge the nations. The Lord will reign forever.

The Jewish philosopher Philo has no conception of a personal Messiah. He expects a restoration of Israelites to the holy land. They will be led by an appearance only visible to the redeemed.[1] This is thought of as a second Exodus in which they will be conducted by a theophany like the pillar of fire and cloud of the earlier Exodus. Philo also describes " a man coming forth leading a host and warring furiously. He will subdue great and populous nations, God sending that assistance which is suitable for pious men."[2] This passage seems to point to a personal Messiah, a victorious chieftain. But this interpretation is against the context; for Philo adds that "this assistance is an intrepid hardihood of soul and an irresistible strength of body, either of which things is formidable to the enemy, and if both qualities are united they are completely invincible." Philo is idealizing and thinking of the supremacy of true manhood, after the Greek fashion, and has no thought of a personal Messiah.

The Hellenistic Jewish Literature gives no trace of a personal Messiah; but represents merely the hope of the prevalence of righteousness in a more ethical and prosperous future.

## THE MESSIANIC IDEAS OF THE JEWISH SECTS.

§ 9. *The Sadducees had no other Messianic idea than the hope of the perpetuity of the temple and the nation. The Essenes sought to realize the kingdom of God in a community of saints by withdrawal from the world and purification of the flesh. The Pharisees of the School of Hillel were devout and ethical, and nearer the genuine Old Testament type. The School of Shammai looked for the res-*

---

[1] *De execrationibus*, §§ 8-9.   [2] *De praemis et poenis*, §§ 15-20.

*toration of the kingdom to Israel through divine intervention. The Zealots perpetuated the heroic spirit of the Maccabees and longed for a Messianic hero.*

The literature already considered reflects to a considerable extent the doctrines of the Jewish sects. But we have other sources of information to guide us in the interpretation of their doctrines.

The Sadducees were a priestly and an aristocratic party with little faith and less hope. It does not appear that they cherished the Messianic ideas of the ancient psalmists and prophets. Denying angels and spirits, the resurrection and the future life, they had no conception of a divine judgment at the end of the world or of a Messianic deliverer. They studied to maintain the temple-worship in its integrity, and to live on good terms with the Roman Empire.

The Essenes were a mystical sect. They had no hope of reform in public life. They sought communion with God by retirement from the world, and they strove for victory over evil by the purification of the flesh. They endeavored to prepare for the kingdom of God by the organization of a community of saints. It does not appear that they had any other Messianic idea.

The Messianic idea lived and was fruitful among the sects of the Pharisees. The School of Hillel was learned and moderate, pious and ethical in its tendencies. It troubled itself but little with political affairs. It was ever opposed to the rebellions against the Roman Empire. To this tendency in Israel we may ascribe such productions as the Psalter of Solomon and the Similitudes of the Book of Enoch.

The School of Shammai was stern, severe, exclusive, and scholastic in tendency. Dogmatic rules prevailed over ethical principles. They ever indulged in political scheming, although hesitating to put their principles in practice. To men of this school we may attribute much of the Palestinian literature that expresses its Messianic hopes for a more glorious future for Israel in the Holy Land, with little or no thought of a Messiah.

The party of the Zealots was a more popular sect of the Pharisees. These perpetuated the spirit of the Maccabean times. They were dissatisfied with the foreign yoke and were ever ripe for rebellion in order to bring in the kingdom of God. Whenever we see this party in action we find alongside of it Pharisees of the school of Shammai. To this party of the people a personal Messiah, a Son of David, a heroic king, was essential, and they were ever ready to follow any one claiming to be a prophet or a Messiah of their sort. Judas, the Gaulonite, in his early rebellion was supported by Zadok, of the School of Shammai.

## CHAPTER II.

### THE MESSIANIC IDEA OF THE FORERUNNERS OF JESUS.

NOTWITHSTANDING the Messianic idea had been so generally deflected from its normal course of development by the various religious parties in Israel subsequent to the Maccabean revolution, there were yet not a few pious souls, both among the learned of the school of Hillel and among the people, who clung with comparative simplicity and purity to the hope of a personal Messiah and of a moral and spiritual redemption through him. A number of these are brought into view who were waiting and looking for the consolation of Israel— such as Zachariah the priest, Joseph and Mary, Simeon and Anna.

These appear in the earlier chapters of the Gospel of Luke. A single incident is reported in the first chapter of the Gospel of Matthew. The Gospel of Mark, which, apart from a few later additions, is the earliest of our gospels, and which presents the earliest account of the life of Jesus, knows nothing of them. The original Aramaic Gospel of Matthew, the Logia,[1] did not include them; for they are not in those portions of the present Gospel of Matthew and the Gospel of Luke, which derived their material from the Logia. They are in

---

[1] McGiffert's *Eusebius*, pp. 152, 153, 173.

those portions of Luke and Matthew which were derived from other sources than the originals of Mark and Matthew. This material is also in the form of poetry embedded in prose narrative. This poetry is of the same kind as the poetry of the Old Testament. It has the same principles of parallelism and measurement of the lines by the beats of the accent, or by the number of separate words. Early Syriac poetry conformed to the same principles.[1] This poetry was translated from Aramaic originals, and was doubtless written when translated by Luke. The Greek translation in some cases destroys the symmetry of the lines of Aramaic poetry, obscures their measurement, and mars their parallelism.[2] It is probable that the prose which encompasses this poetry comes from the authors of the Gospels, the poetry from other and probably several different authors.[3] Therefore we are not to look for an earlier written Gospel of the Infancy of Jesus, but are to think of a number of early Christian poems with reference to that infancy from which the author of our Gospel made a selection. There are many other stories of the infancy of Jesus in the apocryphal gospels, some of which may be genuine, but the most of them appear to be legendary.

These songs, which have been selected for use in the Gospel of Luke, doubtless represent reflection upon these events by Christian poets, who put in the mouths of the angels, the mothers and the fathers, the poems which they composed.[4] But the inspired author of the

---

[1] Grimme, Z. D. M. G., xlvii. s. 276 seq.

[2] The same characteristics appear in the translations of the poetry of the Old Testament which frequently occur in the writings of the New Testament.

[3] The poetry has indeed different measurement of lines. See pp. 47, 57.

[4] It could not have been otherwise unless there had been a stenographer or reporter at hand on each occasion, which the circumstances narrated in the context make impossible. Whether the original authors were guided by divine

Gospel vouches for their propriety and for their essential conformity to truth and fact. We may divide this material into three sections: 1. The Songs of Annunciation. 2. The Songs of the Mothers. 3. The Songs of the Fathers.

### THE SONGS OF ANNUNCIATION.

*§ 10. John will be born of Elizabeth and be filled with the Holy Spirit from his birth. As a second Elijah he will prepare a people for the Lord. Jesus will be conceived and born of the Virgin Mary in theophanies. He will be called the Son of God. He will be the Messiah, and will reign on the throne of his father David forever; and as Saviour he will save his people from their sins.*

The new dispensation was introduced, according to the Gospel of Luke, by angelic appearances making annunciations.

### *The Annunciation to Zacharias.*

Gabriel the archangel comes first to Zacharias the priest, and brings him a divine message while he is ministering in the holy place of the temple, at the golden altar of incense. He was alone in that darkened room, lighted only by the holy lamps, enveloped in the clouds of incense that he was offering to give efficacy to the prayers of the people worshipping in the courts without. In that solemn hour of mediation the angel Gabriel comes from the immediate presence of God to bring him the glad tidings of the birth and ministry of the

---

inspiration or not it matters little. If the author of the canonical Luke was inspired, he is responsible for what he used as well as what he composed, and his inspiration covers their selection as appropriate and as sufficiently accurate for the purpose.

herald of the Messiah. The promise assumes the trimeter movement of Hebrew poetry.

I.

Fear not, Zacharias:
Because thy supplication is heard,
And thy wife Elizabeth shall bear thee a son,[1]
And thou shalt call his name John.
And thou shalt have joy and gladness;
And many shall rejoice at his birth.
For he shall be great in the sight of the Lord,
He shall drink no wine nor strong drink;
And he shall be filled with the Holy Spirit,
Even from his mother's womb.

II.

And many of the children of Israel
Shall he turn unto the Lord their God.
And he shall go before His face
In the spirit and power of Elijah,
To turn the hearts of the fathers to the children,
And the disobedient *to walk* in the wisdom of the just;
To make ready for the Lord a people prepared [for him].
(Luke i. 13-17).

The fear that sprang up in the heart of Zacharias when Gabriel appeared was stilled by the first word. The supplication that was heard was not the public prayer that he was now bringing before God with the efficacious incense, but his private prayers for a child, and possibly also for the advent of the Messiah. The child is to fulfil the prophecy of Malachi:[2] "Behold, I am about to send you Elijah the prophet, before the coming of the great and terrible day of Yahweh. And

---

[1] Such lines in the Greek betray an Aramaic original.

[2] We must interpret κύριος in accordance with the prediction in Malachi as referring to God.

he will turn the heart of the fathers to the children, and the heart of the children to their fathers; lest I come and smite the earth with a ban."[1] John is to become a second Elijah. As such he is to be a Nazarite[2] like Samuel, the founder of the prophetic order. He is to live a life of severity and austerity, in keeping with a ministry whose aim was to call Israel to repentance and prepare thereby for the advent of God. For this purpose he is to be endowed with the Holy Spirit. The Holy Spirit is not to come down upon him and take violent possession of him, as he did in the case of the ancient judges, the saviours of God's people. The Holy Spirit is to enter into him and dwell in him,—fill him and fill all his ministry. He is to be filled with the Spirit even from his mother's womb,—from the moment of birth on through all his life and activity as the herald of God. This will make him great,—the greatest of those born under the Old Testament,[3] and successful in his work of making the last preparation as the immediate precursor of the Messiah.

### *The Annunciation to Mary.*

Gabriel also announces to Mary the birth of the Messiah. The Blessed Virgin was residing in Nazareth of Galilee, betrothed to Joseph of the royal line of David, the heir of the Messianic promises of the Old Testament. The time for marriage had not yet come. God had a higher appointment for her to fulfil as the virgin mother of the Messiah. The annunciation is made by the angel in three little pieces of trimeter poetry, which have become somewhat obscured by the Greek translation. At first Gabriel comes with

---

[1] Mal. iv. 5, 6.  [2] Num. vi. 1-21.  [3] Luke vii. 28.

a salutation (the Ave Maria) in the form of a distich:

> Hail, thou that art endued with grace,
> The Lord is with thee.¹ (Luke i. 28).

Mary seems to have been disturbed by the coming of the angel. His salutation and its mysterious language must have filled her with surprise and excited her emotions to the utmost. The angel in his second piece soothes her fears, and delivers the message from God in a piece of ten lines.

Fear not, Mary:
For thou hast found grace² with God.
And behold, thou shalt conceive in thy womb, and bring forth a son,³
And shalt call his name Jesus.
He shall be great,
And shall be called the Son of the Most High:
And the Lord God shall give unto him
The throne of his father David:
And he will reign over the house of Jacob for ever;
And of his kingdom there will be no end. (Luke i. 30-33.)

This annunciation contains two references to predictions of the Old Testament. The name of the child, "Son of the Most High," which reappears as "Son of God" in the third word (v. 35), brings to mind:

> Let me tell of a decree of Yahweh.
> He said unto me, "Thou art my son,
> I, to-day, have begotten thee." (Ps. ii. 7.)

---

¹ The rendering of the margin "endued with grace" is preferable to the text of the Revised Version, "highly favoured"; for it brings out the full import as well as the usual meaning of the word. The phrase "the Lord is with thee" is a familiar one in the prophetic historians of the Old Testament.

² We should give χάρις and its verb their technical meaning, of *grace*, as in R. V. margin, and not obscure their full significance by "*favour*" and "*highly favoured*" of the A. V.

³ The length of the third line is due to the Greek translation. It would be in better proportion in Aramaic.

The promise that he will be enthroned on the throne of David, have an everlasting kingdom, and reign over the house of Jacob forever, distinctly presents him as the Messianic King of the Old Testament. The promise of an everlasting kingdom was made to David in the prophecy of Nathan.¹ This Messianic King is described in Isaiah.

For a child is born to us, a son is given to us; and the rule is upon his shoulder,
And his name is called Wonderful Counsellor, Divine Hero, Distributor of Spoils, Prince of Peace;
For the increase of his rule and for peace without end upon the throne of David and over his kingdom,
To establish it, and to confirm it in justice and righteousness, from henceforth, even for ever.² (Isaiah ix. 6-7.)

This passage was, doubtless, in the mind of the angel, and underlies the thought of the song. The name "Jesus" is not explained in the context of Luke. The explanation is given in the annunciation to Joseph.

Joseph, thou son of David, fear not to take unto thee Mary thy wife;
For that which is begotten ³ in her is of the Holy Spirit.
And she shall bring forth a son, and thou shalt call his name Jesus;⁴
For it is he that shall save his people from their sins.
(Matt. i. 20-21.)

The annunciation fills the Virgin with surprise and amazement. She was not married. How could she have a son at all, not to speak of giving birth to the heir

---

¹ 2 Sam. vii. 11-16.
² See Briggs' *Messianic Prophecy*, p. 200.
³ The R. V. margin is to be preferred.
⁴ יהושע = Ἰησοῦς = *Yahweh is salvation*.

of David? The angel explains the mystery of the Divine purpose in a third word.

> The Holy Spirit shall come upon thee,
> And the power of the Most High shall overshadow thee:
> Wherefore also that holy thing that is to be born,
> Shall be called the Son of God:[1]
> And behold Elizabeth thy kinswoman,
> She also hath conceived a son in her old age:
> And this is the sixth month with her that was called barren;
> For no word from God shall be void of power.　(Luke i. 35–37.)

This song of the angel begins with the promise of the Holy Spirit, concludes with the assurance that the divine word is all-powerful, and in the midst points to Elizabeth as a sign of the power of God. Elizabeth, the aged and barren wife of Zacharias, has already conceived by the power of God. As in the history of Sarah the wife of Abraham, the barrenness of Elizabeth has been transformed by the power of God into fertility. This will be a sign that God will use the almighty power of his Spirit in enabling Mary to give birth to the Messiah. That which is to be born of her is called holy, because it was to be born of the Holy Spirit. This word of the angel may be regarded as in accord with the prediction of Isaiah:

> And a twig will come forth from the stump of Jesse,
> And a shoot from his roots will be fruitful;
> And the spirit of Yahweh will rest upon him,
> The spirit of wisdom and understanding,
> The spirit of counsel and might,
> The spirit of knowledge and the fear of Yahweh.
> 　(Isa. xi. 1–2.)

---

[1] The poetical structure decides in favor of the A. V. and against R. V. In the third and fourth lines, the Revised Version renders one way in the text and another way in the margin. The rendering I have given is intermediate between them.

The Messianic King was to be endowed with the fulness of the Divine Spirit. This third word of the angel carries the endowment with the Spirit back of the official life into the origin of life itself. It proclaims that the Spirit of God will take possession of the mother of the Messiah, so that she will become a mother by the power of God and the energy of his Spirit. The Messiah will enter the world conceived by the power of the Holy Spirit and born of the Holy Spirit. He will be holy from his conception onwards. Therefore he will be called the Son of God, because of his native holiness, and because of the divine life that begot him as the Messiah.

The virgin conception of Jesus, as here announced by the archangel, is not to be interpreted as if it were a miracle in violation of the laws of nature; but rather as brought about by God Himself present in theophany. The conception of Jesus in the womb of the Virgin Mary differs from all other conceptions of children by their mothers in that there was no human father. The place of the human father was taken by God Himself; not that God appeared in theophany in human form to beget the child after the analogy of the mythologies of the ethnic religions; but that God in a theophany in an extraordinary way, unrevealed to us, and without violation of the laws of maternity, impregnates the Virgin Mary with the holy seed. The words of the angel imply a theophanic presence; for though it might be urged that the coming of the Spirit upon her was an invisible coming after the analogy of many passages of the Old Testament; yet the parallel statement that the divine power overshadowed her cannot be so interpreted. For it not only in itself represents that the divine power covered her with a shadow; but this is to be thought of after the uniform usage of Scripture as a bright cloud of glory, hovering over her, resting upon her, or enveloping her with a halo of divinity, in the moment when the divine energy enabled her to conceive the child Jesus.[1]

This representation is based upon the well-known pillar of cloud lighted with divine glory, of the story of the Exodus,[2] and of the erection of Solomon's temple.[3] The entrance of God into his tabernacle and temple to dwell there in a theophanic cloud would naturally suggest that the entrance of the divine life into the virgin's womb to dwell there, would be in the same form of theophanic cloud. The earthly origin of Jesus in the virgin's womb would thus begin with a theophany, just as a theophany accompanies his birth,[4] his baptism,[5] his transfiguration,[6] his crucifixion,[7] and his resurrection.[8]

This annunciation represents the conception of Jesus as due to a theophany. It does not state the doctrine of his pre-existence; although that doctrine is a legitimate inference. It represents an early stage of New Testament Christology. It does not go a step beyond the Paulinism of the epistles to the Corinthians.[9] It

---

[1] The same verb ἐπισκιάζω is used in the LXX. of Ex. xl. 35, with reference to the cloud of glory of the Tabernacle, and also to the theophanic cloud of the Transfiguration in Matth. xvii. 5; Mark ix. 7; Luke ix. 34. The cloud of glory is always connected with God, and implies more than the agency of the divine Spirit.

[2] Ex. xl. 34-35; Nu. ix. 15. [3] 1 K. viii. 10.
[4] See p. 51. [5] See p. 75. [6] See p. 100. [7] See p. 128. [8] See p. 130.
[9] This annunciation knows nothing of the incarnation of the Logos, of the prologue of the Gospel of John, i. 14; or of the Son of Man from heaven, of the Gospel itself, John iii. 13; or of the effulgence of the glory of God, of Heb. i. 3; or of the first-born of all creation of Col. i. 15; or of the epiphany of the Messiah of 2 Tim. i. 10: or of the Kenosis of Phil. ii. 6; but represents an earlier Christology than any of these writings. Holzmann, *Die Synoptiker*, s. 532, truly states that Rom. i. 3, viii. 3, Gal. iv. 4, do not imply a virgin birth, but may be interpreted of a birth of Joseph and Mary, in accordance with the reference to Joseph as the father of Jesus in the primitive gospels. But as Schmiedel shows (*Die*

implies nothing more than the sending in birth taught by the epistles to the Galatians and to the Romans. It is really a more primitive and more simple christological conception.

The Virgin, in meekness and humility, yields to the heavenly message in a word that assumes the poetic form as a responsive echo from her heart.

> Behold, the handmaid of the Lord;
> Be it unto me according to thy word. (Luke i. 38.)

### *The Annunciation to the Shepherds.*

A third annunciation is reported in the Gospel of Luke. Shepherds were watching their flocks at night on the hillsides near Bethlehem. "The glory of the Lord shone round about them."[1] This glory is the light in which the Lord manifests himself in theophany. It is a theophany to attend the birth of the Messiah, as we have already had a theophany at his conception in the womb of the Virgin. Such theophanies are frequently mentioned in the story of the Exodus.[2] Out of the midst of the heavenly light an angel of the Lord ap-

---

*Briefe an die Thess. und an die Korinther*, s. 168) the epistles to the Corinthians teach an early stage of the doctrine of the pre-existence of Jesus in the second Adam from heaven, 1 Cor. xv. 45-47; the head of humanity, 1 Cor. xi. 3; and especially in the self-impoverishment of the rich Messiah, 2 Cor. viii. 9. This more primitive form of the doctrine of the pre-existence of the Messiah is still in advance of the doctrine of this annunciation. This annunciation of a theophanic birth is really a simpler conception and one more in accordance with the representations of the Old Testament, than the sending of the Son of God when born of a woman, of Rom. viii. 3; Gal. iv. 4. It is true that none of these passages teach a virgin conception and birth; but they teach or imply more than the virgin birth, namely, the pre-existence of the Messiah before his entrance into the world. All these will come into consideration in their proper place in this work.

[1] Luke ii. 9.
[2] Exod. xvi. 10; xxiv. 16-17; Lev. ix. 23; Num. xiv. 10; xvi. 19.

peared and stood by them. He made the annunciation of the birth of the Messiah.

> Be not afraid,
> For behold, I bring you good tidings of great joy
> Which shall be to all the people:
> For a Saviour[1] is born unto you to-day,
> Who is Messiah, Lord,[2] in the city of David:[3]
> And this is the sign unto you;
> Ye shall find a babe wrapped in swaddling clothes,
> And lying in a manger. (Luke ii. 10–12.)

This song of the angel is immediately followed by a refrain in two lines sung by a heavenly choir, "a multitude of the heavenly host."

> Glory to God in the highest,
> And on earth, peace among men in whom he is well pleased.[4] (Luke ii. 14.)

This song of the angel begins, as the other songs, with calming the fears of the agitated shepherds. The message is for them as representatives of Bethlehem, the ancient shepherd city whence David had gone forth to be the shepherd of Israel. But the glad tidings were for all the people; and it was their high calling to take up the angelic message and proclaim it as the first messengers, to Bethlehem, Jerusalem, and the cities of Judah, that the Messiah had come. The Messiah now born in Bethlehem, lying as a babe in the manger,

---

[1] σωτήρ = מוֹשִׁיעַ cf. יְהוֹשׁוּעַ above.

[2] χριστὸς κύριος cf. Psalter of Solomon, xvii. 4, see p. 34; χριστὸν βασιλέα, Luke xxiii. 2; κύριον καὶ χριστὸν, Acts ii. 36.

[3] The order of the Greek and the structure of the lines of the poem force to this rendering. The R. V. disregards both of these guides.

[4] εὐδοκία = רָצוֹן acceptance with God. Jesus at his baptism was the Son of God in whom He was well-pleased εὐδόκησα, Matt. iii. 17; Luke iii. 22.

wrapped in swaddling clothes, was Lord and Saviour. The Messiah was Lord, in accordance with the Psalter:

Utterance of Yahweh to my Lord: Sit enthroned at my right hand
Till I make thine enemies a stool for thy feet:
The rod of thy strength Yahweh sendeth out of Zion:
Rule in the midst of thine enemies. (Ps. cx. 1, 2.)

The Messiah was born in the city of David, but not in the palace of David. He was born of the royal line, but of a house that had been dethroned, and that had now so long lived in obscurity that the heir attracted little, if any, attention. But the promises of God are sure, even if long delayed as to their realization. This babe is the son and heir of David, and a heavenly proclamation and chorus of angels assure them that he is the Lord, the long expected Messiah. He is to be a Saviour. This is an attribute of the Messiah throughout. He was usually looked for as a national Saviour, to subdue all enemies, and reign on the throne of David as King and Lord. The deeper meaning of Saviour these shepherds could hardly understand as yet. The chorus is a proclamation of peace to the world. It was one of the chief features of the Messiah's work, to establish peace, according to the Prophets.

> And I will cut off the chariot from Ephraim,
> And the horse from Jerusalem
> And the battle-bow will be cut off;
> And he will speak peace to the nations
> And his rule will be from sea to sea,
> And from the river unto the ends of the earth. (Zech. ix. 10.)

Isaiah names the Messianic King "Prince of Peace."[1]

---

[1] Is. ix. 6.

But probably it is the prediction of Micah which is chiefly in mind here.

And thou Bethlehem Ephrathah,
Little to be among the thousands of Judah,
Out of thee will come forth for me
One who is to become ruler in Israel,
Whose goings forth are from of old, from ancient days.
. . . . . . . . . .
And he will stand and act as shepherd in the strength of Yahweh,
In the majesty of the name of Yahweh his God,
And they will abide ; for now he will become great
Unto the ends of the earth.
And this one will be Peace. (Micah v. 2, 4.)

The Messiah is the Saviour, and his mission is one of peace. But there can be no peace to the wicked. Peace is for those who recognize Jesus as the Messiah, accept his salvation, and gladly submit in love to his heavenly dominion. All who enter the kingdom of the Messiah, and love and serve him as King, Saviour, and Lord, are well pleasing to God, and enjoy the beatitude of heavenly peace.

### THE SONGS OF THE MOTHERS.

§ 11. *The Virgin Mary is to be the mother of the Lord, Messiah, and is to be pronounced blessed by all nations. God remembers the mercy promised to the seed of the patriarchs.*

The spirit of prophecy entered into the mothers of the Messianic babes, and prophecy in the form of sacred song burst from their lips. The first to sing the songs of the new covenant was the mother of the herald.

### *The Song of Elizabeth.*

The Virgin Mary, in response to the angelic message, departed from Nazareth of Galilee and went to visit her kinswoman Elizabeth in the hill country of Judah. The meeting of the mothers was enveloped in a halo of sanctity and glory by the presence and power of the Holy Spirit, who took possession of both of them, filled their hearts with joy, and gave them utterance in sacred song.

Elizabeth lifted up her voice with a loud cry, and said:

> Blessed art thou among women,
> And blessed is the fruit of thy womb.
> And whence is this to me,
> That the mother of my Lord[1] should come to me?
> For behold, when the voice of thy salutation
> Came into mine ears,
> The babe leaped for joy in my womb.
> And blessed is she who believed
> That there will be a fulfillment
> To those things spoken to her from the Lord.[2] (Luke i. 42–45.)

Elizabeth, under the influence of the Divine Spirit, here sees the Virgin already the mother of the Messiah, and on that account the mother of the lord and king of her babe and of herself. The mother of the Messiah now in her presence is a pledge of his advent and all the joy and blessedness involved therein. The faith of the Virgin is praised, assurance is given her that the word of the angel will be fulfilled, and, in view of that fulfillment, she is recognized as the most blessed among women.

### The Song of the Virgin.

Under the influence of the Divine Spirit the Virgin at once responds to the song of Elizabeth.[3]

---

[1] This as the κύριος above is in the sense of the אֲדֹנִי Ps. cx. 1.

[2] The lines of this piece of poetry are more obscure than usual in the Greek. A re-translation into the original removes the difficulties for the most part and makes the poetry evident.

[3] This song has ever been used in the Christian Church. It is called in the Latin Church the *Magnificat*, in accordance with the custom to name pieces after the word that begins them. *Magnificat* was the first word of the piece in the ancient Latin version of it.

This song of the Virgin is full of the spirit and language of the song of Hannah,[1] the mother of Samuel. It must have been a favorite hymn with Mary. Doubtless the similarity of situation and circumstance recalled its language to her mind and heart.[2]

My soul magnifieth the Lord,
And my spirit doth rejoice in God my Saviour.
For he looked upon the low estate of his handmaiden:
For behold from henceforth all generations shall call me blessed.
For the Almighty doth great things for me;
And Holy is his name.
And his mercy is unto generations of generations
On them that fear him.
He doth work strength with his arm;
He doth scatter the proud in the imagination of their heart.
He doth put down princes from thrones,
And doth exalt the lowly.
The hungry he doth fill with good things,
And the rich he doth send empty away.
He doth help Israel his servant,
That he might remember mercy,
As he spake unto our fathers,
Toward Abraham and his seed forever.  (Luke i. 46-55.)

Mary conceives of redemption after the more ethical manner of the song of Hannah and the more personal relations of the Psalmists.

### THE SONGS OF THE FATHERS.

§ 12. *God remembers his holy covenant, visits and works redemption, and raises up a horn of salvation in the house of David. John is the prophet to prepare the way of the Lord, who will come as a day-spring to guide in the*

---

[1] Sam. ii. 1-10.
[2] See Briggs' *Messianic Prophecy*, pp. 124, 125, for a translation of the song of Hannah.

*way of peace. Jesus will be for the rise and fall of many, a sign to be spoken against.*

The priest Zacharias had remained dumb from the time of the annunciation in the temple until the birth of his son. On the day of the circumcision of the child who was to herald the Advent, and in connection with giving the name of the boy, " his mouth was opened immediately, and his tongue loosed, and he spake, blessing God."[1]

## *The Song of Zacharias.*

The Holy Spirit entered into Zacharias and filled him with the spirit of prophecy.[2]

### I.

Blessed be the Lord, the God of Israel,
For he doth visit, and work redemption for his people,
And raise up a horn of salvation for us, in the house of his servant David.
As he spake by the mouth of the holy ones, his prophets, of old ;[3]
Salvation from our enemies, and from the hand of all that hate us ;
To show mercy toward our fathers, and to remember his holy covenant ;
The oath which he sware, unto Abraham our father,

---

[1] Luke i 64.

[2] He gave utterance to a hymn which has been ever used in the Christian Church as the *Benedictus*. This hymn is difficult to arrange in its lines and strophes because of the changes that have been made in translation, and authorities are somewhat divided. It seems to me that the original was a poem of the pentameter movement. The lines are longer than those in the songs of the angels and the songs of the mothers, and are like the pentameter pieces of the Old Testament, each line having a cæsura, so that the second half of the line is complementary to the first half. Some divide this into five stropes, *e. g.*, vers. 68, 69 ; 70–72 ; 73–75 ; 76, 77 ; 78, 79. See Holzmann, *Die Synoptiker*, s. 36. But it seems better to divide it into two strophes.

[3] The line is not clear in the Greek. There must have been an Aramaic original.

To grant unto us to be without fear, being delivered out of the hand of our enemies,
To serve him in holiness and righteousness before him all our days.[1]

### II.

And thou, child, shalt be called the prophet of the Most High;
For thou shalt go before the face of the Lord, to make ready his ways;
To give knowledge of salvation unto his people, in the remission of their sins,
Because of the tender mercy of our God, whereby the day-spring from on high hath visited us,
To shine upon them that sit in darkness, and in the shadow of death;
To guide our feet into the way of peace. (Luke i. 68–79.)

The first strophe blesses God for the fulfilment of the promise to David, and looks for the fulfilment of the Abrahamic covenant; and the second strophe predicts the ministry of his son John as the herald of the Messiah. Zacharias weaves together the predictions of a number of the psalms and prophets.

In the first strophe [2] Zacharias begins with a line from the doxologies of the Psalter. He then, thinking of the covenant with David, uses the language of the Psalmist:

> There will I cause a horn to sprout for David,
> I have prepared a lamp for mine anointed
> His enemies will I clothe with shame;
> But upon him his crown will be brilliant.
>
> (Ps. cxxxii. 17, 18.)

---

[1] The arrangement of lines in this strophe differs somewhat from that given in the Revised Version. The Revised Version breaks up several pentameters into two lines each. The chief difference is that the Revised Version gives three lines for lines 5 and 6 of this strophe. It attaches the adverb "without fear" to the verb "serve." But the Greek text of Westcott and Hort, which I follow, gives this adverb in the midst of the previous line. This gives a better poetical movement, and makes the cæsuras evident in both lines.

[2] Pss. lxxii. 18; cvi. 48.

The visitation is in answer to the prayer:

O God, Sabaoth turn now, look from heaven,
See and visit this vine;
And protect that which thy right hand planted
And be over the branch thou hast strengthened for thyself.
(Ps. lxxx. 14, 15.)

He then sees the fulfilment of the Abrahamic covenant, which pervades the Old Testament like a golden thread upon which many promises and predictions are hung. The promise was made to Abraham before he migrated to the promised land. It was the charter of his inheritance.

And I will make thee a great nation.
And I will bless thee and make thy name great;
Therefore be thou a blessing,
And I will bless those blessing thee;
And those making light of thee shall I curse:
And all the clans of the earth will bless themselves with thee.
(Gen. xii. 1-3.)

This promise was taken up into a covenant, and sealed with the sign of circumcision,[1] and finally confirmed by a divine oath.

The second strophe is a prediction of the work of his child as a herald of the Messiah. Several passages of the Old Testament give him the basis for his hopes. As the prophet of the Most High, going before the face of the Lord, and preparing his way, he is to fulfil the predictions of Isaiah and Malachi:

Hark! one proclaiming, in the wilderness, Clear the way of Yahweh,
Level in the desert a highway for our God.

---

[1] Gen. xvii.; xxii. 15-18.

Let every valley be lifted up, and every mountain and hill be depressed,
And the crooked place become straight, and the rugged place a plain,
And the glory of Yahweh will be revealed, and all flesh will see it together.  (Is. xl. 3–5.)[1]

The day-spring has been referred by some to the branch[2] of Old Testament prophecy, because branch is rendered in the LXX. Version by the same Greek word that is given in our text and translated here "day-spring." But the original of our song was in the Aramaic language, and the subsequent context favors the more natural reference to the springing up of the light of the sun.[3] The last two lines, referring to the Messiah as the great light, are based upon Isaiah:

The people that walk in darkness do see a great light;
Those dwelling in a land of dense darkness, light doth shine upon them.  (Isa. ix. 2.)

In the context of Isaiah the great light comes from the person of the Messiah—the Prince of Peace—and so, in the song of Zacharias, the shining of the light guides into the way of peace.

## *The Song of Simeon.*

In accordance with the Mosaic law, Jesus, as the first-born son, was presented before God in the temple at Jerusalem.[4] An aged father in Israel is awaiting the advent of the Messiah, having the witness of the Divine Spirit that he will see him before departing this life. The aged Simeon, representing the best type of Old Testament piety, standing on the heights of Messianic

---
[1] Comp. Mal. iii. 1–iv. 5.    [2] Jer. xxiii. 5; xxxiii. 15; Zech. iii. 8.
[3] As in Mal. iv. 2; comp. Is. lx. 1.
[4] Ex. xiii. 12; xxii. 29; Num. xviii. 15, 16.

expectation, receives the child Jesus into his arms, in the court of the temple, and, under the inspiration of prophecy, sings a song of praise and a song of sorrow.[1]

### I.

Now lettest thou thy servant depart, O Lord,
According to thy word, in peace;
For mine eyes have seen thy salvation,
Which thou hast prepared before the face of all peoples;
A light for revelation to the Gentiles,
And the glory of thy people Israel.

### II.

Behold this one is set for the falling,
And the rising of many in Israel;
And for a sign which is spoken against;
Yea, and a sword shall pierce through thine own soul;
That thoughts out of many hearts may be revealed.
(Luke ii. 29–35.)

The Messianic salvation is the theme of the first strophe. This is seen in its double aspect, a light for revelation to the nations of the world, and the glory of Israel. Simeon doubtless had in mind the prophecies of the second Isaiah.

I, Yahweh, have called thee in righteousness,
In order to hold thine hand and to keep thee,
And to give thee for a covenant of the people, for a light of the
    nations. (xlii. 6.)

It is too light a thing that thou shouldest be my servant
To raise up the tribes of Jacob,
And to restore the preserved of Israel;
I will therefore give thee for a light to the nations,
To become my salvation unto the end of the earth. (xlix. 6.)

---

[1] The first part of his song is the *Nunc Dimittis*, so called from the first words of the Latin translation. This has ever been used in the liturgical service of the Christian Church. The second part of the song is usually given as prose in the versions:

I will greatly rejoice in Yahweh,
Let my soul be joyful in my God;
For he hath clothed me with the garments of salvation,
He hath covered me with the robe of righteousness,
As a bridegroom putteth on a priest's turban,
And as a bride adorned herself with her jewels.
For as the earth bringeth forth her increase,
And as a garden causeth that which is planted in it to spring forth,
So will Yahweh cause righteousness to spring forth,
And praise before all nations. (lxi. 10, 11.)

The second strophe unfolds the salvation of the Messiah in the testing that it makes, and in the sorrow that will be involved, especially to the mother. Here Simeon catches a glimpse of the suffering Messiah as the one who takes away the sin of the world. It was indeed only natural that the predictions of the second Isaiah as to the salvation of the Messianic servant, which were at the bases of his song, should lead the mind up to the suffering Messiah who was the centre of them all. The sword that pierces the Virgin's soul was the agony that she was to experience in the passion of our Lord when she saw him

Despised, and forsaken of men;
A man of sorrows, and acquainted with grief;
And as one before whom there is a hiding of the face,
Despised, and we regarded him not!

. . . . . . . .

But he was one pierced because of our transgressions,
Crushed because of our iniquities;
The chastisement for our peace was upon him;
And by his stripes there is healing for us.

. . . . . . . .

And among his contemporaries who was considering,
That he was cut off from the land of the living,
Because of the transgression of my people he had the blow?

With the wicked his grave was assigned,
And with the rich in his martyr death ;
Although he had done no violence,
And there was no deceit in his mouth. (Is. liii. 3, 5, 8–9.)

It seems also that Simeon had in mind the test stone of the first Isaiah.¹

Thus a strain of sorrow mingles with the thanksgiving of the departing saint who represents so well the departing dispensation of the old covenant. It is said that Anna also praised God and spoke of the child Jesus to all who were looking for redemption in Jerusalem.²

## THE HERALD OF THE MESSIAH.

*§ 13. John the Baptist heralded the advent of God and his kingdom. He taught that Jesus was mightier than himself; that he would baptize with the Holy Spirit and with fire, and would wield the fan of judgment on his threshing floor. Jesus was the lamb of God that taketh away the sin of the world.*

Some thirty years after the events underlying these songs, John the Baptist appeared in the wilderness of Judea declaring that the kingdom of God was at hand, that he was the herald of the Messiah, and instituting the baptism of repentance unto the remission of sins. The four evangelists agree in giving an account of this introductory ministry of the Baptist. It belongs to the earliest Christian tradition and the earliest Gospels. Their reports are essentially the same as to the main features, but each of them has material not contained in the others. The new institution of the baptism of repentance is common to them all. The preacher called the people to repentance as the true preparation for

---

¹ Is. xxviii. 16. ² Luke ii. 38.

their God; he baptized them with water as a public solemn testimony and seal of this repentance, and he set before them the remission of sins as the aim of the repentance and the baptism. John the Baptist conceives of the advent as an advent in judgment, for which repentance and remission are the necessary preparations. Hence it is that the Baptist appears as the herald of the divine advent predicted in Malachi and in the great prophet of the exile.

Behold I send my messenger before thy face, who shall prepare thy way. The voice of one crying in the wilderness, make ye ready the way of the Lord, make his paths straight. Every valley shall be filled, and every mountain and hill shall be brought low; and the crooked shall become straight, and the rough ways smooth: and all flesh shall see the salvation of God.[1]

These translations differ from the original text in several important particulars,[2] but not so as in any way to dull the points of the citations. The advent is the advent of Yahweh; it is an advent in the glory of redemption and of judgment. It is an advent of judgment for the wicked, and of redemption for the righteous people. God is to lead them into the holy land, and before him all nature is transformed. This advent is heralded by a

---

[1] These passages are a mosaic from the three evangelists, Matth. iii. 3; Lk. i. 2, 3; Lk. iii. 4, 5; John i. 23. The first sentence is given only by Mark, who cites it from Isaiah. The evangelist, however, mistakes his reference, for it is from Malachi iii. 1. The citation is free, for it differs from the LXX. as well as the Hebrew. It was made probably from an oral Aramaic targum. The second sentence is given by the three synoptists. It is nearer to the LXX. than the Hebrew. John's Gospel condenses this sentence. The last sentence is given only by Luke. It also is closer to the LXX. than to the Hebrew. The two extracts were probably from an Aramaic original. The movement of the Hebrew poetry of the original was destroyed by these translations, and the R. V. is incorrect in its arrangement of the lines which do not correspond with the rhythm of Isaiah xl. 3-5. See Briggs' *Messianic Prophecy*, pp. 375, 473.

[2] See Toy, *Quotations in the New Testament*, p. 16.

special messenger, whose office is to prepare the way, to proclaim the approach of the great king. John the Baptist was this herald, and it is a divine advent that he has in view, an advent chiefly in judgment, but a judgment that implies redemption to the people of God.

In accordance with this conception of his mission, the few discourses of the Baptist that have been preserved in the three synoptic evangelists are words of warning. They assume the poetic form, as was usual with the prophets of the Old Testament:

> Ye offspring of vipers, who warned you
> To flee from the wrath to come?
> Bring forth therefore fruits worthy of repentance;
> And think not to say within yourselves,
> We have Abraham to our father:
> For I say unto you, that God is able
> Of these stones to raise up children unto Abraham.
> And even now is the axe laid unto the root of the trees:
> Every tree therefore that bringeth not forth good fruit
> Is hewn down, and cast into the fire.[1]

This passage of Matthew and Luke had a common source in the original Aramaic Gospel of Matthew. It has all the features of a trimeter poem. Matthew applies it to the Pharisees and Sadducees, to whom, indeed, it seems most appropriate. But Luke gives it a more general reference to the multitudes. This is all the more striking in view of his specification of publicans and soldiers in the warnings of the Baptist preserved by him alone. It seems most probable that the original source contained only the sayings of the

---

[1] Matth. iii. 7–10 is identical with Luke iii. 7–9 with the exception of καρπὸν ἄξιον for καρποὺς ἀξίους and δόξητε for ἄρξησθε ver. 8, and that Luke inserts καὶ in ver. 9. Matthew's text is preferable.

Baptist without the explanatory remarks. The additional sentences given by Luke are:

> He that hath two coats,
> Let him impart to him that hath none;
> And he that hath food,
> Let him do likewise. (Luke iii. 11.)

To the publicans he said:

Extort no more than that which is appointed you.
(Luke iii. 13.)

To the soldiers he said:

Extort from no man by violence, neither accuse any one wrongfully;
And be content with your wages. (Luke iii. 14.)

These sayings were probably derived from another source than the Aramaic Matthew. Luke represents in his introduction that he used many sources.[1] These are specimens given by the Baptist of the fruits of repentance such as were required in preparation for the advent of God in judgment. He sees that the axe is already lying at the root of the dead trees, and is about to cut them down. The fire is ready to consume them. The true children of Abraham, the heirs of the promises of God, will abide; God will provide for that. Even the stones of the wilderness are more likely to produce living children of Abraham than such fruitless trees and venomous serpents as the Pharisees and their disciples. The day of wrath, the Day of Yahweh, predicted by the prophets of the Old Testament, is at hand; and those who do not prepare themselves for it by true repentance have every reason to dread it, and flee away from it.

Matthew,[2] in accordance with his custom, adds another discourse of the Baptist to the previous one with-

---

[1] Luke i. 1–4.   [2] Matt. iii. 11, 12.

out comment or mark of separation. Luke[1] gives it on another occasion in response to the people, who inquired whether John was the Messiah. Mark[2] gives it in an abridged form, as the theme of his preaching. John[3] also gives it in a shortened form, in response to an inquiry of the Pharisees whether he was Elijah, the Messiah, or the expected prophet. A careful study of these four parallel passages makes it probable that the original Aramaic discourse would be as follows:

> I indeed baptize you with water;
> But he that is mightier than I cometh after me,
> Whose shoes I am unworthy to untie:
> He will baptize you with fire.
> Whose fan is in his hand,
> Thoroughly to cleanse his threshing-floor;
> And to gather the wheat into his garner;
> But the chaff he will burn up with unquenchable fire.[4]

In this discourse the Baptist looks again at the judgment of fire. The chaff will be consumed here, as the

---

[1] Luke iii. 16, 17.     [2] Mark i. 7, 8.     [3] John i. 26, 27.

[4] The first four lines are common to the four evangelists. Disregarding the differences in order of words in the sentences, Matthew alone gives "unto repentance." Matthew and John use the preposition "in" before "water." Mark alone uses the aorist "baptized." Luke's text is to be preferred in the first line. In the second line, Matthew and John use the participle "coming," Mark and Luke the present "cometh." All use "after me" but Luke. In the third line, the text of Luke is best. John uses a final clause for the infinitive of Mark and Luke. Mark inserts "stoop down," and Matthew substitutes "to bear." "Latchet" is given by all but Matthew; it is an amplification for greater distinctness. John uses "worthy" for "sufficient" of the three others. Mark and John do not give "and with fire" of Matthew and Luke. "Fire" is best suited to the context. "Holy Spirit" was probably an explanation of the fire, in two of the evangelists substituted for it, in the other two inserted before it. This was due to reflection upon these words in connection with the descent of the Spirit on the day of Pentecost. The last four lines are given by Matthew and Luke. The only differences are in the use of infinitives of Luke for futures of Matthew. We prefer to follow Luke. This difference, as well as differences in order of words, is due to a different translation of the Aramaic original.

dead wood was to be consumed in the previous passage. As the true children of Abraham were to abide there, so the wheat is to be gathered into the garner here. The fan of the threshing-floor takes the place of the axe of the woodman, in the figure of the act of judgment.

The last four lines harmonize with the previous discourse; but the first four lines bring into view the conception of two baptisms: the one with water, the other with fire. The Baptist connects the baptism with fire and the judgment of fire without discrimination in time, just as the Old Testament prophets were accustomed to do.[1] In this particular he seems not to have advanced beyond them. The judgment of fire, with its redemption of the people of God, is the theme of his preaching. Repentance and baptism with water are its preparations. The advent of God is connected, in the mind of the Baptist, with the advent of the Messiah. The Messiah comes to bestow this baptism of fire, and to exercise judgment. The Baptist seems to have in mind the advent of the Son of Man in the cloud with the Ancient of Days and the fiery stream of the apocalypse of Daniel.[2] The evangelists after the day of Pentecost see in the fire the fiery tongues of the Holy Spirit as well as the fiery flame of the lake of fire of the judgment day.

The Gospel of John tells of a closer recognition of Jesus by the Baptist:

And John bare witness, saying, I have beheld the Spirit descending as a dove out of heaven; and it abode upon him. And I knew him not: but he that sent me to baptize with water, he said unto me, Upon whomsoever thou shalt see the Spirit descending, and abiding upon him, the same is he that baptizeth with the Holy Spirit. And I have seen, and have borne witness

---

[1] Cf. Joel iii.; Ezek. xxxix. Briggs' *Messianic Prophecy*, p. 488.
[2] Dan. vii. 9-12.

that this is the Son of God. [And so the Baptist transfers his own disciples to Jesus with the words]: Behold, the Lamb of God, which taketh away the sin of the world! (John i. 29-34.)

The two sides of the work of the Advent were distinctly foretold by the Baptist; namely, the judgment and the redemption. He reiterates the ancient prophecies with reference to the judgment.[1] But in the doctrine of redemption he advances in the line of the annunciations, and of his father Zachariah, and of Simeon, to a still more vivid conception of the Messiah as the victim, the sin-bearing and suffering Lamb of the great prophet of the exile.[2] Here the Baptist combines the judging Son of Man with the rejected prophetic servant. These two Messianic ideas, kept apart in the Old Testament, converge in his representation. His language is brief, enigmatic, and gives no explanation of the remarkable combination in his mind. This conception of the Baptist is given only by the Gospel of John, preserved in the memory of the apostle who had heard it from the lips of the Baptist himself.

These enigmatic words had pointed him to Jesus as in some way both the Messianic servant and the Son of Man, the mediator of the Day of the Lord, of the divine judgment, and of the redemption of the world.

John the Baptist gives to his disciples a final testimony:

> Ye yourselves bear me witness, that I said, I am not the Messiah, but that I am sent before him. He that hath the bride is the bridegroom; but the friend of the bridegroom, who standeth and heareth him, rejoiceth greatly because of the bridegroom's voice; this my joy therefore is made full. He must increase, but I must decrease. (John iii. 28-30.)

---

[1] Isa. xli. 3-11; Mal. iii.      [2] Isa. liii.

# CHAPTER III.

## THE MESSIAH OF MARK.

The Gospels give glimpses of the life and teaching of Jesus from four different points of view. Mark is the simplest and the earliest in composition. Almost all that is given in Mark reappears in Matthew and Luke; both of these Gospels using the earlier Mark. Matthew is distinguished by long discourses of Jesus upon several great themes. We find very much the same matter in other connections in Luke; but only a limited portion of it in Mark. It is evident that the Gospel of Matthew has grouped the words of Jesus about several themes. As it depended chiefly upon Mark for the historical material, it also depended on the Logia of Matthew for these discourses. The Logia of Matthew is the collection chiefly of the sayings of Jesus made by the apostle Matthew in the Aramaic language, according to the testimony of Papias.[1] This Logia was lost at an early date, but the most if not all of its contents are in the Gospels of Matthew and Luke. Luke gives them more in the circumstances of their utterance. The Gospel of Matthew arranged them in a topical order without regard to these circumstances. These discourses of Jesus from the Logia of Matthew are rich and pregnant with Mes-

---

[1] See p. 41.

sianic material. The Gospel of Matthew gives other sayings of Jesus and reports other acts of Jesus, which were taken probably from other sources, written or oral. The Gospel of Luke uses the historical material of Mark, gives the sayings from the Logia of Matthew their original setting, but it also gives original matter not found in the other evangelists. It is probable that this material was chiefly derived from a third written source. It is evident that Luke seeks historic connection for the life and words of Jesus. He arranges in an orderly chronological and geographical method, distinguishing the ministry in Galilee, in Samaria, in Perea, and in Jerusalem.

The Gospel of John is different from the other three, in that the material is chiefly new. It gives us more the esoteric teaching of Jesus and events of a more private and personal character, all bearing the marks of deep and thorough reflection upon the person and life of Jesus.

In the study of the gospels there is a constant advance in conception, in the order, Mark, Matthew, Luke, John. But the advance from Luke to John is much greater than that between the three other evangelists, so much so that the three are grouped by scholars as the synoptics over against John, which stands apart by itself.

The different methods of composition of the evangelists, their difference in conception, and their difference in the order and grouping of material, are not favorable to a systematic study of the Messianic idea of Jesus. There are several methods that might be pursued in dealing with it.

(1). We might inquire how far the Jesus of the Gospels was the Messiah of the Old Testament, and then study his predictions on the basis of that inquiry. The difficulty in this method is that his predictions relate to his own sufferings, death, and resurrection which are included in the evidences of the Messiahship.

(2). We might group the whole question of the Messianic predictions of Jesus and the Messianic fulfilment of Jesus about the Messianic ideals of the Old Testament. This is a tempting method, but in its use there are several disadvantages. The chief of these is that the Messianic idea of Jesus would be dominated by the results of the synthesis of the Old Testament. The Messianic idea of Jesus is so original, extensive, and profound, that it should be studied by itself and shaped by its own internal principles.

(3). We might first study the Messianic idea of Jesus, as it is given in the Gospels, and then in this light inquire how far the Messiah of the Gospels is the Messiah of the Old Testament. We shall construct our material in accordance with this method. But this method might be used in several ways. The material given in the discourses of Jesus in the form of prediction is greater than we find in any prophet of the Old Testament. It is so great in amount and so various in form that it is necessary to divide it into several chapters.

(a). We would prefer some chronological scheme. But such a chronological scheme is sufficiently difficult in the study of the life of the Messiah. It is still more difficult when we have to put his discourses in their historical relations. Any attempt to do this burdens us with numberless questions of historical criticism where it is impossible at present to attain definite results in some of the most important passages. Many attempts have been made to trace a development in the Messianic consciousness of Jesus and in his doctrine of the kingdom of God, but none of these have found favor. It seems impracticable in the present stage of the criticism of the Gospels to give an accurate and comprehensive statement of such a development. It is sufficiently difficult if the study is limited to the synoptics. It is at present impossible if the Gospel of John is included in the study.[1] The Gospel of Luke seems to have tried the chronological method and to have succeeded only in part. We are not likely to be more successful.

(*b*). An effort might be made to group the Messianic material about several great themes, such as the Kingdom of God, the Rejected Messiah, the Messianic Judgment, and the Messiah from Heaven. But this method has its difficulties. These topics cannot be so distinctly separated without injury to the unity of many of the themes. A considerable amount of repetition is unavoidable under the several heads. Omissions and reservations constantly occur. This indeed is the method pursued in the Gospel of Matthew in his use of the sayings of Jesus. But even Matthew did not consistently use it. The other evangelists used other methods. How then can we reduce them all to Matthew's method?

(*c*). The simplest and easiest method seems on the whole to be the best, at least for the purpose of this volume. We shall follow the method of the Gospels themselves and give the Messiah of each by itself. The Messianic idea of the Gospel of Mark will be first studied in Chapter III. This is for the most part the earliest Christian tradition, and it is found likewise in the parallel passages of Matthew and Luke. These parallel passages have been derived by our Matthew and Luke from the original Mark, and have been edited in their larger

---

[1] Wendt, *Lehre Jesu*, ii. s. 318, 319.

gospels, sometimes in new relations and with variations due to explication, or to abridgment, or to subsequent reflection in the light of other circumstances and events. In some cases a Messianic reference is found in one of the parallels that is absent from Mark. In such a case the Messianic reference is probably due to later reflection, or other sources of information. Inasmuch as our purpose at present is to consider the Messianic idea, we propose to use such parallels under the head of that gospel in which the Messianic reference appears. The Apocalypse of Jesus stands out so prominently by itself in Mark and its parallels in Matthew and Luke, and is so important in its exposition, that we shall treat it in Chapter IV. The Messianic idea of Jesus presented in the Gospel of Matthew, so far as it is not included in Mark, will next be considered in Chapter V. This material, not given by Mark, but added by Matthew to the common tradition in Mark, was derived for the most part from the Aramaic Logia of Matthew, and appears with historical setting in the Gospel of Luke. This material has variations in language due in part to different translations of the same Aramaic original, and in part to different conceptions of the meaning and use of the material in these evangelists and to editorial modification of various kinds. It will be convenient to use in this same chapter the Messianic material peculiar to Matthew, for it is not certain how much of it was derived from the Logia and how much of it from other sources. The sixth chapter will be given to the Messianic material peculiar to the Gospel of Luke and derived by him from other sources. A seventh chapter will conclude with the Messiah of the Gospel of John. The material in the Gospels which may be regarded as giving the Messianic ideas of the authors of the Gospels, rather than those of Jesus, will be considered in the eighth chapter, where the question will be determined whether and how far the Jesus of the Gospels fulfilled the Messianic ideals of the Old Testament.

## THE SON OF GOD.

§ 14. *Jesus was recognized at his baptism as the beloved and accepted son of God, the Messiah, by a theophany of the voice of God, and by the descent of the Holy Spirit from heaven in the form of a dove to abide with him.*

The Gospel of Mark begins the life of Jesus with the story of his baptism by John the Baptist, his forerunner and herald. This fundamental event is described in the four evangelists, each one giving additional information, rising from the simpler story of Mark to the fuller story of John. We give them in parallelism for comparison (see p. 76).

The baptism of Jesus with the Holy Spirit was in accordance with the prophet Isaiah, who predicts that the Divine Spirit will rest upon the Messianic king.[1] The great prophecy of the exile also predicts that the Messianic servant will be anointed by the Spirit for his preaching.[2] But the coming of the Spirit upon Jesus was something more than these predictions. It was a coming of the Spirit in theophany, in the form of a dove. This is unique in the history of divine revelation. The dove, as a symbol of peace, was an appropriate form for the Spirit in the consecration of a prophet whose message was a gospel of peace, and of a king whose reign was to result in everlasting peace.

Besides this consecration by the theophany of the dove, there was also a heavenly recognition by the the-

---

[1] Is. xi. 2.    [2] Is. lxi. 1.

ophany of a voice. This voice was the voice of God claiming Jesus as his son, his beloved son, the son with whom he was well pleased. This theophanic recognition is beyond anything predicted in the Old Testament. Nowhere is it said that the Messiah would be claimed by a divine voice. It is commonly supposed that the Son of God is here to be understood in the theological sense of the second person of the Trinity, but this is ex-

---

### *A.* MARK i. 9–17.

And it came to pass in those days, that Jesus came from Nazareth of Galilee, and was baptized of John in the Jordan. And straightway coming up out of the water, he saw the heavens rent asunder, and the Spirit as a dove descending upon him: and a voice came out of the heavens, Thou art my beloved Son, in thee I am well pleased.

### *B.* LUKE iii. 21–22.

Now it came to pass, when all the people were baptized, that, Jesus also having been baptized, and praying, the heaven was opened, and the Holy Spirit descended in a bodily form, as a dove, upon him, and a voice came out of heaven, Thou art my beloved Son; in thee I am well pleased.

### *C.* MATTH. iii. 13–17.

Then cometh Jesus from Galilee to the Jordan unto John, to be baptized of him. But John would have hindered him, saying, I have need to be baptized of thee, and comest thou to me? But Jesus answering said unto him, Suffer *it* now: for thus it becometh us to fulfil all righteousness. Then he suffereth him. And Jesus, when he was baptized, went up straightway from the water: and lo, the heavens were opened unto him, and he saw the Spirit of God descending as a dove, and coming upon him; and lo, a voice out of the heavens, saying, This is my beloved Son, in whom I am well pleased.

### *D.* JOHN i. 32–34.

And John bare witness, saying, I have beheld the Spirit descending as a dove out of heaven; and it abode upon him. And I knew him not: but he that sent me to baptize in water, he said unto me, Upon whomsoever thou shalt see the Spirit descending, and abiding upon him, the same is he that baptizeth in the Holy Spirit. And I have seen, and have borne witness that this is the Son of God.

tremely improbable. It is more probable that the Son of God is here used in the well-known Messianic sense, of the seed of David, and that the theophanic voice attests the Messiahship of Jesus, rather than his divinity. It is improbable that the divinity of Jesus was made known by a divine voice at the beginning of his ministry, to remain unknown during the greater part of his ministry, and only gradually to be manifested toward the close of his life. It is true that we have the voice, the dove, and the son distinguished in this theophany, but this does not imply the divinity of the three. The divinity of the Son may be proven elsewhere; it is not evident here. The Divine Spirit now appears for the first time in the development of divine revelation in a distinct theophanic individuality. In the Old Testament and in the revelations to the Forerunners the Divine Spirit was an energy of God, a mode of divine manifestation. Here the Divine Spirit is theophanic; it has a distinct embodiment in the form of a dove. This heavenly recognition of Jesus by the theophany sets him at once in a unique position as the Son of God, the significance of which will be disclosed in the development of the Messianic idea of Jesus and his apostles. We notice, however, that the relation here emphasized is an ethical relation and not a theocratic one. This then becomes the characteristic feature of the Messianic idea of Jesus. It is essentially ethical throughout. As Wendt well says: "According to the conception of the Jews the Messianic king was also 'Son of God'; according to the conception of Jesus the 'Son of God' was as such the Messianic king."[1]

Matthew answers a later objection to the baptism of

---

[1] *Lehre Jesu*, ii. s. 436.

the Messiah by John, when he tells us of the hesitancy of John to baptize Jesus on account of his recognition of him as the Messiah. The Gospel of John tells us that the theophany of the Spirit was the sign, given John the Baptist by God, which would assure him that Jesus was indeed the Son of God. The reason for the baptism, as given by Matthew, was that the Messiah might "fulfil all righteousness"; that is, the highest of the divine requirements in preparation for the kingdom. The King would lead his people through the preparatory waters of baptism. Standing thus at the highest point of the righteousness of preparation, Jesus receives the recognition of the heavenly Father, and the baptism of the Divine Spirit, which endow him, as the Messiah, with the authority to baptize his disciples with the Holy Spirit.

According to the Gospel of the Infancy, the immaculate conception of Jesus and his birth at Bethlehem were both accompanied by theophanies.[1] We would expect a theophany to inaugurate his public ministry also.

### THE KINGDOM AT HAND.

§ 15. *Jesus declared that the time was fulfilled, and that the kingdom of God was at hand.*

Jesus began his public ministry by declaring the glad tidings already heralded by the Baptist.

> The time is fulfilled, and the kingdom of God is at hand: repent ye, and believe in the gospel. (Mark i. 15.)

The report of Mark is fuller than Matthew[2] for it associates faith with repentance and the fulfilment of the time with the kingdom. Matthew here, and elsewhere

---

[1] See pp. 49, 51.   [2] iv. 17.

in his report of the discourses of Jesus, uses the term kingdom of heaven. From this we might infer that Jesus was in the habit of using both of these terms, kingdom of God and kingdom of heaven, as synonyms. The kingdom of heaven means, in the usage of Matthew, the kingdom that is heavenly in origin and in its seat of dominion. It is synonymous with the kingdom of God whose origin and dominion are in God. Heaven is the seat of the throne, and God is enthroned over this kingdom. It is probable, however, that Matthew is responsible for the variation, and that he either unconsciously or designedly substituted the one for the other, because of his own preference, or because he thought that the kingdom of heaven was a more suitable term for his purpose in setting forth Jesus as the Messiah.[1]

We are not surprised that the terms kingdom of the Messiah or kingdom of David are absent, for the kingdom of God is a larger and more comprehensive term than the others. It was fitting that Jesus should declare the kingdom of God rather than the kingdom of the Messiah, since in the usage of Old Testament prophecy the kingdom of the Son of God is the kingdom of God. Jesus declares that the kingdom of God is at hand. In this term, *at hand*, he takes up the preaching of the Old Testament prophets whose constant refrain is the nearness of the day of Yahweh.[2] This term, in itself, would

---

[1] It is claimed by Schürer, *Gesch. jüd. Volkes*, II. s. 454; Wendt, *Lehre Jesu*, ii. s. 299, *et al*, that the phrase "kingdom of heaven" in Matthew's usage was a substitution by Matthew of "heaven" for "God" after the Jewish fashion in those times, in accordance with the general reluctance to use divine names. Beyschlag, *Neu. Test. Theologie*, I. s. 41, rightly holds that it is the heavenly origin of the kingdom that is thought of in accordance with Dan. ii. 44, vii. 13, 14, but Beyschlag is probably wrong in ascribing the phrase to the words of Jesus in the Logia. It seems improbable that the other gospels and the epistles would uniformly use kingdom of God, if the original words of Jesus in the Logia were kingdom of heaven.    [2] Briggs' *Messianic Prophecy*, p. 53.

not imply any immediateness in the advent of the kingdom, measured in chronological numbers. But the parallel expression given by Mark is more significant, for when Jesus said, *the time is fulfilled*, he means that the time prior to the advent of the kingdom has been filled out and is about to reach its end. The theme of the discourse is therefore the immediate advent of the kingdom. In view of this advent the people of Israel are to repent and have faith in the gospel, the message of the kingdom.[1]

### THE AUTHORITY OF THE SON OF MAN.

§ 16. *Jesus had unique authority as the Son of Man, in his words and deeds, over man, nature, and demons.*

The Gospel of Mark calls attention to the authority of Jesus in connection with his first preaching.

| MARK i. 22. | LUKE iv. 31-32. | MATTH. vii. 28-29. |
|---|---|---|
| And they were astonished at his teaching: for he was teaching them[2] as having authority, and not as the scribes. | And he came down to Capernaum, a city of Galilee, and he was teaching them on the Sabbath day: and they were astonished at his teaching; for his word was with authority. | And it came to pass, when Jesus ended these words, the multitudes were astonished at his teaching: for he was teaching them as having authority, and not as their scribes. |

| MARK i. 23-27. | LUKE iv. 33-36. |
|---|---|
| And straightway there was in their synagogue a man with an unclean spirit; and he cried out, saying, What have we to | And in the synagogue there was a man that had a spirit of an unclean demon, and he cried out with a loud voice, Ah! |

---

[1] Wendt, *Lehre Jesu*, ii. s. 307.

[2] ἦν διδάσκων. The three narratives use the same expression. It is correctly given in the Revised Version of Luke, but neglected in the Revised Version of Mark and Matthew.

do with thee, thou Jesus of Nazareth? Art thou come to destroy us? I know thee who thou art, the Holy One of God. And Jesus rebuked him, saying, Hold thy peace and come out of him. And the unclean spirit, tearing him and crying with a loud voice, came out of him. And they were all amazed, insomuch that they questioned among themselves, saying: What is this? a new teaching! With authority he commandeth even the unclean spirits, and they obey him.

what have we to do with thee, thou Jesus of Nazareth? Art thou come to destroy us? I know thee who thou art, the Holy One of God. And Jesus rebuked him, saying, Hold thy peace, and come out of him. And when the demon had thrown him down in the midst, he came out of him, having done him no hurt. And amazement came upon all, and they spake together, one with another, saying, What is this word? For with authority and power he commandeth the unclean spirits, and they come out.

The people were at the outset impressed by the teaching of Jesus. He taught with authority. He did not appeal to ancient authorities as was the custom of the rabbis in his time,[1] but he spake on his own authority. Mark and Luke call attention to it in connection with the discourse at Capernaum; Matthew after his collection of the teachings of Jesus in the Sermon on the Mount.

With the same authority Jesus wrought his miracles, in this respect differing from Moses and Elijah, who appealed to God or used means appointed by God. The authority of Jesus was especially manifested in his casting out of demons as at Capernaum, and at a later date in raising the dead. He needed not to call to God for help, or to use appointed instruments. His word of command was sufficient. The demons came forth from their wretched victims at the word of one whom they knew to be the Holy One of God.

Jesus still further manifested his authority in granting absolution from sin, which no prophet had ever done

---

[1] Matt. v. 21 *seq.*

before him. This wonderful exhibition of authority is described by Mark in connection with another discourse at Capernaum.

| MARK ii. 1–12. | LUKE v. 17–26. | MATTHEW ix. 1–8. |
|---|---|---|
| And when he entered again into Capernaum after some days, it was noised that he was in the house. And many were gathered together, so that there was no longer room *for them*, no, not even about the door: and he spake the word unto them. And they come, bringing unto him a man sick of the palsy, borne of four. And when they could not come nigh unto him for the crowd, they uncovered the roof where he was: and when they had broken it up, they let down the bed whereon the sick of the palsy lay. | And it came to pass on one of those days, that he was teaching; and there were Pharisees and doctors of the law sitting by, who were come out of every village of Galilee and Judæa and Jerusalem: and the power of the Lord was with him to heal. And behold, men bring on a bed a man that was palsied: and they sought to bring him in, and to lay him before him. And not finding by what *way* they might bring him in because of the multitude, they went up to the housetop and let him down through the tiles with his couch into the midst before Jesus. | And he entered into a boat, and crossed over, and came into his own city. And behold, they brought to him a man sick of the palsy, lying on a bed: |
| And Jesus seeing their faith saith unto the sick of the palsy, Son, thy sins are forgiven. But there were certain of the scribes sitting there, and reasoning in their hearts, Why doth this man thus speak? he blasphemeth: who can forgive sins but one, *even* God? And straight- | And seeing their faith, he said, Man, thy sins are forgiven thee. And the scribes and the Pharisees began to reason, saying, Who is this that speaketh blasphemies? Who can forgive sins, but God alone? But Jesus perceiving their reasonings, answered and said unto | and Jesus seeing their faith said unto the sick of the palsy, Son, be of good cheer; thy sins are forgiven. And behold, certain of the scribes said within themselves, This man blasphemeth. And Jesus knowing their thoughts, said, Wherefore think ye evil in your hearts? |

| | | |
|---|---|---|
| way Jesus, perceiving in his spirit that they so reasoned within themselves, saith unto them, Why reason ye these things in your hearts? Whether is easier, to say to the sick of the palsy, Thy sins are forgiven; or to say, Arise, and take up thy bed, and walk? But that ye may know that the Son of Man hath authority on earth to forgive sins (he saith to the sick of the palsy), I say unto thee, Arise, take up thy bed, and go unto thy house. And he arose, and straightway took up the bed, and went forth before them all; insomuch that they were all amazed, and glorified God, saying, We never saw it on this fashion. | them, What reason ye in your hearts? Whether is easier, to say, Thy sins are forgiven thee; or to say, Arise and walk? But that ye may know that the Son of Man hath authority on earth to forgive sins (he said unto him that was palsied), I say unto thee, Arise, and take up thy couch, and go unto thy house. And immediately he rose up before them, and took up that whereon he lay, and departed to his house, glorifying God. And amazement took hold on all, and they glorified God; and they were filled with fear, saying, We have seen strange things to-day. | For whether is easier, to say, Thy sins are forgiven; or to say, Arise, and walk? But that ye may know that the Son of Man hath authority on earth to forgive sins (then saith he to the sick of the palsy), Arise, and take up thy bed, and go unto thy house. And he arose, and departed to his house. But when the multitudes saw it, they were afraid, and glorified God, who had given such authority unto men. |

This assumption of the divine prerogative of forgiveness of sins was blasphemous in the eyes of the Pharisees. They could not deny the miracle, but they could refuse the miracle worker as a blasphemer working his miracles through evil supernatural influences. The authority to forgive sins, as here claimed and exercised by Jesus, must have struck the common people unpleasantly. It was an authority which no one but God could exercise. Even the Messianic prediction of the Old Testament did not ascribe to the Messiah such authority. The Messianic King judges and punishes the wicked,[1] but nowhere does he forgive sins. The Messianic prophet is a sin-bearer, a trespass-offering,[2] the means of forgiveness; but the authority of forgiveness is ever retained by God. The Son of Man of Daniel comes on the clouds of heaven to receive the kingdom from the Ancient of Days, but he has no earthly ministry.[3] The Son of Man of the Similitudes of Enoch has a heavenly pre-existence, but there is nothing to suggest a previous earthly life.[4] But Jesus here claims for the Son of Man an earthly ministry, and in that ministry the authority to forgive sins. Here for the first time, according to Mark, Jesus names himself the Son of Man. There can be little doubt that he used the name as a Messianic title, and that that title is based on its use in the Apocalypse of Daniel and probably also in the Apocalypse of Enoch. Jesus uses the term as his own familiar Messianic title, partly because it did not necessarily imply a Messianic meaning, and therefore was less likely to arouse prematurely opposition against his ministry,[5] but chiefly because it was the term most suited to his earthly ministry. He used it with a new meaning, but that meaning easily attached itself to the Apocalyptic meaning which Jesus also uses later on in his ministry. Jesus indeed carries out the idea of the pre-existent Son of Man implied in Daniel; but instead of teaching a heavenly pre-existence as in the Apocalypse of Enoch, he shows in his life and teachings a pre-existence in an earthly life, prior to his advent on the clouds of heaven. The advent on the clouds he subsequently referred to a second advent—the pre-existent Son of Man he unfolds in his own life on earth.

---

[1] Is. xi. 3, 4.   [2] Is. liii.   [3] Dan. vii. 13.   [4] See p. 27
[5] "*An incognito*," Bruce, *Kingdom of God*, p. 177. See also Wendt, *Lehre Jesu*, ii. s. 450; Adeney, *Theology of the New Testament*, p. 32.

Such authority to forgive sins either makes Jesus a blasphemer, as the Pharisees claimed, or else he was a Messiah of even greater authority than any presented in the Messianic ideals of the Old Testament. The Messianic Son of Man has an earthly ministry prior to his advent on the clouds, and an earthly ministry transcending all Messianic ideals of the Old Testament.

Jesus himself knew that it was as easy to forgive sins as to heal the paralytic, and that the authority to do the one involved the authority to do the other. It was not so much the healing as the authority with which it was accomplished. This witnessed to an authority which might even forgive sins also. It was the authority given in Daniel and Enoch to the enthroned Messiah, exercised in miracle-working, in teaching, and in forgiveness of sins by the Son of Man on earth, in the form of a meek and gentle prophet.

The synoptists agree in another saying of Jesus respecting the authority of the Son of Man in connection with the narrative of the disciples plucking grain on the Sabbath.[1] "*The Son of Man is Lord of the Sabbath.*"

The Son of Man is Lord of the Sabbath because he has authority over the Sabbath. This authority is, from the context of Mark, an authority to determine how the law of the Sabbath is to be interpreted in particular cases, and how it must yield to the higher law of the welfare of man. The authority of the Son of Man is thus exalted above the authority of the doctors of the law and of the traditional teaching of the rabbinical schools, because he was the Son of Man with divine

---

[1] Mark ii. 23-28; Matthew xii. 1-8; Luke vi. 1-3.

authority over the institutions and laws of the people of God.[1]

It was just this authority of Jesus in word and deed that troubled the Pharisees and stirred them up against him. In his last days in Jerusalem they demanded of him his warrant.

| MARK xi. 27–33. | MATT. xxi. 23–27. | LUKE xx. 1–8. |
|---|---|---|
| And they come again to Jerusalem; and as he was walking in the temple, there come to him the chief priests, and the scribes, and the elders; and they said unto him, By what authority doest thou these things? or who gave thee this authority to do these things? And Jesus said unto them, I will ask of you one question, and answer me, and I will tell you by what authority I do these things. The baptism of John, was it from heaven, or from men? an- | And when he was come into the temple, the chief priests and the elders of the people came unto him as he was teaching, and said, By what authority doest thou these things? and who gave thee this authority? And Jesus answered and said unto them, I also will ask you one question, which if ye tell me, I likewise will tell you by what authority I do these things. The baptism of John, whence was it? from heaven or from men? And they reasoned | And it came to pass, on one of the days, as he was teaching the people in the temple, and preaching the gospel, there came upon him the chief priests and the scribes with the elders; and they spake, saying unto him, Tell us: By what authority doest thou these things? or who is he that gave thee this authority? And he answered and said unto them, I also will ask you a question; and tell me: The baptism of John, was it from heaven or from men? And |

---

[1] It is urged by Baldensperger (*Das Selbstbewusstsein Jesu*, s. 179 *seq.*) that these passages in which Jesus claims to be the Son of Man and asserts his authority as such, must be later than the confession of Peter. He thinks that Jesus would not have distinctly claimed to be the Messiah so long before the apostles recognized him as such. Accordingly, Baldensperger thinks the evangelists have put these incidents too early in the life of Jesus. There is no other evidence of such displacement than the theory which Baldensperger proposes. The title Son of Man was a Messianic title; but it was not so clearly such as the Son of God, the Messiah; and it was difficult for any one to associate the Son of Man of Daniel with an earthly life. Therefore Jesus used this Messianic term in the training of the twelve, to lead them up to the ultimate combination of the Son of Man with the Son of God, the Messiah. Until they made that combination they could hardly make the confession he desired from them.

swer me. And they reasoned with themselves, saying, If we shall say, From heaven; he will say, Why then did ye not believe him? But should we say, From men — they feared the people; for all verily held John to be a prophet. And they answered Jesus and say, We know not. And Jesus saith unto them, Neither tell I you by what authority I do these things.

with themselves, saying, If we shall say, From heaven; he will say unto us, Why then did ye not believe him? But if we shall say, From men; we fear the multitude; for all hold John as a prophet. And they answered Jesus, and said, We know not. He also said unto them, Neither tell I you by what authority I do these things.

they reasoned with themselves, saying, If we shall say, From heaven; he will say, Why did ye not believe him? But if we shall say, From men; all the people will stone us: for they are persuaded that John was a prophet. And they answered, that they knew not whence *it was*. And Jesus said unto them, Neither tell I you by what authority I do these things.

The insincerity of the question of the Pharisees was developed by a counter question. Such insincerity receives no answer. Jesus' authority might be questioned by the insincere and the enemies of the truth, but it needed no other warrant than its own exercise in words of blessing and deeds of mercy. Such warrant Jesus had given every day of his ministry. Such authority had its own credentials wrapped up in itself. It had been observed early in His ministry. It was a constant feature of his ministry. Any sincere inquirer would receive ample illustrations of it. Any sincere doubter would be overcome by invincible evidence. But for the insincere and the hostile no evidence is so convincing as to convict them of their insincerity, hostility, and inconsistency. This Jesus does, and the very authority they question is discovered in the ease and grace with which he overcomes them.

THE PARABLES OF THE KINGDOM.

§ 17. *The kingdom is good seed sown in the field of the world by the preaching of the Gospel. It grows in a secret, gradual, and orderly manner from planting to harvest. It has the smallest beginnings, but an abundant harvest.*

Mark gives three parables of the kingdom—those of the sower, the seed growing secretly, and the grain of mustard seed; the middle one being peculiar to his gospel.[1] Luke gives the sower alone in this connection,[2] but the grain of mustard seed in another connection.[3] Matthew gives the two in a larger group of nine, seven of which we shall consider in Chapter V.[4]

The parable of the sower is essentially the same in the three evangelists, only the details differ in their reports. This parable was interpreted to them by Jesus, and his interpretation of this parable is a model for the interpretation of others.

| MARK iv. 14-20. | MATT. xiii. 19-23. | LUKE viii. 11-15. |
|---|---|---|
| The sower soweth the word. And these are they by the wayside, where the word is sown; and when they have heard, straightway cometh Satan, and taketh away the word which hath been sown in them. And these in like manner are they that are sown upon the rocky *places*, who, when they have heard the word, straightway receive it with joy; and they have no root in themselves, but endure for a while: | When any one heareth the word of the kingdom, and understandeth it not, *then* cometh the evil *one*, and snatcheth away that which hath been sown in his heart. This is he that was sown by the wayside. And he that was sown upon the rocky places, this is he that heareth the word, and straightway with joy receiveth it; yet hath he not root in himself, but endureth for a while; and when tribulation | Now the parable is this: The seed is the word of God. And those by the wayside are they that have heard; then cometh the devil, and taketh away the word from their heart, that they may not believe and be saved. And those on the rock *are* they who, when they have heard, receive the word with joy; and these have no root, who for a while believe, and in time of temptation fall away. And that |

---

[1] iv. 1-32.      [2] viii. 4-13.      [3] xiii. 18-19.
[4] xiii. 1-52. See A. B. Bruce, *Parabolic Teaching of Christ*, for an admirable study of this group of parables.

then, when tribulation or persecution ariseth because of the word, straightway they stumble. And others are they that are sown among the thorns; these are they that have heard the word, and the cares of the age and the deceitfulness of riches, and the lust of other things entering in, choke the word, and it becometh unfruitful. And these are they that were sown upon the good ground; such as hear the word, and accept it, and bear fruit thirtyfold, and sixtyfold, and a hundredfold.

or persecution ariseth because of the word, straightway he stumbleth. And he that was sown among the thorns, this is he that heareth the word; and the care of the age, and the deceitfulness of riches, choke the word, and he becometh unfruitful. And he that was sown upon the good ground, this is he that heareth the word, and understandeth it; who verily beareth fruit, and bringeth forth, some a hundredfold, some sixty, some thirty.

which fell among the thorns, these are they that have heard, and as they go on their way they are choked with cares and riches and pleasures of *this* life, and bring no fruit to perfection. And that in the good ground, these are such as in an honest and good heart, having heard the word, hold it fast, and bring forth fruit with patience.

The kingdom of God is here conceived as a grain field. The seed is the word of the kingdom. The field consists of the hearers of the Gospel, men differing as a field differs to the sower. These different classes deal with the word in various manners. The superficial, the obdurate, the preoccupied—these are the three classes with whom the word of the kingdom is not fruitful. There is, however, a class of men who are attentive, receive the word, and are exceedingly fruitful.

This parable teaches that the kingdom is to be established by means of preaching the Gospel, and that it is composed of men of various kinds, who receive it, although only one kind of men really gain the benefits of it. These benefits are benefits of character, and not of carnal possession and temporal advantages. The kingdom is a spiritual kingdom, which grows from seed to fruit; a kingdom of grace and not a kingdom of mere sovereignty; a kingdom of truth and not a kingdom of physical force.

Mark gives us a parable which is a suitable companion to that of the *Sower:*

> And he said, So is the kingdom of God, as if a man should cast seed upon the earth; and should sleep and rise night and day, and the seed should spring up and grow, he knoweth not how. The earth beareth fruit of herself; first the blade, then the ear, then the full corn in the ear. But when the fruit is ripe, straightway he putteth forth the sickle, because the harvest is come. (Mark iv. 26–29.)

The parable takes up the fruitful seed of the previous parable and sets forth its gradual, silent, and sure growth. There are successive stages—sowing, the blade, the ear, the full grain in the ear, the harvest. This is the growth of the fruitful members of the kingdom; and the growth of the kingdom itself as made of such members. This parable teaches us to distinguish several stages in the growth and development of the kingdom. At its origin it is planted. Some considerable time elapses before the blade becomes visible. Then it has to grow until it reaches its maturity. Growth gradual, secret, and certain is the law of the kingdom of God. It is not a kingdom of armies, but of truth; its victories are not by violence, but by persuasion. It advances by growth in the apprehension and practice of the truth of God. Patient waiting is needed in that long interval between the Sowing and the Reaping.

Matthew and Mark attach to this group of parables the parable of the Grain of Mustard Seed, which is given by Luke in another connection. It may be appropriately considered here.

| MARK iv. 30–32. | MATT. xiii. 31, 32. | LUKE xiii. 18, 19. |
|---|---|---|
| And he said, How shall we liken the kingdom of God? or in what parable shall we set it forth? It is like a grain of mustard seed, which, when it is sown upon the earth, though it be less than all the seeds that are upon the earth, yet when it is sown, groweth up, and becometh greater than all the herbs, and putteth out great branches; so that the birds of the heaven can lodge under the shadow thereof. | Another parable set he before them, saying, The kingdom of heaven is like unto a grain of mustard seed, which a man took, and sowed in his field: which indeed is less than all seeds; but when it is grown, it is greater than the herbs, and becometh a tree, so that the birds of the heaven come and lodge in the branches thereof. | He said therefore, Unto what is the kingdom of God like? and whereunto shall I liken it? It is like unto a grain of mustard seed, which a man took, and cast into his own garden: and it grew, and became a tree; and the birds of the heaven lodged in the branches thereof. |

The parable of the Sower brought out the darker side of the fortunes of the kingdom. This parable confines itself to the brighter side. It contrasts the smallness of the kingdom in its origin with the greatness of its fruition. It takes up the doctrine of the growth of the kingdom set forth in the parable of the growing seed. The good seed here is not a grain seed, but a mustard seed, exceedingly small. The seed does not here represent the members of the kingdom, but the kingdom itself. The parable reminds us of the cedar twig of Ezekiel and its marvelous growth,[1] and of the spreading vine of Asaph.[2]

The contrast between the origin of the kingdom and its fruition is very striking. In its origin it is a very small seed. Its planting and its early development will

---

[1] Ezek. xvii. 22–24. [2] Ps. lxxx.

not attract attention. But when it is rapidly reaching its maturity then it will attract the attention of all.

## JESUS RECOGNIZED AS MESSIAH.

§ 18. *Jesus was recognized as the Messiah, the Son of God, on several occasions by demons and at last by his own apostles.*

The Gospel of Mark gives an account of a recognition of the Messiahship of Jesus by a demon in connection with his first miracle of casting out demons in Capernaum.

What have we to do with thee, thou Jesus of Nazareth? Art thou come to destroy us? I know thee who thou art, the Holy One of God. (Mark i. 24.)[1]

Jesus is here declared to be "the holy one of God," holy not so much in contrast with the unclean spirit, but in the sense that he was the one consecrated by God as the Messiah, he was anointed with the Holy Spirit of God.

At a later period Mark reports:

And the unclean spirits, whensoever they beheld him, fell down before him, and cried, saying, Thou art the Son of God. (Mark iii. 11.)

The Son of God is here the epithet of Jesus as the Messiah, in accordance with Messianic usage.

At another time, in the country of the Gerasenes, we have a similar recognition by demons.

| MARK v. 6, 7. | MATTH. viii. 29. | LUKE viii. 28. |
|---|---|---|
| And when he saw Jesus from afar, he ran and worshipped | And behold, they cried out, saying, What have we to do | And when he saw Jesus, he cried out, and fell down before |

---

[1] The report of Luke iv. 34 is the same.

| | | |
|---|---|---|
| him; and crying out with a loud voice, he saith, What have I to do with thee, Jesus, thou Son of the Most High God? I adjure thee by God, torment me not. | with thee thou Son of God? Art thou come hither to torment us before the time? | him, and with a loud voice said, What have I to do with thee, Jesus, thou Son of the Most High God? I beseech thee, torment me not. |

Here Jesus is recognized by the demons as "the Son of the Most High God," according to Mark and Luke, and as "the Son of God," according to Matthew. The thought of God as "the Most High" was possibly suggested by the demons' fear of the depths of the abyss.

In the meanwhile the people were disputing among themselves, who Jesus might be, and even Herod was disturbed. The people doubted whether he was Elijah, the herald of the prophecy of Malachi, or a prophet like one of the prophets of the Old Testament. Herod's guilty conscience led him to fear in Jesus the risen John the Baptist.[1] In all these conjectures they were erring, for they did not understand that John the Baptist was the second Elijah, the herald of Jesus the Messiah. The faith of the apostles was tested by a direct question of Jesus in the region of Cæsarea Philippi.

| MARK viii. 27–30. | MATT. xvi. 13–16, 20. | LUKE ix. 18–21. |
|---|---|---|
| And Jesus went forth, and his disciples, into the villages of Cæsarea Philippi: and in the way he asked his disciples, saying unto them, Who do men say that I am? And | Now when Jesus came into the parts of Cæsarea Philippi, he asked his disciples, saying, Who do men say that the Son of Man[2] is? And they said, Some *say* John the Baptist; | And it came to pass, as he was praying alone, the disciples were with him: and he asked them, saying, Who do the multitudes say that I am? And they answering said, John |

---

[1] Mark vi. 14–16; Matth. xiv. 1, 2; Luke ix. 7–9.

[2] Matthew's "Son of Man" seems inappropriate here. The text of Mark and Luke is to be preferred. It is not likely that Jesus would have asserted that he was the Messianic Son of Man when he was asking his disciples what they thought of him.

|  |  |  |
|---|---|---|
| they told him, saying, John the Baptist: and others, Elijah; but others, One of the prophets. And he asked them, But who say ye that I am? Peter answereth and saith unto him, Thou art the Messiah. And he charged them that they should tell no man of him. | some Elijah: and others, Jeremiah, or one of the prophets. He saith unto them, But who say ye that I am? And Simon Peter answered and said, Thou art the Messiah, the Son of the living God. . . . Then charged he the disciples that they should tell no man that he was the Messiah. | the Baptist; but others *say*, Elijah; and others, that one of the old prophets is risen again. And he said unto them, But who say ye that I am? And Peter answering said. The Messiah of God. But he charged them, and commanded *them* to tell this to no man. |

The people were confounding Jesus with the prophetic herald of Malachi and of the great prophet of the exile,[1] but the apostles had now learned that Jesus himself was the Messiah, and they express their faith in him through their spokesman Peter.

The term, the Christ, is equivalent to the Messiah.[2] Mark reports this simple word, "the Messiah"; Luke, "the Messiah of God"; Matthew, "the Messiah, the son of the living God." It is clear that Jesus here accepted the recognition of himself as the Messiah by his apostles, and that he claimed to be the Son of God, the Messianic king of the Old Testament.

### THE RESURRECTION AND THE SECOND ADVENT.

§ 19. *Jesus will be rejected by the rulers, and put to death. He will rise again after three days. His disciples must follow him in self-denial and cross-bearing. He will come in his kingdom in the lifetime of some of his hearers. He will also come in the glory of his Father to reward every one according to his works.*

After the profession of faith on the part of Peter and

---

[1] Is. xl. 3; Mal. iii. 1; iv. 5.     [2] χριστός = מָשִׁיחַ. See pp. 34, 52.

the other apostles, Jesus taught them very distinctly that he must die and rise again.

| MARK viii. 31. | MATTHEW xvi. 21. | LUKE ix. 22. |
|---|---|---|
| And he began to teach them, that the Son of Man must suffer many things, and be rejected by the elders, and the chief priests, and the scribes, and be killed, and after three days rise again. | From that time began Jesus to show unto his disciples, how that he must go unto Jerusalem, and suffer many things of the elders and chief priests and scribes, and be killed, and the third day be raised up. | The Son of Man must suffer many things, and be rejected of the elders and chief priests and scribes, and be killed, and the third day be raised up. |

Jesus now for the first time, according to Mark, tells his apostles of his impending passion. He is a suffering Messiah. He has not come to reign, but first to suffer and die and rise again in order to come a second time to set up his kingdom and reign over it. He is to be persecuted by the rulers at Jerusalem and to be put to death. But he will rise again on the third day after a brief abode in the grave. This conception of the suffering Messiah is based on the predictions of the suffering prophet of the great prophet of the exile.[1] Jesus saw therein the way of the cross to the throne. He combines with the faithful prophet of the second Isaiah, the Son of Man of Daniel. As in a previous passage he had set forth the authority of the Son of Man to forgive sins on earth during an earthly ministry, he here advances to the conception that the Son of Man must suffer and die and rise again. He is to rise again to be the Son of Man on the clouds, of Daniel. His earthly life is a life prior to that advent. The three days here are doubtless a symbolic number to represent a short time, and are not

---
[1] Is. liii.

a precise and definite prediction of the time spent by Jesus in the abode of the dead. Furthermore the resurrection is here not so much the manifestation to his apostles, as the resurrection in all its fulness to be the Son of Man on the clouds.[1]

This prediction of the death and resurrection was a great disappointment to the apostles. They saw the near future, and that obscured the remote future. They caught at Jesus' prediction of his sufferings and death; they seem not to have understood the prediction of his resurrection. And yet that resurrection was to be the great Messianic testing to that generation and to all generations. It is not strange that Peter stumbled at these words of Jesus, and presumed to rebel against such an outcome of his Messianic hopes.

The spokesman of the apostles did not apprehend the rashness of his interference. He did not know that he was tempting Jesus to abandon his Messianic calling and cease to be the Messiah of prophecy in order to become the Messiah of the vain hopes and fanciful conceits of the zealots of his time. The Messiah rebukes his hasty disciple with stern words which set him right. Peter had forsaken his true position as a disciple to become a stumbling-block in the way of his Master. He had assumed the attitude of Satan, the great adversary of Jesus and his kingdom.

The Messiah soon after gives his disciples in general a lesson based upon his prediction. Not only is the Son of Man to undertake a work of suffering and humiliation unto death, but his disciples must follow him in the same path.

---

[1] Wendt, *Lehre Jesu*, ii. s. 545.

| MARK viii. 34—ix. 1. | MATT. xvi. 24-28. | LUKE ix. 23-27. |
|---|---|---|
| And he called unto him the multitude with his disciples, and said unto them, If any man would come after me, let him deny himself, and take up his cross, and follow me. For whosoever would save his self[1] shall lose it; and whosoever shall lose his self for my sake and the gospel's, shall save it. For what doth it profit a man, to gain the whole world, and forfeit his self? For what should a man give in exchange for his self? For whosoever shall be ashamed of me and of my words in this adulterous and sinful generation, the Son of Man also shall be ashamed of him, when he com- | Then said Jesus unto his disciples, If any man would come after me, let him deny himself, and take up his cross, and follow me. For whosoever would save his self[1] shall lose it: and whosoever shall lose his self for my sake shall find it. For what shall a man be profited, if he shall gain the whole world, and forfeit himself? or what shall a man give in exchange for himself? For the Son of Man shall come in the glory of his Father with his angels; and then shall he render unto every man according to his deeds. Verily, I say unto you, There be some of them that stand here, which shall in | And he said unto all, If any man would come after me, let him deny himself, and take up his cross daily, and follow me. For whosoever would save his self[1] shall lose it; but whosoever shall lose his self for my sake, the same shall save it. For what is a man profited if he gain the whole world, and lose or forfeit his own self? For whosoever shall be ashamed of me and of my words, of him shall the Son of Man be ashamed, when he cometh in his own glory, and *the glory* of the Father and of the holy angels. But I tell you of a truth, There be some of them that stand here, |

---

[1] The interpretation of this passage depends in a measure upon the meaning of the Greek ψυχή here. The Greek term ψυχή like נֶפֶשׁ of the Old Testament has a variety of meanings. The versions differ in their rendering here. Some take the meaning life, others the meaning soul. Whichever of these meanings is accepted should be uniformly used. But neither of these renderings seems to be correct. The contrast is not between body and soul. Jesus is not thinking of the loss of the soul as distinguished from the death of the body, as if he would save the soul at the risk of the body. The contrast is not between life and death, as if Jesus meant to teach the paradox that the sacrifice of life is the only way to gain life, which would then be explained by the contrast between life in this world and life in the world to come. It seems better to use the meaning self which is common to ψυχή in the New Testament and נֶפֶשׁ in the Old Testament.

| eth in the glory of his Father with the holy angels. And he said unto them, Verily, I say unto you, There be some here of them that stand *by*, which shall in no wise taste of death, till they see the kingdom of God come with power. | no wise taste of death, till they see the Son of Man coming in his kingdom. | which shall in no wise taste of death, till they see the kingdom of God. |
|---|---|---|

The contrast is between the man himself and the world about him. His aim should not be circumscribed by this world; he should fix his attention upon himself as outlasting all temporal things. It is the man himself who is to account to the Son of Man in the day of judgment, and it is of supreme importance that he should attach himself to the Son of Man as soon as possible ere that day. He must be one with the Son of Man and follow him in his humiliation unto death in order to share with him in the glory of his kingdom. Self-denial, cross-bearing, following the Son of Man, are indispensable for discipleship. They must so deny themselves that they follow their Master in humiliation and shame even to the malefactor's death. The life of self-denial and cross-bearing on the part of the disciple, in imitation of the Son of Man, will ultimately gain its reward. The Son of Man will go on to a malefactor's death, and they must follow him, if need be, to the gallows. But he will not abide in a malefactor's tomb. He will rise and come again as the Son of Man of prophecy to set up his kingdom and reward the faithful. Hence it is that the prediction of the resurrection of the Son of Man now passes over into a prediction of a second Advent of the Son of Man.

The terms used by the evangelists referring to the

Advent are somewhat different, and on this account give great difficulty in their interpretation and reconciliation. The three agree in telling us of the coming of the Son of Man in the glory of his Father with the holy angels to reward the faithful and shame the unfaithful, every man according to his works. This evidently is the Advent in glory and judgment at the close of the dispensation, and gives no difficulty, for it is the final scene of Old Testament prophecy. It is the Son of Man on the clouds of Daniel. The difficulty arises in connection with the closing words, that some of his hearers who were standing by him on that occasion would not taste of death until they saw "the kingdom of God," according to Luke; "the kingdom of God coming with power," according to Mark; and "the Son of Man coming in his kingdom," according to Matthew. In these words it is definitely taught that within the lifetime of some of his hearers the kingdom of God would come, the Son of Man would come in it, and they would see its power. Is this coming in the kingdom the same as the coming in the glory of the Father of the previous context, or is it a different coming? There is nothing in the text or context to distinguish them. And yet they might be different events if evidence were produced from other predictions of Jesus. Indeed there is nothing in the context to show what is the relation between the resurrection of the Son of Man and these advents, whether these are all one and the same event or two different events, or three stages in the Messianic work of Jesus. If there is the mingling in the same picture of different events far apart in time, Jesus is simply following the method of the predictions of the Old Testament. We are guided to separate the advent to establish the kingdom from the Advent in glory to reward the faithful disciples, by the parables of the kingdom already considered. These teach us that the kingdom was to be established in the world as good seed and to grow in several stages from a small beginning until it attained a great and glorious fruition. Accordingly the advent of the Son of Man in his kingdom during the lifetime of his hearers may refer to the setting up of his kingdom in the world, an advent to be carefully distinguished from his Advent in glory and in judgment, which cannot take place until the kingdom is ripe for judgment and glory. The prediction of the resurrection of the Son of Man is a third event, distinct from the other two, as will appear in the prophecies that follow. We accordingly have here three distinct Messianic events predicted by Jesus—(1) the resurrection of the Son of Man ; (2) his advent to set up his kingdom in the lifetime of his hearers ; and (3) his Advent in glory for judgment.

### THE TRANSFIGURATION.

§ 20. *Jesus manifests his glory in the Christophany of the Transfiguration which is connected with the theophanic voice claiming him as the beloved and accepted Son of God, and is associated with the witness of Moses and Elijah.*

In the midst of the earthly life of Jesus, a theophany marks the second stage of his Messianic career. This event is reported by the synoptists, and is also mentioned in the epistle of Peter.[1]

And after six days Jesus taketh with him Peter, and James, and John, and bringeth them up into a high mountain apart by themselves : and he was transfigured before them : and his garments became glistering, exceeding white ; so as no fuller on earth can whiten them. And there appeared unto them Elijah

---

[1] Mark ix. 2–8 ; Matt. xvii. 1–8 ; Luke ix. 28–36 ; 1 Peter i. 16–18.

with Moses: and they were talking with Jesus. And Peter answereth and saith to Jesus, Rabbi, it is good for us to be here: and let us make three tabernacles; one for thee, and one for Moses, and one for Elijah. For he knew not what to answer; for they became sore afraid. And there came a cloud overshadowing them: and there came a voice out of the cloud, This is my beloved Son: hear ye him. And suddenly looking round about, they saw no one any more, save Jesus only with themselves.
(Mark ix. 2–8.)

There are three things that demand our attention in this central event. (1) The Theophany is essentially the same as that at the Baptism. The voice of God claims Jesus as the Son of God, beloved and well-pleasing to Him. This puts the seal of divine approval upon the first part of the ministry of Jesus as the Messianic Son of God, and expresses confidence in its future. (2) The place of the Theophany of the dove at the Baptism is taken by the manifestation of Moses and Elijah. These two representatives of the old dispensation come forth from their abode in the world of the departed to bear witness to Jesus. Luke tells us that they spake of the departure which Jesus was about to make in Jerusalem. Their witness to his Messiahship and their testimony as to his work, strengthened Jesus for the passion which he was henceforth to face. (3) But the most important thing was the transfiguration of Jesus himself. Here for the first time the immanent glory of the Messiah shines forth in Christophany. This sign he grants his three favored apostles, and this comfort he takes to himself ere he sets his face towards the cross.

### THE KINGDOM OF THE CHILDLIKE.

§ 21. *The kingdom is open to the childlike and the penitent but difficult of access by the rich. Those who have given up all for the Messiah will be rewarded a hundredfold.*

There are several discourses that set forth a kingdom

into which there is immediate access by those who have the proper qualifications.

| MATT. xviii. 1–5. | MARK ix. 33–37. | LUKE ix. 46–48. |
|---|---|---|
| In that hour came the disciples unto Jesus, saying, Who then is greatest in the kingdom of heaven? And he called to him a little child, and set him in the midst of them, and said, Verily I say unto you, except ye turn, and become as little children, ye shall in no wise enter into the kingdom of heaven. Whosoever therefore shall humble himself as this little child, the same is the greatest in the kingdom of heaven. And whoso shall receive one such little child in my name receiveth me. | And they came to Capernaum: and when he was in the house he asked them, What were ye reasoning in the way? But they held their peace: for they had disputed one with another in the way, who *was* the greatest. And he sat down, and called the twelve; and he saith unto them, If any man would be first, he shall be last of all, and minister of all. And he took a little child, and set him in the midst of them: and taking him in his arms, he said unto them, Whosoever shall receive one of such little children in my name, receiveth me: and whosoever receiveth me, receiveth not me, but him that sent me. | And there arose a reasoning among them which of them was the greatest. But when Jesus saw the reasoning of their heart, he took a little child, and set him by his side, and said unto them, Whosoever shall receive this little child in my name receiveth me: and whosoever shall receive me receiveth him that sent me: for he that is least among you all, the same is great. |

The parallels in Mark and Luke make no mention of the kingdom, but in other respects are essentially the same as Matthew. This discourse was held in Capernaum, the scene of so much of the activity of Jesus.

The kingdom of the Messiah was the great object of their anxieties and hopes. The question of rank in the kingdom was one that would naturally arise in the minds of the apostles, for they could not get beyond the conception of a kingdom of power and rank in the land of Palestine. Jesus gives them a lesson that was most striking in its contrasts. The little child is the model of the great in the kingdom of the Messiah, and childlikeness the measure of excellence. Men must put aside all questions of rank and power in order to enter the kingdom and share its blessings. They must turn about and become transformed into little children ere they can enter into the kingdom of the Messiah, and then after they have entered it, their growth must still be in the direction of childlikeness in order to the attainment of higher degrees of excellence and rank in the kingdom.

The apostles could not understand this strange doctrine. Jesus soon afterwards repeats it with slight differences:

| MARK x. 13-15. | MATT. xix. 13, 14. | LUKE xviii. 15-17. |
|---|---|---|
| And they were bringing unto him little children, that he should touch them: and the disciples rebuked them. But when Jesus saw it he was moved with indignation, and said unto them, Suffer the little children to come unto me; forbid them not; for to such belongeth the kingdom of God. Verily I say unto you, whosoever shall not receive the kingdom of God as a little child, he shall in no wise enter therein. | Then were there brought unto him little children, that he should lay his hands on them, and pray: and the disciples rebuked them. But Jesus said, Suffer the little children, and forbid them not, to come unto me: for to such belongeth the kingdom of heaven. | And they were bringing unto him also their babes, that he should touch them: but when the disciples saw it, they rebuked them. But Jesus called them unto him, saying, Suffer the little children to come unto me, and forbid them not: for to such belongeth the kingdom of God. Verily I say unto you, Whosoever shall not receive the kingdom of God as a little child, he shall in no wise enter therein. |

Jesus here teaches his disciples that the kingdom belongs to little children. They have a title to it, not indeed by birthright, but because of the appropriateness of their childlike natures for the life of the kingdom. In the previous discourse only the childlike could enter the kingdom. Here they are conceived as already in it and as entitled to its privileges. Accordingly all who would enter the kingdom must be childlike.

In the previous discourse men were to be transformed into children in order to enter the kingdom. Here the kingdom is represented as coming to them, as being offered to them, and they are privileged to receive it in a childlike spirit. This doctrine of the kingdom is in accordance with the lessons of the parables of the kingdom. The good seed are the attentive, receptive hearers. Such are the childlike. These are the true members of the kingdom, the heirs of its rights and privileges. Its growth is in the development of such childlike characters.

This doctrine is enforced by the experiment with the rich young ruler, who is taught that something more than scrupulous obedience to the moral law is required. The high standard of Christlike perfection is held up to him. A counsel of Christian perfection is given by Jesus. This man is called to sacrifice his property and wealth, to make himself poor, and to follow Jesus in his life of poverty and self-sacrifice for the good of men. The rich young man cannot rise to this call of Jesus, which might have made him another apostle. He is hindered by his riches from learning the lesson of Jesus. He thus affords a striking contrast between the rich and strong of the world and the childlike poor of the kingdom. This is given by the three synoptists in essentially the same report, with the single exception that Matthew inserts a word of Jesus, verse 28, which is given by Luke in a later and better historical connection.[1]

| MARK x. 23-31. | MATTH. xix. 23-27, 29, 30. | LUKE xviii. 24-30. |
|---|---|---|
| And Jesus looked round about, and saith unto his disciples, How hardly shall they that have riches enter into the kingdom of God! And the disciples were amazed at his words. But Jesus answereth again, and saith unto them, Children, how hard is it for them that trust in riches to enter into the kingdom of God! It is easier for a camel to go through a needle's eye, than for a rich man to enter into the kingdom of God. And they were astonished exceedingly, saying unto him, Then who can be saved? Jesus looking upon them saith, With men it is impossible, but not with God: for all things are possible with God. Peter began to say unto him, Lo, we have left all, and have followed thee. Jesus said, Verily I say unto you, There is no man that hath | And Jesus said unto his disciples, Verily I say unto you, It is hard for a rich man to enter into the kingdom of heaven. And again, I say unto you, It is easier for a camel to go through a needle's eye, than for a rich man to enter into the kingdom of God. And when the disciples heard it, they were astonished exceedingly, saying, Who then can be saved? And Jesus looking upon *them* said to them, With men this is impossible; but with God all things are possible. Then answered Peter and said unto him, Lo, we have left all, and followed thee; what then shall we have? And Jesus said unto them: . . . . . And every one that hath left houses, or brethren, or sisters, or father, or mother, or children, or lands, for my name's sake, shall receive a hun- | And Jesus seeing him said, How hardly shall they that have riches enter into the kingdom of God! For it is easier for a camel to enter in through a needle's eye, than for a rich man to enter into the kingdom of God. And they that heard it said, Then who can be saved? But he said, The things which are impossible with men are possible with God. And Peter said, Lo, we have left our own, and followed thee. And he said unto them, Verily I say unto you, There is no man that hath left house, or wife, or brethren, or parents, or children, for the kingdom of God's sake, who shall not receive manifold more in this time, |

---

[1] Luke xxii. 30.

| left house, or brethren, or sisters, or mother, or father, or children, or lands, for my sake, and for the gospel's sake, but he shall receive a hundredfold now in this time, houses, and brethren, and sisters, and mothers, and children, and lands, with persecutions; and in the world to come eternal life. But many *that are* first shall be last; and the last first. | dredfold, and shall inherit eternal life. But many shall be last *that are* first; and first *that are* last. | and in the world to come eternal life. |

The doctrine of this passage is sufficiently clear. The contrast is here between the rich and the poor, as in previous discourses it had been between men and children. The Master does not contrast the rich and poor as such, but the rich as seeking and trusting in riches, with the poor as giving up riches in houses and lands, in relations and friends, for the sake of the Messiah. Such rich men can no more enter the kingdom of the Messiah than a camel can pass through the needle's eye. It is impossible. And yet the kingdom of the Messiah has an entrance through which men can pass. As in the previous discourse men must become children, so in this discourse the rich must become poor by divesting themselves of their riches. Only in this way can they enter through the needle's eye of the kingdom. Our Saviour does not mean to teach that all men must become poor in order to enter his kingdom in any mechanical or external sense any more than he meant in the previous discourse that men must be transformed in their bodies into boys. But men must become childlike in their dispositions and characters. Men must give up their trust in riches and use them as the riches of God for the sake of the kingdom of God. They must become poor in their dispositions and characters, poor in spirit. Thus the kingdom of heaven is a kingdom of the childlike and the poor, and in this respect entirely different from the kingdom of the world, where manly strength, and power, and riches have the highest places of rank and glory.

### THE SON OF MAN IS A RANSOM.

§ 22. *The Son of Man will be betrayed, cruelly abused and delivered by the rulers of the Jews to the Gentiles to be crucified. He will rise again after three days. The apostles must follow the Master in sufferings, and will be rewarded in the kingdom; but the highest places will be assigned by the Father. The Son of Man is a ransom.*

Jesus gave his disciples a second prediction of his death and resurrection.

| Mark ix. 30-32. | Matt. xvii. 22, 23. | Luke ix. 43-45. |
|---|---|---|
| And they went forth from thence, and passed through Galilee; and he would not that any man should know it. For he taught his disciples, and said unto them, The Son of Man is delivered up into the hands of men, and they shall kill him; and when he is killed, after three days he shall rise again. But they understood not the saying, and were afraid to ask him. | And while they abode in Galilee, Jesus said unto them, The Son of Man shall be delivered up into the hands of men; and they shall kill him, and the third day he shall be raised up. And they were exceeding sorry. | But while all were marvelling at all the things which he did, he said unto his disciples, Let these words sink into your ears; for the Son of Man shall be delivered up into the hands of men. But they understood not this saying, and it was concealed from them, that they should not perceive it: and they were afraid to ask him about this saying. |

In this discourse Jesus renews the prediction of the death of the Son of Man and his resurrection after three days, and adds that he would be betrayed. This troubles his disciples, for they cannot understand it.

The third prediction of his death and resurrection reported by Mark was in connection with his last journey to Jerusalem with the apostles. It seems to have been occasioned by the request of the mother of James and John, that her sons might occupy the two highest places in the kingdom, nearest the Master. This request showed on the one side great faith in the Messiahship of Jesus and in the advent of his kingdom; but on the other side a great ignorance of the doctrine of the kingdom he had been teaching them. A kingdom of service and grace must precede the kingdom of reward and glory. The incident gives occasion for once more teaching the disciples that their Master must soon be put to death, and that they must share in his sufferings. It is true that the evangelists give the prediction before the request. But it is probable that this is a logical rather than a chronological order.

| MARK x. 32–34. | MATT. xx. 17–19. | LUKE xviii. 31–34. |
|---|---|---|
| And they were in the way, going up to Jerusalem; and Jesus was going before them: and they were amazed; and they that followed were afraid. And he took again the twelve, and began to tell them the things that were to happen unto him, *saying*, Behold, we go up to Jerusalem; | And as Jesus was going up to Jerusalem, he took the twelve disciples apart, and in the way he said unto them, Behold, we go up to Jerusalem; and the Son of Man shall be delivered unto the chief priests and scribes: and they shall condemn him to death, and shall deliver him | And he took unto him the twelve, and said unto them, Behold, we go up to Jerusalem, and all the things that are written by the prophets shall be accomplished unto the Son of Man. For he shall be delivered up unto the Gentiles, and shall be mocked, and shamefully entreated, and spit |

and the Son of Man shall be delivered unto the chief priests and the scribes; and they shall condemn him to death, and shall deliver him unto the Gentiles: and they shall mock him, and shall spit upon him, and shall scourge him, and shall kill him; and after three days he shall rise again.

unto the Gentiles to mock, and to scourge, and to crucify: and the third day he shall be raised up.

upon: and they shall scourge and kill him: and the third day he shall rise again. And they understood none of these things; and this saying was hid from them, and they perceived not the things that were said.

This prediction differs from the previous two in its detailed statement of the sufferings of the Son of Man. Jesus is first to be delivered to the chief priests and scribes. These in council assembled are to condemn him to death. They are then to deliver him into the hands of the Gentiles. He is to be mocked, spit upon, scourged, and finally crucified. Thus Jesus clearly told his disciples that he was to die as a malefactor, an outcast from the nation. His sufferings were to be the greatest conceivable. His death was to be a shameful one. This hard fact, this stern event, confronts them. The only relief is the promise of the resurrection on the third day. This emphasis upon the sufferings of the Son of Man is a fitting prelude to the prediction of the sufferings of the apostles.

MARK x. 35-45.

And there came near unto him James and John, the sons of Zebedee, saying unto him, Master, we would that thou shouldest do for us whatsoever we shall ask of thee. And he said unto them, What would ye that I should do for you? And

MATTH. xx. 20-28.

Then came to him the mother of the sons of Zebedee with her sons, worshipping *him*, and asking a certain thing of him. And he said unto her, What wouldest thou? She saith unto him, Command that these my two sons may they said unto him, Grant unto us that we may sit, one on thy right hand, and one on *thy* left hand, in thy glory. But Jesus said unto them, Ye know not what ye ask. Are ye able to drink the cup that I drink? or to be baptized with the baptism that I am baptized with? And they said unto him, We are able. And Jesus said unto them, The cup that I drink ye shall drink; and with the baptism that I am baptized withal shall ye be baptized: but to sit on my right hand or on *my* left hand, is not mine to give: but *it is for them* for whom it hath been prepared. And when the ten heard it, they began to be moved with indignation concerning James and John. And Jesus called them to him, and saith unto them, Ye know that they who are accounted to rule over the Gentiles lord it over them; and their great ones exercise authority over them. But it is not so among you: but whosoever would become great among you, shall be your minister: and whosoever would be first among you, shall be servant of all. For the Son of Man also came not to be ministered unto, but to minister, and to give his self a ransom for many.

sit, one on thy right hand, and one on thy left hand, in thy kingdom. But Jesus answered and said, Ye know not what ye ask. Are ye able to drink the cup that I am about to drink? They say unto him, We are able. He saith unto them, My cup indeed ye shall drink: but to sit on my right hand, and on *my* left hand, is not mine to give, but *it is for them* for whom it hath been prepared of my Father. And when the ten heard it, they were moved with indignation concerning the two brethren. But Jesus called them unto him, and said, Ye know that the rulers of the Gentiles lord it over them, and their great ones exercise authority over them. Not so shall it be among you: but whosoever would become great among you shall be your minister; and whosoever would be first among you shall be your servant: even as the Son of Man came not to be ministered unto, but to minister, and to give his self a ransom for many.

The report of Mark is fullest here. Luke does not mention this incident. Jesus sets forth his sufferings as a bitter cup and a baptism of suffering. The apostles will have to share in them. Jesus came at this time to minister and not to reign. They, like their master, are first to minister; those who become great must excel in service. The Son of Man came to give his life, or rather his self, a ransom for many. And the disciples are to follow his example. It is well for them that they learn their duty of service. They will not go unrewarded. They will receive the rank due to sufferings and service. But the highest places in the kingdom are so high that they are beyond the gift of the Son of Man himself. They are the award of the Father who gives the Son of Man his reward, and associates the most deserving with him.

In this passage Jesus teaches his disciples the redemptive meaning of his self-sacrifice. His life, which he gives up in death, or rather his self, his entire person and service which he gives in ministry, is a ransom for many. Ransom[1] may be interpreted of the redemptive covering price of the Old Testament usage which purchases freedom from bondage. So Wendt thinks of the bondage to death[2] and Beyschlag of the bondage to sin, from which the Son of Man delivers the disciples by his self-sacrificing death.[3] Although Jesus uses the term Son of Man, he is thinking of the prophetic servant of the second Isaiah here as in the previous passages. The term itself was probably derived from the second Isaiah:

> I have given Egypt as thy ransom,
> Cush and Seba in thy stead.
> Since thou art precious in mine eyes;
> Thou art honoured, and I love thee;
> And I will give mankind in thy stead,
> And peoples instead of thy life. (Is. xliii. 3, 4).

Egypt, Cush, and Seba are heathen ransom prices for Israel. They are given to the conqueror of Babylon to induce him to restore Israel to his land. Israel is redeemed from bondage by this ransom price.[4]

As these nations are the ransom price there, so Jesus, the Son of Man, is the ransom price here. This concep-

---

[1] λύτρον.
[2] *Lehre Jesu*, s. 516.
[3] *Neutest. Theologie*, s. 149.
[4] Briggs' *Messianic Prophecy*, p. 350.

tion of the Son of Man as the ransom price is based on another passage of the same prophet.

The servant of Yahweh interposed as a mediator for his people; he himself made the trespass-offering. He justified many.¹ So the son of Man here interposes as a ministering servant between his disciples and their enemies. He takes upon himself the sin, the evil, and the death which were threatening them. He paid the ransom price by offering himself as victim instead of them. Jesus does not intimate to whom the price was paid, nor from what the ransom was made. He makes a comprehensive statement which we should beware of limiting.² He not only gives his life up in death, but he gives himself in his entire ministry prior to death and subsequent to death. He is to be the ransom, not only on the cross, but during his life of interposition, which leads to the cross, and in his mediatorial life, which was subsequent to the cross. He interposes and gives himself as the ransom, in that he is and continues to be the Son of Man, the mediating, interposing servant of God, until his entire redemptive work has been accomplished. The ransom price was not paid to God, who claimed no such ransom. The Son of God was on a mission from God. It was not paid to the devil, because the devil was not entitled to it and his authority was never recognized by Jesus. It was paid to sin and evil as their ransom price, in order to deliver his disciples from the penalty of sin and evil, which threatened them from the whole order of nature and the whole constitution of human affairs.

## THE MESSIAH CLAIMS HIS OWN.

§ 23. *Jesus enters Jerusalem as the king of peace. He is recognized by the multitudes, but is rejected by the Pharisees.*

---

¹ Is. liii.   ² Adeney, *Theology of the New Testament*, p. 66.

As the time for his passion draws nigh, Jesus departs from his previous custom and makes a public entry into Jerusalem and claims recognition as the Messiah.

### A. MARK xi. 7-10.

And they bring the colt unto Jesus, and cast on him their garments; and he sat upon him. And many spread their garments upon the way; and others branches, which they had cut from the fields. And they that went before, and they that followed, cried, Hosanna; Blessed *is* he that cometh in the name of the Lord: Blessed *is* the kingdom that cometh, *the kingdom* of our father David: Hosanna in the highest.

### B. MATTHEW xxi. 7-11, 15, 16

And brought the ass, and the colt, and put on them their garments; and he sat thereon. And the most part of the multitude spread their garments in the way; and others cut branches from the trees, and spread them in the way. And the multitudes that went before him, and that followed, cried, saying, Hosanna to the Son of David: Blessed *is* he that cometh in the name of the Lord; Hosanna in the highest. And when he was come into Jerusalem, all the city was stirred, saying, Who is this? And the multitudes said, This is the prophet, Jesus, from Nazareth of Galilee. . . . . But when the chief priests and the scribes saw the wonderful things that he did, and the children that were crying in the temple and saying, Hosanna to the Son of David; they were moved with indignation, and said unto him, Hearest thou what these are saying? And Jesus saith unto them, Yea: did ye never read, Out of the mouth of babes and sucklings thou hast perfected praise?

### C. LUKE xix. 35-40.

And they brought him to Jesus: and they threw their garments upon the colt, and set Jesus thereon. And as he went, they spread their garments in the way. And as he was now drawing nigh, even at the descent of the Mount of Olives, the whole multitude of the disciples began to rejoice and praise God with a loud voice for all the mighty works which they had seen; saying, Blessed *is* the King that cometh in the name of the Lord: peace in heaven, and glory in the highest. And some of the Pharisees from the multitude said unto him, Master, rebuke thy disciples. And he answered and said, I tell you that, if these shall hold their peace, the stones will cry out.

### D. JOHN xii. 12, 13.

On the morrow a great multitude that had come to the feast, when they heard that Jesus was coming to Jerusalem, took the branches of the palm-trees, and went forth to meet him, and cried out, Hosanna: Blessed *is* he that cometh in the name of the Lord, even the King of Israel.

This public entry into Jerusalem and the temple is so different from his ordinary methods that it marks a crisis in the life of Jesus. He allows his Messianic dignity to shine forth upon the nation, and for a few moments, possibly for a few hours, is recognized by the people as the Messiah. The multitude heap up Messianic terms in their acclamations. "The kingdom that cometh, that of our father David" is the acclaim reported by Mark. It seemed as if the kingdom of David of the prophets was now to be inaugurated. "The son of David" is the word preserved by Matthew; "The king of Israel," by John. These are titles of the Messianic king whom they see in Jesus. Luke reports the words, "The king that cometh in the name of the Lord." They see in Jesus the king predicted in the prophecies of the Old Testament. This public recognition of the Messiah by the multitudes is displeasing to the Pharisees, who would have Jesus command their silence. But Jesus does not refuse the recognition he has for once courted. He replies that the multitude could not do otherwise. His Messianic dignity was so transparent that even the stones would cry out if the multitude were silent.

### THE REJECTED CORNER-STONE.

§ 24. *The rulers of Israel have rejected the prophets and they are about to reject the Messiah, the corner-stone of the kingdom. The kingdom will be taken from them and given to a faithful nation.*

During his last week in Jerusalem Jesus contends with the Pharisees who are seeking to entrap him and put him to death. Mark reports a parable which Jesus gives them, in which he sets forth that his rejection is but the culmination of their rejection of all the prophets.

And on this basis he claims to be the corner stone, of the prophecy of the Old Testament.

| MARK xii. 1-11. | MATT. xxi. 33-42. | LUKE xx. 9-17. |
|---|---|---|
| A man planted a vineyard, and set a hedge about it, and digged a pit for the winepress, and built a tower, and let it out to husbandmen, and went into another country. And at the season he sent to the husbandmen a servant, that he might receive from the husbandmen of the fruits of the vineyard. And they took him, and beat him, and sent him away empty. And again he sent unto them another servant; and him they wounded in the head, and handled shamefully. And he sent another; and him they killed: and many others; beating some, and killing some. He had yet one, a beloved son: he sent him last unto them, saying, They will reverence my son. But those husbandmen said among themselves, This is the heir; come, let us kill him, and the inheritance shall be ours. And they took him, and killed him, and cast him forth | There was a man that was a householder, which planted a vineyard, and set a hedge about it, and digged a winepress in it, and built a tower, and let it out to husbandmen, and went into another country. And when the season of the fruits drew near, he sent his servants to the husbandmen, to receive his fruits. And the husbandmen took his servants, and beat one, and killed another, and stoned another. Again he sent other servants more than the first: and they did unto them in like manner. But afterward he sent unto them his son, saying, They will reverence my son. But the husbandmen, when they saw the son, said among themselves, This is the heir; come, let us kill him, and take his inheritance. And they took him, and cast him forth out of the vineyard, and killed him. When therefore the lord of the vineyard shall | A man planted a vineyard, and let it out to husbandmen, and went into another country for a long time. And at the season he sent unto the husbandmen a servant, that they should give him of the fruit of the vineyard: but the husbandmen beat him, and sent him away empty. And he sent yet another servant: and him also they beat, and handled him shamefully, and sent him away empty. And he sent yet a third: and him also they wounded, and cast him forth. And the lord of the vineyard said, What shall I do? I will send my beloved son: it may be they will reverence him. But when the husbandmen saw him, they reasoned one with another, saying, This is the heir: let us kill him, that the inheritance may be ours. And they cast him forth out of the vineyard and killed him What therefore will the lord of the vine- |

out of the vineyard. What therefore will the lord of the vineyard do? he will come and destroy the husbandmen, and will give the vineyard unto others. Have ye not read even this scripture;

The stone which the builders rejected,
The same was made the head of the corner:
This was from the Lord,
And it is marvellous in our eyes?

come, what will he do unto those husbandmen? They say unto him, He will miserably destroy those miserable men, and will let out the vineyard unto other husbandmen, which shall render him the fruits in their seasons. Jesus saith unto them, Did ye never read in the Scriptures,

The stone which the builders rejected,
The same was made the head of the corner:
This was from the Lord,
And it is marvellous in our eyes?

yard do unto them? He will come and destroy these husbandmen, and will give the vineyard unto others. And when they heard it, they said, God forbid. But he looked upon them, and said, What then is this that is written,

The stone which the builders rejected,
The same was made the head of the corner?

In the parable of the wicked husbandmen Jesus takes up the figure of the vineyard which is familiar in the usage of the Old Testament[1] as a representation of the kingdom of God. God made Israel his kingdom and gave it in charge of rulers who were in covenant to yield the fruits to their Lord. They were unfaithful to their covenant. The servants, sent from time to time reminding them of their obligations and demanding fruits, are the prophets calling to repentance. These they persecute and slay. At last the Son, the Messianic prophet, is sent with the same prophetic call, and he is slain. This is the last hour of waiting on the part of God. The climax of guilt has been reached. The doom of the rulers of Israel has come. The vineyard, the kingdom

---

[1] Isa. v.

of God, will be taken from them, and will be given to a nation who will yield the fruits of repentance and good works. This parable is the basis upon which Jesus puts forth his claim to be the corner-stone of the kingdom in the representations of the prophecy of the Old Testament.[1] They are about to reject the precious corner-stone of God. But their rejection will not avail. That stone will become the head of the corner. Here the rejection of the Messiah is represented as the casting away of the corner-stone, and the resurrection as the lifting of the corner-stone to its place in the building. In this parable Jesus shows the relation of the kingdom of the Messiah to the kingdom of God in the Old Testament. The kingdom of the Messiah is a continuation of the kingdom of God under the Old Testament. Then God had ruled through kings and priests. These had proved unfaithful to him. The rule of God was still carried on through the priests and scribes who had control of the religion of Israel. These were unfaithful as their predecessors had been. They had rejected the warnings of the prophets; they now reject the Messiah himself. This rejection of the Messiah brings the kingdom of God under the Old Testament to an end. It is to die with its Messiah. But a new kingdom is to rise up in its place with the resurrection of the Messiah. He is to be the corner-stone of the new kingdom of God, in which Israel, as a nation, and the rulers, as descendants of the ancient authorities appointed of God, will have no place; but a new and spiritual Israel with new and spiritual rulers, will occupy the vineyard and constitute the kingdom under the sway of the Messiah.

---

[1] Isa. xxviii. 14-18; Ps. cxviii. 22, 23. See Briggs' *Messianic Prophecy*, p. 208.

## THE LORD OF DAVID.

§ 25. *Jesus is the Messianic king, the son of David and his Lord.*

Jesus in his contest with the Pharisees and rulers, in the last week of his ministry, presses upon them his claims to be the Messiah. The Synoptists unite in an account of the words of Jesus claiming to be the Messiah of Psalm cx.

| MARK xii. 35-37. | MATT. xxii. 41-45. | LUKE xx. 41-44. |
|---|---|---|
| And Jesus answered and said, as he taught in the temple, How say the scribes that the Messiah is the son of David? David himself said in the Holy Spirit, The Lord said unto my Lord, Sit thou on my right hand, till I make thine enemies the footstool of thy feet. David himself calleth him Lord; and whence is he his son? | Now while the Pharisees were gathered together, Jesus asked them a question, saying, What think ye of the Messiah? Whose son is he? They say unto him, *The son of David.* He saith unto them, How then doth David in the Spirit call him Lord, saying, The Lord said unto my Lord, Sit thou on my right hand, till I put thine enemies underneath thy feet? If David then calleth him Lord, how is he his son? | And he said unto them, How say they that the Messiah is David's son? For David himself saith in the book of Psalms, The Lord said unto my Lord, Sit thou on my right hand, till I make thine enemies the footstool of thy feet. David therefore calleth him Lord, and how is he his son? |

Jesus here cites a Messianic passage from Ps. cx.[1] in which the poet describes the conquering king after the order of Melchizedek. If David be the author of this psalm, as the Pharisees supposed,[2] this conquering king

---

[1] See Briggs' *Messianic Prophecy*, p. 132.

[2] It does not follow from this that Jesus held to the Davidic authorship of the psalm. He was arguing from the position of his opponents, not from his own; he was pressing them with an apparent inconsistency in their position which they could not explain or remove. He was not called upon to state his own views of the authorship of this psalm.

is his son and at the same time his lord. This seems to be contrary to nature. It raises the question whether the Messiah may not be something more than the son and heir of David. He must be not only a greater monarch, but greater in office and in dignity than David in order to fulfil the ideal. This was indicated in the psalm so far as the Messiah was a king after the order of Melchizedek. That was something more than the dynasty of David; for it involved the priestly as well as the royal office, and it suggested the thought that as Melchisedek was higher in office than Abraham, so the Messiah was to be higher in office than David,—his lord as well as his son. The priests and scribes were not prepared to explain this mystery. They could not answer the inquiry of Jesus. Their inability to answer this question ought to have opened their minds to see and to admit that the Messiah when he came would be something different from what they expected, and that they ought not to stumble at Messianic attributes that seemed to them strange and difficult to understand. Jesus was himself this priest-king and lord of the psalmist, but he was also something more, namely, the suffering prophet, and the rejected corner-stone. The reconciliation of all these apparent inconsistencies could not be made to them by Jesus at that time, but only by the progress of events when history would be the true interpreter of prophecy. These Pharisees were silenced by the words of Jesus. They would have acted wisely if they had awaited in silence the unfolding of the life of Jesus, which would gradually have unveiled his Messiahship and set forth his reconciliation of the varying features of Old Testament prophecy in the higher harmonics of its historic fulfilment.

### ERE ANOTHER COMMUNION-MEAL.

**§ 26.** *Jesus instituted the Lord's Supper as the sacrificial meal of the new covenant, and promised that the kingdom of God would come ere another communion-meal.*

Jesus in his earlier ministry preached the speedy advent of the kingdom. He again took up this subject when he instituted the Lord's supper.

There are two important sayings of Jesus on this occasion which are pregnant with Messianic meaning. The first of these is the saying of Jesus when he gave the cup to his disciples:

> This is my blood of the covenant which is shed for many.[1]
> (Mark xiv. 22-25.)

It is clear that Jesus represents here that his blood, which was about to be shed on the cross, was blood shed for his disciples for the purpose of establishing a new covenant relation. Jesus was doubtless thinking of the new covenant of Jeremiah[2] and Ezekiel,[3] and especially of the second Isaiah, where the new covenant is connect-

---

[1] See also Matt. xxvi. 26-29; Luke xxii. 18-20; 1 Cor. xi. 23-26. This simple saying of Jesus, as reported in Mark, is explained in Matthew by the addition "unto remission of sins." That was one of the aims of the shedding of the blood of the Messiah. This is a correct statement, as is clear from other passages of the New Testament, but it is not probable that Jesus uttered these words, for Matthew alone gives them. Luke and Paul add "new" to covenant. This also is explanatory, to bring out clearly the antithesis between the old covenant sacrifice at Horeb and the new covenant sacrifice at Calvary. But this antithesis is really implied in the simple statement that the blood was blood of the covenant. Luke and Paul use the explanatory "this cup" for "this" of Matthew and Mark, and change "my blood of the covenant" into "covenant in my blood" which do not change the meaning. See Jülicher, *Zur Geschichte der Abendmahlsfeier in der ältesten Kirche*, in the *Theologische Abhandlungen Weizsäcker gewidmet*, 1892, s. 237 *seq.*, and Spitta, *Urchristenthum*, I., s. 318 *seq.*

[2] Jeremiah xxxi. 31-37.      [3] Ezekiel xxxiv. 25-31; xxxvii. 26-28.

ed with the servant of Yahweh.¹ It is this connection of the new covenant with the suffering and dying servant which leads to the thought of the covenant sacrifice. This covenant sacrifice is an antithesis to the covenant sacrifice of Horeb.² The blood of the covenant was in the old covenant sprinkled upon those who entered into covenant relations. Here the blood was shed for many, but it was to be drunk in a cup under the form of wine. Participation by drinking is more expressive than participation by sprinkling. The flesh of the victim was eaten in the sacrifice of the old covenant; the flesh of Jesus was eaten in the form of bread in the new covenant. Here Jesus plainly teaches that his impending death is the death of a sacrificial victim; that it is to be of the nature of a peace-offering, and especially a sacrifice instituting the new covenant, which was to take the place of the initial sacrifice of the old covenant with all that was involved therein. In accordance with the predictions of the prophets, the suffering servant was to introduce a new dispensation based on a covenant sacrifice, which was to take the place of the old dispensation with all its institutions of law and prophecy which were based upon the covenant sacrifice at Horeb.³

The report of Mark and Matthew would give us nothing more than the institution of a covenant in which those who partook of the victim would represent all their successors. But Luke gives the additional words, "This do in remembrance of me," which seem to imply

---

¹ Isaiah xlii. 6; liv. 10-17; lv. 3; lix. 21; lxi. 8, 9. See Briggs' *Messianic Prophecy*, pp. 496, 497.

² Exodus xxiv. 1-12.

³ This sacrifice is specifically a covenant sacrifice which belongs to the class of peace offerings. It is incorrect to think of a sin-offering here, which is of an entirely different class, and where the blood is never applied to persons, but always to altars. See Wendt, *Lehre Jesu*, s. 586.

a command to repeat the celebration as a memorial meal and also the substitution of a Christian Passover for a Jewish Passover.[1] Paul not only gives this sentence of Jesus, but also adds another more explicit, "This do, as oft as ye drink *it*, in remembrance of me." Jesus, according to Paul, looked forward to constant and oft-repeated observances of the Lord's supper as a Christian Passover. If it was to be oft repeated, it implied something more than the covenant sacrifice of Horeb. That sacrifice was the only covenant sacrifice for the Old Testament dispensation and needed no renewal. It was partaken of by the people for themselves and all their successors. But it was also at the foundation of all the sacrificial system of the old covenant legislation and history. The oft-repeated participation in the Lord's supper, however, carried with it the conception of a continuous sacrifice. The death of the victim was but once, but the provision of flesh and blood eaten and drunk, in which the entire meaning of the covenant sacrifice is always found, implied a continual provision of the sacrificial victim.

Paul adds an explanatory word of his own:

For as often as ye eat this bread, and drink the cup, ye proclaim the Lord's death till he come. (1 Cor. xi. 26.)

According to this teaching the Lord's supper is to be celebrated until the Advent of the Lord, until the close of the dispensation. This implies that Jesus remains the sacrificial victim throughout the entire period between his death and his second Advent—ever present on the altar-table of his Church. This is an elaboration of the conception of the covenant sacrifice of Jesus by the

---

[1] Ex. xii. 14. See Spitta, *l. c.*, s. 232.

apostle Paul, and is not contained in the words of institution.[1]

It may be doubted how far these supplementary words of Jesus given by Luke and Paul, and the interpretation of them by Paul, have been influenced by the second saying of Jesus reported by the synoptists.

I will no more[2] drink of the[3] fruit of the vine, until that

---

[1] Jülicher, *l. c.*, s. 238 *seq.*, and Spitta, *l. c.*, s. 238 *seq.*, are doubtless correct in their opinion that the earliest Christian tradition represented by Mark and Matthew, knew nothing of an institution of the Lord's supper by Jesus on the night of his betrayal, as a sacrament to be observed continuously in the future. But they admit that Paul and Luke are sustained by the earliest Christian usage in representing it as a permanent institution. Jülicher explains this change from the facts that the apostles and earliest disciples when they met at their Christian meals were reminded of their last meal with their Lord, and that Jesus seems to have manifested himself to them after his resurrection at such meals. Spitta maintains that Jesus did not eat the passover with his disciples, but that he was crucified on Passover day, and that therefore his disciples could not eat the passover until the next month, and he suggests that Jesus appeared to them at that secondary passover meal and thereby associated himself with the passover in their minds. If we are to go so far with Jülicher and Spitta, it is easier to suppose that the risen Lord in connection with these manifestations commanded the perpetual observance of the holy supper just as he gave the apostles their commission to preach and baptize, and explained the mystery of his life and death (Luke xxiv. 25–49). Paul and Luke would then combine the words of Jesus on two different occasions, just as Paul did in his discourse in the book of Acts (xxvi 15–18). All such explanations, however, are conjectural. It must be recognized that the covenant sacrifice of the New Testament of Mark and Matthew would not of itself need repeated eating and drinking any more than the covenant sacrifice of the Old Testament, which was partaken of, once for all, on the day of its institution (Ex. xxiv. 6–11). The combination of the annual passover meal with the initial meal of the covenant, such as we find in Paul and Luke (cf. 1 Cor. v. 7, 8, with xi. 23 *seq.*) would make an annual celebration appropriate. But it is necessary to go further and connect these with the love-feasts of the early Christians, and see in them the continuation of the sacrificial meals of the ordinary peace offerings of the Jews and Gentiles alike. This combination is given in the antithesis between the communion-meals of Christians and the communion-meals of idols (1 Cor. x. 14–22), and in the joint celebration of the Lord's supper and the love-feast in the apostolic church. Thus the Lord's supper is also the fulfilment of the thank-offerings and free-will offerings of the Old Testament.

[2] Matthew and Luke substitute "henceforth," which may be only a different translation of the same Aramaic original.

[3] Matthew is more specific by substituting "this" for "the."

day when I drink it new in the kingdom of God.[1] (Mark xiv. 25.)

This is a prediction of a return of Jesus subsequent to his death. The return and the drinking of the cup are to be in the kingdom of God. Most interpreters think of the kingdom here as the kingdom of glory of the second Advent,[2] or of the heavenly reunion with the Messiah.

This would be favored by the fact that Paul may have made his reference to the second Advent on the basis of these words. But it does not appear that Paul had these words in mind. He is rather expounding the words "as oft as ye drink it" in order to teach an oft-repeated observance of the supper until the second Advent. The evangelists, however, emphasize the drinking from the cup. There are two drinkings in antithesis, the one at present at the institution of the supper, the other in the kingdom of God. They teach not the absence of the Lord during an indefinite number of feasts or an indefinite number of Lord's suppers until the Advent in glory; but a speedy advent of the kingdom, such as we have seen in previous predictions. At first the kingdom was proclaimed as at hand, then as planted in the ministry of our Lord as good seed springing up and growing secretly, then as coming in the lifetime of some of his hearers, then as open to the childlike and the poor in spirit. All this reaches its culmination in the prediction that ere another communion-meal came, before there was another opportunity to partake of the wine cup, the kingdom of God would be set up. The next feast would be celebrated by Jesus and his apostles within the Messianic kingdom, in a communion feast which would be no more

---

[1] Matthew adds "with you" and substitutes "in my Father's kingdom." Luke condenses the clause into "until the kingdom of God shall come."

[2] Weiss, *Marcusevangelium*, s. 452; Wendt, *Lehre Jesu*, ii., s. 170.

predictive of his covenant sacrifice, but would be based upon it as an historical event, the turning-point of a new age of the world.

## THE REJECTED SHEPHERD.

§ 27. *Jesus as the Messianic shepherd was rejected and his flock was scattered.*

The doctrine of the rejected Messiah reaches its culmination in the words of Jesus on the way to Gethsemane.

And Jesus saith unto them, All ye shall be offended: for it is written, I will smite the shepherd, and the sheep shall be scattered abroad. Howbeit, after I am raised up, I will go before you into Galilee.[1] (Mark xiv. 27–28.)

The crisis of the Messiah is now at hand. The predictions of his sufferings and death have now reached their climax as the events are about to fulfil them.

Here Jesus definitely represents himself as the Messianic shepherd of the prophecy of Zechariah,[2] and warns his disciples of his impending death. He tells them that they will be scattered abroad. But he comforts them with the promise that he will not only rise again, but that he will meet them in Galilee.

The apostles ought now to be prepared for the sad events that await them, by the interpretation given to them by Jesus of the neglected prophet, of the rejected corner-stone, and of the rejected shepherd,[3] as well as by his own thrice repeated prediction that his death would be followed by a speedy resurrection and the establishment of his kingdom.[4]

---

[1] Matthew xxvi. 31–32 is essentially the same. The differences are that Matthew adds for explanation to "offended" "in me this night," and to "sheep," "of the flock," and uses δέ for the stronger ἀλλά. In all these respects Mark is nearer the Aramaic original.

[2] Zechariah xiii. 7.     [3] See pp. 112, 114.     [4] See pp. 95 *seq.*, 107 *seq.*

## THE REJECTED MESSIAH.

§ 28. *The Messiah takes the oath before the Sanhedrin that he is the Messiah and predicts his Advent on his throne. He is mocked and crucified as the Messiah.*

The arrest of Jesus and his trial give occasion for solemn inquiry before the Sanhedrin, the highest tribunal of the nation, where he was called upon to take the oath by the high priest, whether he was the Messiah or not.

| MARK xiv. 61–64. | MATT. xxvi. 63–66. | LUKE xxii. 66–71. |
|---|---|---|
| Again the high priest asked him, and saith unto him, Art thou the Messiah, the Son of the Blessed? And Jesus said, I am: and ye shall see the Son of Man sitting at the right hand of power, and coming with the clouds of heaven. And the high priest rent his clothes, and saith, What further need have we of witnesses? Ye have heard the blasphemy: what think ye? And they all condemned him to be worthy of death. | And the high priest said unto him, I adjure thee by the living God, that thou tell us whether thou be the Messiah, the Son of God. Jesus saith unto him, Thou hast said: nevertheless I say unto you, Henceforth ye shall see the Son of Man sitting at the right hand of power, and coming on the clouds of heaven. Then the high priest rent his garments, saying, He hath spoken blasphemy: what further need have we of witnesses? behold, now ye have heard the blasphemy: what think ye? They answered and said, He is worthy of death. | And as soon as it was day, the assembly of the elders of the people was gathered together, both chief priests and scribes; and they led him away into their council, saying, If thou art the Messiah, tell us. But he said unto them, If I tell you, ye will not believe: and if I ask *you*, ye will not answer. But from henceforth shall the Son of Man be seated at the right hand of the power of God. And they all said, Art thou then the Son of God? And he said unto them, Ye say it, for I am. And they said, What further need have we of witness? for we ourselves have heard from his own mouth. |

The official claim of Jesus to be the Messiah was rejected by the Sanhedrin as blasphemous and he was condemned to death for making the claim. Jesus not only makes the claim to be the Messiah, but he predicts that the Sanhedrin will see the enthronement of the Son of Man. He has not come at present with power, authority, and dominion. He has not been enthroned. His throne is not an earthly throne, but a heavenly throne. His second Advent will be from heaven upon the clouds as his chariot of power and victory.

His claim to be at once the Messianic king and the Messianic Son of Man, thus becomes the ground for his persecution and death. Jesus is mocked by Pilate, Herod, and their soldiery as the Messiah.[1] Pilate presents him to the Pharisees and the people as their Messiah, crowned with thorns, with a reed sceptre and with royal attire, and they reject him and demand his crucifixion.[2] Jesus is then crucified with the title on his cross, "*The King of the Jews.*"[3] He is mocked by Pharisees and people, and even one of the crucified robbers, as the false Messiah.[4]

There can be no doubt, therefore, that Jesus claimed to be the Messianic king, and that he was rejected as a false Messiah by the Jews and crucified as such by the Romans at the solicitation of the Jews.

---

[1] Mark xv. 16-19; Matth. xxvii. 27-30; Luke xxiii. 11; John xix. 2, 3.
[2] Mark xv. 6-15; Matth. xxvii. 15-26; Luke xxiii. 13-25; John xviii. 39, 40, xix. 4-16.
[3] Mark xv. 26. *This is Jesus, the King of the Jews,* Matth. xxvii. 37. *This is the King of the Jews,* Luke xxiii. 38. *Jesus of Nazareth, the King of the Jews,* John xix. 19-22.
[4] Mark xv. 31, 32; Matth. xxvii. 41-43; Luke xxiii. 35-37.

## THE MESSIAH'S DEATH AND RESURRECTION.

**§ 29.** *The theophanies that accompany the crucifixion of Jesus and his own resurrection in fulfilment of his predictions show him to be the everliving Messianic Son of God.*

The crucifixion of Jesus was accompanied with theophanic signs.

| MARK xv. 33-39. | MATT. xxvii. 45-54. | LUKE xxiii. 44-47. |
|---|---|---|
| And when the sixth hour was come, there was darkness over the whole land until the ninth hour. And at the ninth hour Jesus cried with a loud voice, *Eloi, Eloi, lama sabachthani?* which is, being interpreted, My God, my God, why hast thou forsaken me? And some of them that stood by, when they heard it, said, Behold, he calleth Elijah. And one ran, and filling a sponge full of vinegar, put it on a reed, and gave him to drink, saying, Let be; let us see whether Elijah cometh to take him down. And Jesus uttered a loud voice, and gave up the ghost. And the veil of the temple was rent in twain from the top to the bottom. | Now from the sixth hour there was darkness over all the land until the ninth hour. And about the ninth hour Jesus cried with a loud voice, saying, *Eli, Eli, lama sabachthani?* that is, My God, my God, why hast thou forsaken me? And some of them that stood there, when they heard it, said, This man calleth Elijah. And straightway one of them ran, and took a sponge, and filled it with vinegar, and put it on a reed, and gave him to drink. And the rest said, Let be; let us see whether Elijah cometh to save him. And Jesus cried again with a loud voice, and yielded up his spirit. And behold, the veil of the temple was rent in twain from the top to the bottom; and the earth did quake; | And it was now about the sixth hour, and a darkness came over the whole land until the ninth hour, the sun's light failing: and the veil of the temple was rent in the midst. And when Jesus had cried with a loud voice, he said, Father, into thy hands I commend my spirit: and having said this, he gave up the ghost. |

| And when the centurion, which stood by over against him, saw that he so gave up the ghost, he said, Truly this man was the Son of God. | and the rocks were rent; and the tombs were opened; and many bodies of the saints that had fallen asleep were raised; and coming forth out of the tombs after his resurrection they entered into the holy city and appeared unto many. Now the centurion and they that were with him watching Jesus, when they saw the earth quake, and the things that were done, feared exceedingly, saying, Truly this was the Son of God. | And when the centurion saw what was done, he glorified God, saying, Certainly this was a righteous man. |

The three evangelists unite in reporting the darkness and the earthquake. The darkness at midday, from noon until three o'clock in the afternoon, or total eclipse of the sun, was followed by an earthquake, that rent the rocks and tombs and the veil of the temple. Such transformations of nature are the usual accompaniment of theophanies. They are predicted in the Old Testament as accompaniments of the divine advent. They indicate the presence and power of God in nature. The presence and power of God were nowhere more to be expected than at the crucifixion of the Messiah. The rending of the veil of the temple was a sign that the temple at Jesusalem was rejected by God. His people had rejected their Messiah. God had likewise rejected them and theirs.

The three evangelists also agree in the following account of the resurrection of Jesus:

| MARK xvi. 1–8. | MATT. xxviii. 1–8. | LUKE xxiv. 1–9. |
|---|---|---|
| And when the Sabbath was past, Mary Magdalene, and Mary the *mother* of James, and Salome, bought spices, that they might come and anoint him. And very early on the first day of the week, they come to the tomb when the sun was risen. And they were saying among themselves, Who shall roll us away the stone from the door of the tomb? and looking up, they see that the stone is rolled back: for it was exceeding great. And entering into the tomb, they saw a young man sitting on the right side, arrayed in a white robe; and they were amazed. And he saith unto them, Be not amazed: ye seek Jesus, the Nazarene, which hath been crucified: he is risen; he is not here: behold, the place where they laid him! But go, tell his disciples and Peter, He goeth before you into Galilee: there shall ye see him, as he said unto you. And they went out, and fled from the tomb; for trembling and astonishment had come upon them. | Now late on the sabbath day, as it began to dawn toward the first *day* of the week, came Mary Magdalene and the other Mary to see the sepulchre. And behold, there was a great earthquake; for an angel of the Lord descended from heaven, and came and rolled away the stone, and sat upon it. His appearance was as lightning, and his raiment white as snow: and for fear of him the watchers did quake, and became as dead men. And the angel answered and said unto the women, Fear not ye: for I know that ye seek Jesus, which hath been crucified. He is not here; for he is risen, even as he said. Come, see the place where the Lord lay. And go quickly, and tell his disciples, He is risen from the dead; and lo, he goeth before you into Galilee; there shall ye see him: lo, I have told you. And they departed quickly from the tomb with fear and great joy, and ran to bring his disciples word. | And on the sabbath they rested according to the commandment. But on the first day of the week, at early dawn, they came unto the tomb, bringing the spices which they had prepared. And they found the stone rolled away from the tomb. And they entered in, and found not the body of the Lord Jesus. And it came to pass, while they were perplexed thereabout, behold, two men stood by them in dazzling apparel: and as they were affrighted, and bowed down their faces to the earth, they said unto them, Why seek ye the living among the dead? He is not here, but is risen: remember how he spake unto you when he was yet in Galilee, saying that the Son of Man must be delivered up into the hands of sinful men, and be crucified, and the third day rise again. And they remembered his words, and returned from the tomb, and told all these things to the eleven, and to all the rest. |

Mark and Luke tell us that the women found the stone door rolled away from the entrance of the tomb of Jesus.

Matthew tells us that this was accomplished by a great earthquake and the descent of an angel from heaven, filling the watch with terror. The three agree in a report that an angel announced to the women the resurrection of Jesus. Matthew and Mark state that he showed them that the tomb was vacant, and told them to report to the disciples that they were to meet Jesus in Galilee. With this brief witness to the resurrection the Gospel of Mark comes to an end.[1]

---

[1] The remaining verses of the sixteenth chapter are a later addition to the original Gospel, as critics agree. They are separated in the Revised Version by a space with a note stating that they are not found in the two oldest MSS. We shall compare them in a subsequent chapter in their parallelism with Matthew and Luke.

# CHAPTER IV.

### THE APOCALYPSE OF JESUS.

The discourse of Jesus, given by the Synoptists in Matt. xxiv., Mark xiii., and Luke xxi., is an Apocalypse. It is intermediate between the Apocalypse of Daniel and the Apocalypse of John. As it depends upon the former and advances upon the Messianic idea contained therein, so it is the prelude to the latter and the key to its interpretation.

The discourse is enlarged in Matt. xxiv. by the insertion of two sections: vers. 26–28, 37–41, that belong to another discourse given in a different connection in Luke,[1] and by the use of two parables, vers. 43–51, that are given by Luke[2] at an earlier date. Furthermore, Matthew adds chap. xxv., which contains two parables and a judgment scene which have no exact parallels in the other evangelists, although there are similar parables in Luke.[3]

These sections have all been added by Matthew in accordance with his custom to group the words of Jesus spoken at different times and under various circumstances, about a central theme. That which remains after the elimination of these sections is, with few exceptions, essentially the same in the three Synoptists, and is a discourse complete in itself, a real apocalypse.

---

[1] xvii. 22–37.  [2] xii. 39–46.  [3] xii. 35, 36, xix. 11–27.

This apocalypse resembles in many respects the Jewish pseudepigraphical apocalypses. This resemblance and the method of Matthew raise the question whether the critical knife should not go deeper and eliminate also the lesser sections that are peculiar to Mark and Luke, and even dissect the material that is common to the three evangelists. Accordingly, Colani[1] proposed the theory that the apocalypse of Jesus contained a Jewish-Christian apocalypse which was used by Mark in connection with genuine words of Jesus, and probably was the same as the oracle mentioned by Eusebius,[2] which warned Christians to leave the doomed city of Jerusalem. This opinion was adopted by Weizsäcker,[3] with the modifications that it was a Jewish apocalypse and that it had been taken from a lost section of the apocalypse of Enoch, in accordance with the citation in Barnabas.[4] Pfleiderer[5] and Keim[6] held that it was a Jewish-Christian apocalypse. Weiffenbach[7] gave the whole subject a more elaborate treatment, and by a very careful analysis distinguished three parts of this original Jewish-Christian apocalypse: (1) Mark xiii. 7-3, $a$ = Matt. xxiv. 6-8 = Luke xxi. 9-11, giving the $ἀρχή ὠδίνων$; (2) Mark xiii. 14-20 = Matt. xxiv. 15-22, giving the $θλίψις$; (3) Mark xiii. 24-27 = Matt. xxiv. 29-31 = Luke xxi. 25-27, giving the $παρουσία$. Wendt[8] and Vischer[9] have also given their adhesion to the theory.

---

[1] *Jesus Christ et les croyances messianiques de son temp*, 2 ed., 1864.
[2] *Hist. Eccl.* iii 5, 3.
[3] *Untersuchungen*, 1864, s. 121-26.
[4] Barnabas, c. iv.
[5] *Jahrb. f. d. Theologie*, xiii., 1868, S. 134, 149.
[6] *Jesu v. Naz.*, iii., s. 200-206.
[7] *Wiederkunftsgedanke Jesu*, 1873.
[8] *Lehre Jesu*, 1886, s. 161.
[9] *Die Offenbarung Johannis*, 1886. See also *The Presbyterian Review*, 1888, p. 112.

It is true that these three sections which have been separated by Weiffenbach are apocalyptic in character. They resemble in many respects the Jewish pseudepigraphical apocalypses. But this is because they all depend on the apocalypse of Daniel, and use the language of the judgment scenes of the Old Testament Prophets. There is no sufficient reason why Jesus himself should not have used the Old Testament in the same manner. We ought to expect that Jesus in his predictions would bridge the time between the apocalypse of Daniel and the apocalypse of John, and give an intermediate stage in the development of the apocalyptic prophecy, if, as we believe, these apocalypses give us genuine prediction. Weiffenbach's elimination of this older apocalypse from the discourse of Jesus enabled him to propose the theory that Jesus' prediction of his second Advent was only another phase of his prediction of his resurrection, and that anything in the gospels that teaches a different doctrine does not belong to Jesus, but to the misconceptions of his disciples.

The apocalypse of Jesus has been much discussed in recent years. J. S. Russell,[1] an English scholar, in 1878 proposed the theory that our Lord's predictions as to his Parousia were fulfilled in connection with the destruction of Jerusalem. Israel P. Warren,[2] an American divine, maintained that the Parousia is not an event, but a dispensation, embracing the spiritual presence of Jesus during the entire period from the establishment of the kingdom at Pentecost until the transformation of nature at the end of the world. Professor Willibald Beyschlag, of Halle, thinks that our Lord embraces in his conception of his advent the reunion

---

[1] *The Parousia*, 2d ed., 1887.     [2] *The Parousia*, 2d ed., 1884.

with his disciples begun at the resurrection, renewed at Pentecost, and maintained in spiritual presence during the entire period of the world, yes, even to eternity.[1]

These recent theories have greatly enlarged and improved the discussion, for they have been based upon a comprehensive study of New Testament prophecy. They have all been defective in their apprehension of the fundamental importance of the Old Testament prophecy. The theory of Weiffenbach and his associates removes the apocalyptic features from the discourse of Jesus and attaches them to a Jewish-Christian apocalypse. The theories of Russell, Warren, and Beyschlag agree in making them symbolical, the drapery or the scenery of the prediction.

§ 30. *Jerusalem is to be destroyed after a siege and trodden under foot of the Gentiles. The temple is to be destroyed and there will be a short time of extraordinary distress. The signs of these events are armies laying siege and a desecration of the temple. False Messiahs and prophets will arise, and there will be wars, rumors of wars, insurrections, famines, pestilences, earthquakes, terrors, and great signs from heaven; the beginnings of the birth-throes of the End of the Age. There will be signs of the Advent of the Son of Man in the darkening of the sun, moon, and stars; the shaking of earth, heaven, and sea; distress of nations, perplexity, and fear. All these will transpire in the generation of Jesus and show that the End is near. There will be a Gospel Age for the preaching of the gospel to the nations. This will be accompanied by persecutions and false prophets and apostacy. Patience and perseverance will be required until the End. There will be a Gentile Age during which Jerusalem will be held*

---

[1] *Das Leben Jesu*, i., s. 357–64.

*in subjection. The Son of Man will come on the clouds with the holy angels and the trumpet blast for the redemption of the elect, who will be gathered by angels from all parts. It will be for the completion of the age and the establishment of the kingdom of glory. The time of the Advent is not known even to the Son, but to the Father only. It may be early or late. It is near and impending, sure to come, but uncertain as to time, requiring all to watch and pray.*

### (1) *The Prelude.*

| MARK xiii. 1, 2. | MATT. xxiv. 1, 2. | LUKE xxi. 5, 6. |
|---|---|---|
| And as he went forth out of the temple, one of his disciples saith unto him, Master, behold, what manner of stones and what manner of buildings! And Jesus said unto him, Seest thou these great buildings? there shall not be left here one stone upon another, which shall not be thrown down. | And Jesus went out from the temple, and was going on his way; and his disciples came to him to show him the buildings of the temple. But he answered and said unto them, See ye not all these things? verily I say unto you, There shall not be left here one stone upon another, that shall not be thrown down. | And as some spake of the temple, how it was adorned with goodly stones and offerings, he said, As for these things which ye behold, the days will come, in which there shall not be left here one stone upon another, that shall not be thrown down. |

The Synoptists agree closely in the prelude which gives the circumstances under which the Apocalypse was uttered. The temple which the disciples so greatly admired for its magnificence and beauty, was to be destroyed so utterly that there would not be left one stone upon another. This prediction of the destruction of the temple is similar to the prediction with reference to the *city* of Jerusalem—"The days shall come upon thee, when thine enemies shall cast up a bank about thee, and compass thee round, and keep thee in on every side, and shall dash thee to the ground, and thy children within thee; and *they shall not leave in thee one stone upon another.*"[1] The destruction of the *temple here* is to be as the destruction of the *city there—total.*

### (2) *The Inquiry.*

| MARK xiii. 3, 4. | MATT. xxiv. 3. | LUKE xxi. 7. |
|---|---|---|
| And as he sat on the mount of Olives over against the temple, Peter and James and John and Andrew asked him privately, Tell us, when shall these things be? and what *shall be* the sign when these things are all about to be accomplished? | And as he sat on the mount of Olives, the disciples came unto him privately, saying, Tell us, when shall these things be? and what *shall be* the sign of thy coming, and of the End of the Age? | And they asked him, saying, Master, when therefore shall these things be? and what *shall be* the sign when these things are about to come to pass? |

The disciples have been deeply impressed by the prediction with respect to the destruction of the temple. They take advantage of their being apart on the Mount of Olives to inquire more deeply into this matter. According to Mark, the question seems to have been asked by four apostles only. We have first to inquire as to the scope and matter of their question. According to Mark, it is simply as to "*these things*" which the context refers to the destruction of the temple. The same is true of Luke, save that the phrase, "There shall not be left here one stone upon another," used with reference to the *temple*, would remind them of the same prediction made a few days before in the vicinity overlooking Jerusalem, with reference to the *city*; and the subsequent context of Luke evidently includes the destruc-

---

[1] Luke xix. 43, 44.

tion of the *city* in the answer to the questions. It is, therefore, probable that it was included in the inquiry, in the minds of the apostles as well as of Jesus. Furthermore, as Weiss [1] says: "The ταῦτα refers primarily to the destruction of the temple, but the plural would not have been used if it had not been regarded as including a series of decisive events whose final accomplishment was comprehended in the πάντα." When now we look to Matthew we find that he represents the inquiry as more specific—"*thy coming*" and "*the End of the Age.*" He gives us two technical terms of New Testament prophecy, the παρουσία and the συντέλεια τοῦ αἰῶνος. It is necessary for us to determine their meaning, and also to learn how these events come to be included in the question according to Matthew. These questions are entwined to some extent. It seems that, in the mind of the Evangelist Matthew, Jesus has been leading his apostles through the events and discourses of the week in Jerusalem to the climax of this discourse. He had already predicted that the nation, with its holy city and temple, would be destroyed by armies, that all the woes for the rejected prophets and the Messiah would come upon that generation, and that the Messiah would come again and be greeted with hosannas. It also seems likely that it was in the mind of the evangelist that Jesus would now give his chosen apostles an esoteric key to the mysteries of his Messianic future, as the culmination of all his discourses on the subject, and from this point of view Matthew does not hesitate to combine other discourses of Jesus with this main one, and to gather a group of parables about the central theme.

The παρουσία is the technical term for the second

---

[1] *Marcusevangelium*, s. 411, 412.

Advent of Jesus himself.¹ Συντέλεια τοῦ αἰῶνος is "completion of the age." We might think of the age of the Old Testament dispensation coming to completion in the age of the Messiah.² This would be proper from the point of view of the Old Testament itself, and possibly of the apostles also. It is usually rendered "completion of the age of the world" or "End of the world." But this involves the theory that Jesus is here predicting events at the end of the world. This may be so, but it is hardly proper to put this theory into the translation of a phrase which does not in itself have so definite a meaning. It seems clear from the context and the parallelism of the question that the disciples and Jesus understood in this phrase the age that would be completed by the *Parousia*, so that everything depends upon our interpretation of the latter. The additional feature of Matthew is an inquiry as to the second Advent of the Messiah. With regard to the matter of the inquiry, there are two events which differ in form, if not in substance. The one is common to the three evangelists, and relates to the destruction of the temple; the other is peculiar to Matthew, and relates to the second Advent of the Messiah.

There are two distinct questions as to these events given by the three evangelists: (1) "*When* shall these

---

¹ I do not see that it makes any very important difference whether we translate it " coming," as in the text of the R. V., or " presence," as in the margin of the R. V., and I think that the polemic of Dr. Warren (*Parousia*, p. 25) against the former, and the term " second advent," is without justification; for it still remains to determine what is the nature of that " coming " or " presence " or " advent " which is here predicted. Even a " presence " must have its point of beginning, and that is the real question, after all. It is not denied that the advent is followed by a long-continued presence of the Messiah with his people, and even if we lay the stress on the presence, we must distinguish between it and the earthly life of Jesus, and use the term second presence.

² Russell, *Parousia*, p. 59.

things be?"[1] (2) *What shall be the sign?*[2] The sign of what? Mark gives "when *these things* are all about to be accomplished"; Luke, "when *these things* are about to come to pass." This is most naturally to be interpreted of the same things as the previous question—namely, the destruction of the temple, with the other events that clustered about it in the mind of Jesus and his apostles. Matthew specifies the second Advent. This raises the question whether Matthew regarded the second Advent and the judgment of Jerusalem as the same,[3] or whether he designs to lay stress upon the second Advent as an altogether different event. This question will be determined as we proceed. It is sufficient here to remark that the prediction of Jesus in the prelude favors the form of the question in Mark and Luke; but the answer of Jesus to the question in the subsequent context favors the form of the question given by Matthew.

There are two questions which determine the answers of Jesus and the analysis of the discourse; (1) the *time*, (2) the *signs*.

(3) *The Negative Answer as to the Time.*

| MARK xiii. 5-8. | MATT. xxiv. 4-8. | LUKE xxi. 8-11. |
|---|---|---|
| And Jesus began to say unto them, Take heed that no man lead you astray. Many shall come in my name, saying, I am he; and shall lead many astray. [And when ye shall hear of wars and rumors of wars, be not | And Jesus answered and said unto them, Take heed that no man lead you astray. For many shall come in my name, saying, I am the Messiah; and shall lead many astray. [And ye shall hear of wars and rumors | And he said, Take heed that ye be not led astray: for many shall come in my name, saying, I am he; and The time is at hand: go ye not after them. [And when ye shall hear of wars and tumults, be not terrified: for |

---

[1] πότε ταῦτα ἔσται.   [2] τί τὸ σημεῖον.   [3] Russell, *Parousia*, p. 82.

| troubled: *these things* must needs come to pass; but the End is not yet. For nation shall rise against nation, and kingdom against kingdom; there shall be earthquakes in divers places; there shall be famines: these things are the beginning of travail.] | of wars: see that ye be not troubled; for *these things* must needs come to pass; but the End is not yet. For nation shall rise against nation, and kingdom against kingdom: and there shall be famines and earthquakes in divers places. But all these things are the beginning of travail.] | these things must needs come to pass first; but the End is not immediately. Then said he unto them, Nation shall rise against nation, and kingdom against kingdom: and there shall be great earthquakes, and in divers places famines and pestilences; and there shall be terrors and great signs from heaven.] |

Jesus answers the first question as to the *time when*, and, first of all, negatively. (*a*) They are in peril of being led astray by false Messiahs. Men will come claiming to be the Messiah, and they will have followers. These will come with the words, "I am the Messiah" (Matthew) and "the time is at hand" (Luke). In this respect they will repeat the message of Jesus and John the Baptist. This will happen in the interval prior to the time of the apostles' question. It is clear, then, that Jesus has here chiefly in mind his παρουσία, and not the destruction of the city and temple. He warns his disciples that they be not deceived by false Messiahs who will come, and may mislead them to think that the *Parousia* of Jesus is in them.[1]

(*b*) There will be wars (Mark, Matthew, Luke) and rumors of wars (Mark and Matthew) and tumults (Luke). It is necessary that these should occur in the interval.

---

[1] Weiss (*Marcusevangelium*, s. 413) thinks that it is incredible that Jesus should have begun his answer to the question of the disciples in this way, and draws the inference that the entire introduction, with the exception of vers. 6, 8, 9, did not belong to the Apocalypse itself, which was originally a discourse to the apostles.

They will precede the End: "The End is not yet"[1] (Matthew and Mark); "The End is not immediately"[2] (Luke). The End is the equivalent of the End or completion of the age. This term used by the three evangelists shows that Matthew's specification of this event in the question was involved in the more general terms used by the other evangelists. The time of the second advent of Jesus is therefore subsequent to these false Messiahs and wars. It cannot take place until these events have happened; it is not immediate (Luke); it is not *yet* (Mark and Matthew).

(*c*) There will be not only wars widespread and general, but also earthquakes and famines. These are represented as "the beginning of travail," $ἀρχὴ\ ὠδίνων$ (Mark and Matthew). The time or age is conceived as a woman in the pangs of child-birth, who is to bring forth the end. These distresses are the beginnings of the birth throes; others are to follow before the birth of the last hour, in which the Messiah will come.

(*d*) In addition to the distresses already referred to, Luke mentions pestilences, terrors, and great signs from heaven. By great signs from heaven he probably means commotions in the heavenly bodies, comets, eclipses, and the like.

All these things must come to pass, and after they have transpired it will appear that the End, the completion of the age, the Advent of the Messiah are not immediate, are not yet. There are other birth throes to follow. Thus we have a definite answer to the question as to the time of the Advent from the negative side. Jesus tells them when it is *not* to be.[3]

---

[1] $οὔπω\ (ἐστὶν)\ τὸ\ τέλος.$    [2] $οὐκ\ εὐθέως\ τὸ\ τέλος.$

[3] It is urged by Weiffenbach that *b, c, d*, enclosed in parentheses above, constitute the first section of the Jewish Christian Apocalypse. The disturbances

## (4) *The Positive Answer as to the Time.*

| MARK xiii. 9–13. | MATT. xxiv. 9–14.[1] | LUKE xxi. 12–19. |
|---|---|---|
| But take ye heed to yourselves: for they shall deliver you up to councils; and in synagogues shall ye be beaten; and before governors and kings shall ye stand for my sake, for a testimony unto them. And the gospel must first be preached unto all | Then shall they deliver you up unto tribulation, and shall kill you: and ye shall be hated of all the nations for my name's sake. And then shall many stumble, and shall deliver up one another, and shall hate one another. And many false prophets shall arise, | But before all these things, they shall lay their hands on you, and shall persecute you, delivering you up to the synagogues and prisons, bringing you before kings and governors for my name's sake. It shall turn unto you for a testimony. Settle it therefore in |

here described are such as we would expect to find in such a writing, but they are also such as we might expect to find in an apocalypse of Jesus, and they are not at all discordant with *a*, but rather harmonious with the coming of the false Messiahs. All these are woes, birth throes. That this idea is found in Jewish pseudepigrapha amounts to nothing. It was derived by them from the Old Testament, the common source of the Christian apocalypses as well as the Jewish, the canonical and uncanonical as well, and there is no sufficient reason why Jesus should not have used it. (Comp. Isa. xiii. 8, xxvi. 18; Jer. xiii. 21, xxii. 23; Hos. xiii. 13; Mic. iv. 9, 10.)

[1] Matthew here differs from Mark and Luke, because he has already used Mark xiii. 11–13 in connection with the sending forth of the twelve (x. 17–22). The passage very much resembles this section of the Apocalypse in Mark. It is given here for comparison.

"But beware of men: for they will deliver you up to councils, and in their synagogues they will scourge you; yea and before governors and kings shall ye be brought for my sake, for a testimony to them and to the Gentiles. But when they deliver you up, be not anxious how or what ye shall speak: for it shall be given you in that hour what ye shall speak. For it is not ye that speak, but the Spirit of your Father that speaketh in you. And brother shall deliver up brother to death, and the father his child: and children shall rise up against parents, and cause them to be put to death. And ye shall be hated of all men for my name's sake: but he that endureth to the End, the same shall be saved."

It would appear that the author of Matthew has confounded this extract with a sentence of Jesus spoken on another occasion in Luke xii. 11, 12. This is replaced by brief or general statements of a more comprehensive character relating to the preaching of the gospel to the nations. Weiss thinks that this was an independent prediction of the apostles' work that is not in its correct place in any of the evangelists, but belonged to the close of the life of Jesus. (*Marcusevang.*, s. 416.)

| | | |
|---|---|---|
| the nations. And when they lead you *to judgment*, and deliver you up, be not anxious beforehand what ye shall speak; but whatsoever shall be given you in that hour, that speak ye: for it is not ye that speak, but the Holy Spirit. And brother shall deliver up brother to death, and the father his child; and children shall rise up against parents, and cause them to be put to death. And ye shall be hated of all men for my name's sake: but he that endureth to the End, the same shall be saved. | and shall lead many astray. And because iniquity shall be multiplied, the love of the many shall wax cold. But he that endureth to the End, the same shall be saved. And this gospel of the kingdom shall be preached in the whole world for a testimony unto all the nations; and then shall the End come. | your hearts, not to meditate beforehand how to answer: for I will give you a mouth and wisdom, which all your adversaries shall not be able to withstand or to gainsay. But ye shall be delivered up even by parents, and brethren, and kinsfolk, and friends; and *some* of you shall they cause to be put to death. And ye shall be hated of all men for my name's sake. And not a hair of your head shall perish. In your patience ye shall win your souls. |

The evangelists differ somewhat in their statements as to time. Mark begins with the positive statement: "And the gospel must first be preached unto all the nations," and closes with: "He that endureth to the End, the same shall be saved." Matthew brings both of these statements to the close of the section, and changes their order—"But he that endureth to the End, the same shall be saved. And this gospel of the kingdom shall be preached in the whole world for a testimony unto all the nations; and then shall the End come." These are positive statements that the End, the completion of the age, the second Advent, will come after the accomplishment of the preaching of the gospel to the world. The End ($τὸ\ τέλος$) is the time when the endurance of the preachers will be completed, when their ministry will have been accomplished. The gospel must first be preached to all the nations is the statement of Mark. After this preaching of the gospel has been accomplished "then shall the End come" is the statement of Matthew.

Luke's language is different in form, but the same in substance. He represents Jesus as saying, "Before all these things." This cannot refer to the immediate context, but goes back upon the original question, and affirms that before all these things relating to the Advent of the Messiah, the preaching of the gospel to the world must take place. It is similar, therefore, to Mark. The teaching of this section is that the age prior to the second Advent is an age of the preaching of the gospel. The circumstances of this preaching are given with considerable detail.

(*a*) There is the commission to preach the gospel "unto all the nations" (Mark); "to all the nations"; "in the whole world" (Matthew). These terms are general, if not universal. There is nothing in the text or context to limit them even to the Roman Empire.[1] It is not necessary to suppose that they are so universal as to include every nation without exception, or the entire extent of the habitable globe, without the omission of any part whatever. But the language is as general and universal as possible. The gospel was to be preached to the nations and to the whole habitable globe, that the nations and the world might be saved and not be condemned in the judgment of the world. This is the scope of the preaching of the gospel. Until this has been accomplished, the second Advent cannot come. So soon as this has been accomplished the second Advent will come.[2]

---

[1] So Russell would have it, relying upon Col. i. 6, 23 (in l. c., p. 70 *seq.*).

[2] Weiffenbach thinks that this verse was inserted from another connection, and finds a discrepancy between the thought of a speedy advent and an age of the world-wide preaching of the gospel (in l. c., s. 138 *seq.*). This discrepancy is evident if we fail to make the proper discriminations.

(*b*) This preaching of the gospel is "for a testimony," εἰς μαρτύριον—not that all the nations will be saved, or that all the world and every person will embrace the gospel, but that the gospel may be offered to the world, and so be the test of the world in the judgment of the world.

(*c*) The promise is made of the presence and power of the Holy Spirit to direct them in their testimony. They are not to be anxious in preparation of what they are to say, but to trust in the Holy Spirit and utter what he speaks through them. This is a promise of the immanent presence and power of the Holy Spirit, made to the apostles during their ministry of preaching the gospel to the world.

(*d*) The apostles will preach in synagogues, before the Sanhedrin, and before governors and kings, and will suffer persecution (Mark and Luke).

(*e*) Relatives and friends will turn against them (Mark and Luke).

(*f*) False prophets will arise to counteract their influence (Matthew).

(*g*) Lukewarmness and apostasy will be found among the disciples (Matthew).

(*h*) They will be hated by all men (Mark, Matthew, and Luke).

(*i*) They will require endurance and patience (Mark, Matthew, and Luke).

Many of these circumstances were peculiar to the work of the apostles. The most of them represent very well the condition of the preachers during the martyr age. But there are several features that have always accompanied the preaching of the gospel, even until the present time. And we can hardly say that the preaching of the gospel to the whole world has yet been accomplished.

Jesus in this section teaches that the παρουσία is to be preceded by a gospel age, and that the whole time previous to it is occupied by the preaching of his gospel. Inasmuch as this preaching is to be accompanied by the presence and power of the Holy Spirit, it is evident that the παρουσία of this discourse is something different from the gift of the Holy Spirit, and that it is an advent that brings to an end a period which has been characterized by the presence and power of the Holy Spirit in the preaching of the gospel.

Jesus thus far has answered the question as to the *time*. He answered it negatively, that there would be false Messiahs, wars, earthquakes, famines, pestilences, terrors, and signs from heaven, the first of the birth throes of the End, but that the End was not immediate, was not yet. He then answered the question positively, and said that the End would come after the gospel had been preached to all nations, to the habitable globe.

It is noteworthy that in these answers Jesus makes no reference whatever to the destruction of the temple,—the chief thing apparently in the form of the question according to Mark and Luke; but he refers entirely to the End, the completion of the age, in the form of the question given by Matthew.

(5) *The Sign of the Destruction of Jerusalem and the Temple.*

| MARK xiii. 14–20.[1] | MATT. xxiv. 15–22. | LUKE xxi. 20–24. |
|---|---|---|
| But when ye see the abomination of desolation standing | When therefore ye see the abomination of desolation, which | But when ye see Jerusalem compassed with armies, |

---

[1] This section, as given by Mark and Matthew, is regarded by Weiffenbach as the second section of the original Jewish-Christian apocalypse which has been used by the Evangelist Mark and taken from him by Matthew.

where it ought not (let him that readeth understand), then let them that are in Judæa flee unto the mountains: and let him that is on the housetop not go down, nor enter in, to take anything out of his house: and let him that is in the field not return back to take his cloke. But woe unto them that are with child and to them that give suck in those days! And pray ye that it be not in the winter. For those days shall be tribulation, such as there hath not been the like from the beginning of the creation which God created until now, and never shall be. And except the Lord had shortened the days, no flesh would have been saved: but for the elect's sake, whom he chose, he shortened the days.

was spoken of through Daniel the prophet, standing in the holy place (let him that readeth understand), then let them that are in Judæa flee unto the mountains: let him that is on the housetop not go down to take out the things that are in his house: and let him that is in the field not return back to take his cloke. But woe unto them that are with child and to them that give suck in those days! And pray ye that your flight be not in the winter, neither on a sabbath: for then shall be great tribulation, such as hath not been from the beginning of the world until now, no, nor ever shall be. And except those days had been shortened, no flesh would have been saved: but for the elect's sake those days shall be shortened.

then know that her desolation is at hand. Then let them that are in Judæa flee unto the mountains; and let them that are in the midst of her depart out; and let not them that are in the country enter therein. For these are days of vengeance, that all things which are written may be fulfilled. Woe unto them that are with child and to them that give suck in those days! for there shall be great distress upon the land, and wrath unto this people. And they shall fall by the edge of the sword, and shall be led captive into all the nations: and Jerusalem shall be trodden down of the Gentiles, until the times of the Gentiles be fulfilled.

Our Saviour now directs the attention of his apostles to the *signs*.

According to Mark and Matthew, he refers to the "abomination of desolation."[1] Mark gives "standing

---

[1] τὸ βδέλυγμα τῆς ἐρημώσεως. This is represented by Matthew as the שִׁקּוּץ שֹׁמֵם of Daniel xii. 11, cf. ix. 27, xi. 31.

where it ought not."[1] Matthew is more explicit, "standing in the holy place."[2] Here Jesus gives the sign predicted by Daniel as the sign heralding the destruction of the temple. The holy place is the holy place of the temple which was to be desecrated by this abomination of desolation standing there where it ought not to be. Daniel represents the desolator as a gigantic vulture, a bird of prey who comes down with his foul and abominable wings to defile and destroy the sacred places; and predicts the removal of the continual burnt-offering and the setting up of the abomination that maketh desolate in its place. Jesus uses this prediction of Daniel, and points to its fulfilment as a sign of warning, giving little time for escape from ruin. Accordingly, the view of Weiss[3] that the abomination of desolation is the Roman army, and that the holy place is the holy land, though it brings Matthew and Mark into closer connection with Luke, is to be rejected as not in accordance with the specific reference to Daniel and the most natural interpretation of the passage. Pfleiderer[4] rightly insists that the passages in Daniel and 1 Maccabees i. 54 force to the conclusion that it was a desecration of the temple while it was still in existence.

The days are days of extraordinary affliction,[5] so unprecedented, and so unique for future time that, in order to the salvation of the elect, God shortened them. This shortening of the days in connection with the abomination of desolation of Daniel, reminds us of the statement of Daniel: "And he will confirm the covenant with many for one week; and in the middle of the week he will cause peace offering and vegetable offering to cease; and upon the wing of abomination will be a desolator."[6]

---

[1] ὅπου οὐ δεῖ.     [2] ἑστὼς ἐν -όπῳ ἁγίῳ.
[3] *Marcusevangelium*, s. 421.     [4] *Jahr. f. d. T.*, 1868, s. 137
[5] θλίψις μεγάλη     [6] ix. 27.

"And from the time that the continual *burnt offering* shall be taken away, and the abomination that maketh desolate set up, there will be 1,290 days. Blessed is he that waiteth, and cometh to the 1,335 days."[1] There is a week at the end of the Old Testament dispensation, in the middle of which the affliction culminates, the holy place is desecrated, and the holy city and its institutions destroyed.[2]

Luke is so different here that it looks like part of another discourse, save that the movement of thought is essentially the same as in the discourse given in Mark and Matthew. We have already noticed that the question of the disciples seems to have the temple chiefly in view. Accordingly, Matthew and Mark give words of Jesus that have to do with a sign in the temple. But Luke gives a sign that has to do with the city—"When ye see Jerusalem compassed with armies, then know that her desolation is at hand." This preparation to lay siege to Jerusalem is a sign already referred to: "Thine enemies will cast up a bank about thee, and compass thee round, and keep thee in on every side."[3]

Accordingly, Jesus predicts the destruction of the city, and warns Christians to flee from it and not enter it. All that has been written will be fulfilled upon her, in Luke, takes the place of the prediction of Daniel, in Mark and Matthew. The land and people are to suffer great distress, the people are to be put to the sword and carried away into captivity, and Jerusalem will be trodden down by the nations.

In place of the shortened time of Matthew and Mark, Luke mentions the times of the Gentiles. The latter is much more comprehensive than the former. It is no shortened time, but a time during which the Gentiles

---

[1] xii. 11, 12.  [2] Briggs' *Messianic Prophecy*, pp. 424 *seq.*  [3] Luke xix. 43.

keep Jerusalem in subjection. It corresponds with the times of the gospel of the previous context, for the times of the Gentiles are the times of their supremacy until the judgment upon the Gentiles. The destruction of Jerusalem and the Jewish nation was a judgment upon the Jews inflicted by the Gentiles. The Gentiles were now to have their time until their judgment came. The discourse in Luke is here much wider in its sweep and longer in its outlook than in the parallel passages of Matthew and Mark. Luke has essentially the same thing, but he presents it from the point of view of the Gentiles; while Mark and Matthew give it from the Jewish-Christian point of view. The latter give us a short time, a broken week of tribulation, which carries on the thought of the beginning of the birth throes in section (3). The former gives us a time of the Gentiles which corresponds with the preaching of the gospel to the Gentiles in section (4). Taking the two representations together, we are taught that the time of the beginning of the birth throes will be followed by a short time of tribulation and the destruction of the city and temple; and that there is also a period of the preaching of the gospel to the Gentiles and of the supremacy of the Gentiles, that will extend until the time of the Gentiles has reached its end, and the time for the *Parousia* has come.[1]

### (6) *The Sign of the Second Advent.*[2]

| MARK xiii. 24-27. | MATT. xxiv. 29-31. | LUKE xxi. 25-27. |
|---|---|---|
| But in those days, after that tribula- | But immediately, after the tribulation | And there shall be signs in s u n  a n d |

---

[1] The section that follows in Mark (xiii. 21-23) and Matthew (xxiv. 23-28) does not belong to the apocalypse. It is given by Luke (xvii. 22-37) in connection with another discourse respecting the Advent, where it is more appropriate. (Weiss, *Marcusevangelium*, s. 424.)

[2] This section is the third section of the original Jewish apocalypse, according to the theory of Weiffenbach.

| tion, the sun shall be darkened, and the moon shall not give her light, and the stars shall be falling from heaven, and the powers that are in the heavens shall be shaken. And then shall they see the Son of Man coming in clouds with great power and glory. And then shall he send forth the angels, and shall gather together his elect from the four winds, from the uttermost part of the earth to the uttermost part of heaven. | of those days, the sun shall be darkened, and the moon shall not give her light, and the stars shall fall from heaven, and the powers of the heavens shall be shaken: and then shall appear the sign of the Son of Man in heaven: and then shall all the tribes of the earth mourn, and they shall see the Son of Man coming on the clouds of heaven with power and great glory. And he shall send forth his angels with a great sound of a trumpet, and they shall gather together his elect from the four winds, from one end of heaven to the other. | moon and stars; and upon the earth distress of nations, in perplexity for the roaring of the sea and the billows; men fainting for fear, and for expectation of the things which are coming on the world: for the powers of the heavens shall be shaken. And then shall they see the Son of Man coming in a cloud with power and great glory. |
|---|---|---|

We now have a second answer to the question as to the sign. As the previous section answers the question so far as to give the sign of the destruction of the temple and Jerusalem, this section gives the signs of the Advent of the Messiah. These signs are the usual ones of Old Testament prophecy.

(1) The sun shall be darkened; (2) the moon shall not give her light; (3) the stars shall fall from heaven; (4) the powers of the heavens shall be shaken (Matthew, Mark, Luke); (5) upon the earth distress of nations; (6) roaring of the sea and the billows; (7) men fainting for fear and expectation of what is coming (Luke); (8) the sign of the Son of Man in heaven; (9) all the tribes of the earth mourning (Matthew).

Joel uses 1, 2, 3, and 4 with reference to the judgment of the nations in the vale of Jehoshaphat,[1] and with reference to the day of Yahweh, which he represents as near.[2] Another prophet[3] declares that the day of Yahweh is near, with special mention of the judgment of Babylon, and uses signs 1, 2, 3, 4, and 7, and adds, 10 : "The earth will be shaken out of her place." A prophet of the exile[4] refers to the judgment of the earth, and uses 1, 2, and 10. Another prophecy[5] uses similar language with reference to the judgment of the nations :

> And all the host of heaven will consume away,
> And the heavens will be rolled together as a scroll :
> And all their host will fade away,
> As the leaf fadeth from off the vine,
> And as a fading *leaf* from the fig-tree.[6]

Thus these are the familiar theophanic signs that accompany the Day of Yahweh and the Advent of Yahweh, which the prophets ever represent as near.

Matthew differs from the other evangelists in giving *the sign of the Son of Man in heaven*, and the mourning of all the tribes of the earth. There is here a reference to the prediction in Zechariah[7] which represents Israel as bitterly wailing because of their rejected Messiah. Herein Jesus shows that he himself is that rejected Shepherd. The Evangelist Matthew probably refers to some special sign of the second Advent in the clouds that would bring the nations to mourning over the great sin of the rejection of the Messiah. The original passage has in view only the house of David and inhabitants of Jerusalem. It is possible that the " tribes of the earth " also refers to Israel alone,[8] but it is probable that

---

[1] iii. 15, 16.  [2] ii. 1, 10.  [3] Isa. xiii. 6 *seq.*  [4] Isa. xxiv. 18 *seq.*
[5] Isa. xxxiv.  [6] Briggs' *Messianic Prophecy*, pp. 311, 312.
[7] xii. 10–14.  [8] Russell, in *l. c.*, p. 77.

with the broader conception of the gospel the tribes are those of the earth who have become equally guilty with Israel in the rejection of their common Messiah. The context has to do with the nations, and not with Israel alone.

Having considered the signs of the Advent and found them to be the usual theophanic signs, we are now prepared to look at the Advent itself. It is here given in the style of Daniel: "The Son of Man coming on the clouds of heaven with great power and glory." The three evangelists agree essentially in these words. Jesus here distinctly makes himself the "Son of Man" of Daniel, and proclaims that he will come in the same manner, enthroned upon the clouds. This advent is here conceived, as in Daniel, as an advent not for Israel alone, but also for the nations. The angels are sent forth to gather the elect from all parts of the earth (Mark and Matthew). The redemption of the elect is in the mind of Jesus here. He passes over the condemnation of the nations, which is the prominent feature in Daniel.

Many scholars regard these signs and the advent in the clouds as purely symbolical, and of the nature of drapery or scenery to set forth more distinctly and graphically an advent which is essentially not visible and physical, but spiritual. Russell says: "The moral grandeur of the events which such symbols represent may be most fitly set forth by convulsions and cataclysms in the natural world."[1] Warren says: "It was in terms thus hallowed by association with the founding of their own divine monarchy, and familiarized to the Jews as the technical phraseology denoting the accession

---

[1] In *l. c.*, p. 81.

of kings to their thrones—*the court language of inauguration*, so to speak, that Christ described his coming to men in his kingdom."[1] Beyschlag recognizes that Jesus had in mind the renovation of heaven and earth, but he also insists that Jesus thought also of the spiritual renovation of humanity,[2] and that the cosmical features are the dress of the spiritual substance, and that both the spiritual and the cosmical find their fulfilment in their order, although they were not discriminated in the mind of Jesus.

This combination of the cosmical and the spiritual in the representation of Beyschlag is tempting in some respects, but not satisfying. These cosmical disturbances belong not only to the theophanies and the Christophanies of prophecy, but also to the theophanies and Christophanies of history in both the Old Testament and the New. They represent the response of the creature to the presence of the Creator. They cannot be symbolical in the prophecy without destroying their force in the history. These signs are theophanic signs, and they show that a Christophany or Advent of the Messiah is impending.

We are now prepared to consider the question of time. Luke gives us nothing on this subject. Mark says: "In those days, after that tribulation." Matthew is more definite: "But immediately after the tribulation of those days." The statement is that *immediately* after that shortened time of tribulation the signs heralding the advent appear. What meaning are we to ascribe to εὐθέως? It is certainly no stronger than the קָרוֹב of Old Testament prophecy used in connection with similar advents to judgment. It represents that to the mind of the prophet

---

[1] *Parousia*, p. 127.   [2] *Leben Jesu*, ii. s. 312 *seq*.

Jesus, as to the prophets that preceded him, the Advent was *near*. It was near in the prophetic sense—that is, the event was certain, but the time uncertain.

It is noteworthy that Mark and Matthew have now given us in their order the birth throes, the tribulation and the *Parousia* with its signs, which is $εὐθέως$ to the tribulation. These are the three sections of the original Jewish-Christian Apocalypse, according to Weiffenbach. It is also manifest that the period of the preaching of the gospel to the nations of the three Synoptists, and the times of the Gentiles, of Luke, are not in the same order of events as these. If they are to be brought into chronological relation with the other series, it would seem that while the preaching of the gospel may be to some extent parallel with the tribulation, it cannot be limited by that shortened time, but must extend beyond it and be parallel with the times of the Gentiles, which were certainly subsequent to the destruction of the holy city, and therefore intervene between the tribulation and the *Parousia*, and must be covered by the expression $εὐθέως$ of Matthew. To take the $εὐθέως$ strictly, or in any other way than the apocalyptic sense of the Old Testament advent scenes, is to introduce a glaring inconsistency between the two representations.[1]

### (7) *The Relation of the Signs to the Advent.*

| MARK xiii. 28–32. | MATT. xxiv. 32–36. | LUKE xxi. 28–33. |
|---|---|---|
| Now from the fig tree learn her parable: when her branch is now become tender, and putteth forth its leaves, ye know that | Now from the fig tree learn her parable: when her branch is now become tender, and putteth forth its leaves, ye know that the sum- | But when these things begin to come to pass, look up, and lift up your heads; because your redemption draweth nigh. And he spake |

---

[1] Briggs' *Messianic Prophecy*, pp. 52 *seq*.

| | | |
|---|---|---|
| the summer is nigh; even so ye also, when ye see these things coming to pass, know ye that he is nigh, *even* at the doors. [Verily I say unto you, This generation shall not pass away, until all these things be accomplished. Heaven and earth shall pass away; but my words shall not pass away.][1] But of that day or that hour knoweth no one, not even the angels in heaven, neither the Son, but the Father. | mer is nigh; even so ye also, when ye see all these things, know ye that he is nigh, *even* at the doors. [Verily I say unto you, This generation shall not pass away, till all these things be accomplished. Heaven and earth shall pass away, but my words shall not pass away.] But of that day and hour knoweth no one, not even the angels of heaven, neither the Son, but the Father only. | to them a parable: Behold the fig tree and all the trees: when they now shoot forth, ye see it and know of your own selves that the summer is now nigh. Even so ye also, when ye see these things coming to pass, know ye that the kingdom of God is nigh. [Verily I say unto you, This generation shall not pass away, till all things be accomplished. Heaven and earth shall pass away: but my words shall not pass away.] |

Having given the signs of the destruction of Jerusalem and the temple, and then of the Advent, in their order, Jesus now answers the question in the form of showing the inter-relation of the two questions as to the time and the signs, or of the relation of the signs to the End in the matter of time. He uses the symbol of the fig tree (Matthew, Mark) and trees in general (Luke). The putting forth of leaves shows that summer is nigh. As the leaves of the tree are to the summer, so are the signs to the Advent of the Messiah.

1. "When ye see these things coming to pass, know ye that he is nigh, even at the doors" (Mark).

2. "When ye see all these things, know ye that he is nigh, even at the doors" (Matthew).

3. "But when these things begin to come to pass, look up and lift up your heads, because your *redemption*

---

[1] The parts of this section enclosed in brackets are regarded by Weiffenbach as the close of the original Jewish-Christian Apocalypse.

draweth nigh. .... Even so, ye also, when ye see these things coming to pass, know ye that the *kingdom of God* is nigh " (Luke).

Luke is much fuller and more definite here than Mark or Matthew. There are two questions: (1) the reference of "these things" of Mark and Luke, and "all these things" of Matthew. The context and the parable make it clear that they are the *signs* of the Advent, which are like the putting forth of leaves by the trees. "When these things begin to come to pass" (Luke)—that is, in their order from the beginning; or "when ye *see* these things coming to pass" (Mark)—that is, during their progress; or "when ye see all these things," when they have transpired (Matthew)—that is, all these signs from beginning to end; then it may be known that the great event is "nigh" (Mark, Matthew, Luke), "at the doors" (Mark, Matthew). (2) This great event is left indefinite in the statement of Matthew and Mark, so that interpreters differ whether it is the Messiah himself, or the *Parousia*, or "the completion of the age," depending upon the question whether we are to look to the Son of Man of the immediate context, which is most natural, or go back to the original question in Matthew. Luke states definitely what it is. He gives two clauses of explanation, which enclose the symbol of the trees. The former represents that *redemption* draweth nigh, the latter that it is the *kingdom of God* that is nigh. These are parallel expressions, and must refer to the same event. The redemption of the disciples is that which they are to expect at the end of their labors in preaching the gospel. They are exhorted, having this end in view: "In your patience ye shall win your souls";[1] "But he

---

[1] Luke xxi. 19.

that endureth to the End, the same shall be saved."[1] It is the salvation at the completion of the age, and not the salvation of believers by faith; for it could not be said of that "it draweth nigh," inasmuch as it was already in their possession. Accordingly the kingdom of God is not the kingdom that cometh without observation, and that was already among them,[2] or the kingdom in any of its stages of growth; but it was the kingdom of glory, the fruition of the kingdom at the completion of the age. The expressions given in Luke, redemption and kingdom of God, are really equivalent to Matthew's Parousia and completion of the age, and the Son of Man coming in the clouds, which is essentially common to the three evangelists. Accordingly the statement is, that all these closing events are near and at the doors when the signs appear.

The next sentence, which is common to the three evangelists, is of great difficulty in its context—"This generation shall not pass away until all (these) things be accomplished." The question again arises as to the reference of "all these things." Shall we give to them the same reference as to the same expression in the previous verse—namely, to the *signs;* or shall we refer them to the Parousia as well as the signs? It is not easy to decide from the context. It seems to me that the former interpretation is the most natural one, and that "all these things" should have the same reference in both verses, if they are regarded as parts of the same section. This is strengthened by the fact that the terms "that day, or that hour" of Mark and Matthew clearly refer to the day of the Advent and the closing events of the previous context; and it would seem that we have a

---

[1] Matt. xxiv. 13.   [2] Luke xvii. 20, 21.

parallel statement to that of the previous verses, so that the two things, the signs and the Advent, are distinguished here as there. We have thus an advance in the three parallel statements. (1) It is said with reference to the *signs:* (*a*) The tree "putteth forth its leaves"; (*b*) "When ye see these things coming to pass"; (*c*) "This generation shall not pass away until all these things be accomplished." (2) And with reference to the *Advent:* (*a*) "Summer is nigh"; (*b*) "he (your redemption, the kingdom of God) is nigh (at the doors)"; (*c*) "but of that day or that hour knoweth no one, not even the angels in heaven, neither the Son, but the Father."

The signs would all transpire in *that generation;* but the event itself, although near and at the doors of that generation, could not be determined as to the day or the hour, even by the Messiah himself. With regard to that, he could only say what all prophets before him had said, It is near, εὐθέως, קרוב.

The most natural interpretation of γενεά is generation, the duration of human life, the lifetime of those then living, which would not extend beyond the first Christian century. Dr. Edward Robinson [1] urges that it is here used for one hundred years, and thinks that the time should then be extended to the war of Hadrian. He bases his interpretation on his exegesis of Gen. xv. 13. Accordingly, he sees the Advent of Jesus in his kingdom in the establishment of Christianity on the ruins of Judaism.[2]

Dorner, in an early writing on this discourse of Jesus,

---

[1] *Bibliotheca Sacra*, 1843, iii., pp. 540 *seq.*

[2] "Jesus first points out what was to happen after his departure, the trials and dangers to which his followers would be exposed. Then comes the 'abomination of desolation'; Jerusalem is 'compassed by armies,' and is 'trodden down of the Gentiles'; all this referring to its desolation by Titus in A.D. 70. Imme-

reminds us that Jesus used an Aramaic word,[1] and thinks of a lengthened period or age.[2] But we have no sufficient reason for departing from the ordinary meaning of the Greek terms.

The closing statement of this section is very important. It limits the knowledge of the time of the Advent to God the Father. It expressly excludes the knowledge of it from the Messiah. He could not give his disciples the knowledge of the day or the hour; he did not know it himself. This reacts upon the interpretation of the previous context. He who knew not the day or the hour could hardly say that it would be in his own generation, for that would be a knowledge of the day and hour within quite narrow limits.[3] It would amount to saying, It will be in this generation, before all of you have passed away; but I cannot give you the precise day or hour. It seems to me that such an interpretation greatly weakens the words of Jesus. He certainly did not mean to say: I know not the day or hour, but I do know the time in other respects. I can give you the week, month, year, and I choose to give you the generation or the time within thirty or forty years. On the other hand, the statement is very strong. It amounts to this: He did not know the day or hour at all. He makes no restrictions to himself. He could not say, therefore, that it would be in one of the days and hours of the lifetime of some of his hearers. There seems to be such an inconsistency here, if we think that Jesus

---

diately afterward the Lord would come and establish more fully his spiritual kingdom, by crushing in terrible destruction the last remnants of the power and name of Judaism, and this within the general limits of a generation of a hundred years from the time when he was speaking." (*Bib. Sac.*, 1843, p. 532.)

[1] דור
[2] *Orat. Chr. Eschat.*, p. 81.
[3] Beyschlag, *Leben Jesu*, i, s. 353.

represented that he knew not the day and hour, and yet said that it would be within thirty or forty years, that Weiffenbach,[1] and those who hold to the same theory, feel justified in ascribing the former statement of Mark to Jesus, and the latter to the Jewish-Christian apocalypse, these two pieces having different events in view. There can be no doubt that the former statement accords with the representation of Mark and Matthew, that after the beginning of birth throes and the tribulation, the Parousia was εὐθέως, and if we had only these passages to deal with, it would remove all difficulty; for the things happening in that generation would be the beginning of birth throes and the tribulation, and the Parousia would then be at the doors in the apocalyptic sense here as in the εὐθέως there. On the other hand, it seems impossible to limit the gospel age and the times of the Gentiles to that generation. And the parable, and the closing words as to the ignorance of the time on the part of the Messiah, seem to accord quite well with this larger conception. Accordingly, we cannot yield to Russell,[2] who presses the theory that the second Advent must have occurred in connection with the destruction of Jerusalem, or else Jesus made a false prediction. We are compelled by the context to make certain discriminations. There cannot be glaring inconsistencies in such close juxtaposition as we have here. The authors of the gospels would have seen them, and would not have left them unguarded. The indefinite terms need qualification from the larger context and the general teaching of Jesus. We must first distinguish between the events and their signs, and then consider that, in the combination of the signs and the time, Jesus

---

[1] In *l. c.*, s. 152.    [2] In *l. c.*, pp. 544 *seq.*

is summing up and giving his final answer to the question of his disciples. The events have been discriminated as two: (1) the destruction of Jerusalem and the temple with its signs, and (2) the *Parousia* with its signs. The parable suits both events in their relation to the signs. As the leaves of the tree indicate the approach of summer, these signs herald, each series of them, the nearness of the great event which they precede. The last half of the section now returns to the answer as to the time. There was, first, the negative answer that it was not immediate after the beginning of birth throes, and that it was immediate after the tribulation. Now, it is just these two things that are connected with the signs, and it is likely that these things were in the mind of Jesus in these words; whereas the time of the preaching of the gospel and the times of the Gentiles that follow the tribulation were in the mind of Jesus as the basis of his statement as to the Parousia itself, that "of that day or that hour knoweth no one, not even the angels of heaven, neither the Son, but the Father."

(8) *Exhortation to Watch.*

| MARK xiii. 33-37. | MATT. xxiv. 42. | LUKE xxi. 34-36. |
|---|---|---|
| Take ye heed, watch and pray: for ye know not when the time is. *It is* as *when* a man, sojourning in another country, having left his house, and given authority to his servants, to each one his work, commanded also the porter to watch. Watch therefore: for ye know not when the lord of | Watch therefore: for ye know not on what day your Lord cometh. | But take heed to yourselves, lest haply your hearts be overcharged with surfeiting, and drunkenness, and cares of this life, and that day come on you suddenly as a snare: for *so* shall it come upon all them that dwell on the face of all the earth. But watch ye at every season, making supplica- |

the house cometh, whether at even, or at midnight, or at cockcrowing, or in the morning; lest coming suddenly he find you sleeping. And what I say unto you I say unto all, Watch.[1]

tion, that ye may prevail to escape all these things that shall come to pass, and to stand before the Son of Man.

Matthew gives us a brief closing statement based upon the previous verse—"Ye know not on what day your Lord cometh." He knows not, he cannot tell you, you cannot know; therefore watch. He then adds several parables[2] which are given by Luke[3] more fully in another connection. Matthew then gives a chapter of parables and a concluding discourse. They seem not to have been a part of the apocalypse of Jesus, but to introduce other, though kindred matters.

Luke gives us a general exhortation to watchfulness, with a warning that the "day" will come suddenly as a snare. They are, therefore, to watch "at every season," and not only to watch, but to pray that they may escape the signs, "all these things that shall come to pass," and come to the Advent, and "stand before the Son of Man." This is appropriate to the discourse, but seems to have been an independent discourse originally given under other circumstances.

Mark gives a closing exhortation which has essentially the material of Luke and Matthew. The exhortation: "Take ye heed, watch and pray: for ye know not when the time is," includes the watching of Mat-

---

[1] Matthew now inserts vers. 38–41, which are given by Luke (xvii. 26–37) more fully in another connection where they belong. They are appropriate here for giving a fuller statement of the words of Jesus on this theme, but they do not belong to the apocalypse itself. Weiss thinks that the closing parable of Mark is a brief form of the parable of the talents in Matt. xxv., mixed with the parable of Luke xii. 36–38; but Weiffenbach correctly thinks that it was the original close of the apocalypse of Jesus.

[2] xxiv. 43–51.      [3] xii. 39–48.

thew and the watching and praying of Luke. The little parable of Mark[1] enforces it. We there have a warning: "Watch therefore: for ye know not when the lord of the house cometh, whether at even, or at midnight, or at cockcrowing or in the morning." Here the night is divided into four watches, from the earliest at even to the break of day. The time of the Advent is so uncertain that it may take place at any hour of the night; it may be early or it may be late. The night prior to the Advent may be a very short one, a moderate one, a long one, or the Advent may be postponed till the very last moment. These are forcible words, and exceedingly appropriate to the statement that no one knows the advent day but God the Father. They certainly do not mean to imply that Jesus knew the night, but not the watch of the night; they correspond with the previous statement that he knew not the day or the hour, and they imply that the time was as uncertain in the length of the interval to the Advent as the uncertainty whether a master will come in the first hours of the night, or at any time during its interval, or not till its closing moments. This reacts upon all the previous statements as to time, and shows that the $εὐθέως$ must be flexible enough to comprehend all this enormous uncertainty. And if our Lord has delayed his Advent until the closing hours of a long night of history, and has not come in its early hours, as his disciples hoped, this is not against the warning of the Lord that they should watch or that his Advent is $εὐθέως$; for he warned them of the uncertainty, and we are to do as all who have gone before us—remain in the like uncertainty and WATCH.

---

[1] xiii. 34-36.

# CHAPTER V.

### THE MESSIAH OF MATTHEW.

WE have considered in the previous chapters the Messiah of the Gospel of Matthew so far as the report is in accord with Mark. We have now to consider the Messianic idea of the Gospel of Matthew so far as it depends upon other sources than Mark. The chief of these sources is the Aramaic Logia of Matthew. Luke gives us a large proportion of this material. These two evangelists differ, in that Matthew prefers topical arrangement, whereas Luke prefers a geographical and chronological order. It is best therefore to follow Luke's order, while we use Matthew's words as the basis of our study.

### JESUS SUPERIOR TO TEMPTATION.

§ 31. *Jesus was tempted by the devil to assume his Messianic authority and dominion at once; but he declines to do anything more than to serve God as a pious man.*

The synoptists report that the official anointing of the Messiah was followed by a conflict with the devil. This conflict Jesus undertakes under the influence of the divine Spirit, who abode with him. The temptation in the wilderness is conceived as the counterpart of the temptation of our first parents in the garden of Eden. This is true not by mere coincidence or from a literary point of view, but by design, by necessity and in fact. If the Messiah was to accomplish the Messianic predictions of the Old Testament he could not neglect the fundamental one of the protevangelium.¹ As the son and heir of Adam, the woman's seed, he must conquer the serpent and overcome all the forces of evil. The three synoptists unite in making this the first act of the Messiah after his baptism. But Mark merely mentions it as an event without bringing out its Messianic significance. Accordingly we have reserved it for treatment here in connection with the Messianic idea of Matthew.

| MATT. iv. 1–11. | MARK i. 12, 13. | LUKE iv. 1–13. |
|---|---|---|
| Then was Jesus led up of the Spirit into the wilderness to be tempted of the devil. And when he had fasted forty days and forty nights, he afterward hungered. And the tempter came and said unto him, If thou art the Son of God, command that these stones become bread. But he answered and said, It is written, Man shall not live by bread alone, but by every word that proceedeth out of the mouth of God. Then the devil taketh him into the holy city; and he set him on the pinnacle of the temple, and saith unto him, If thou art the Son of God, cast thyself down: for it | And straightway the Spirit driveth him forth into the wilderness. And he was in the wilderness forty days tempted of Satan; and he was with the wild beasts; and the angels ministered unto him. | And Jesus, full of the Holy Spirit, returned from the Jordan, and was led in the Spirit in the wilderness during forty days, being tempted of the devil. And he did eat nothing in those days: and when they were completed, he hungered. And the devil said unto him, If thou art the Son of God, command this stone that it become bread. And Jesus answered unto him, It is written, Man shall not live by bread alone. And he led him up, and shewed him all the kingdoms of the world in a moment of time. And the devil said unto him, To thee will I give all this authority, |

---

¹ See Briggs' *Messianic Prophecy*, p. 71.

is written, He shall give his angels charge concerning thee: and on their hands they shall bear thee up, lest haply thou dash thy foot against a stone. Jesus said unto him, Again it is written, Thou shalt not tempt the Lord thy God. Again, the devil taketh him unto an exceeding high mountain, and showeth him all the kingdoms of the world, and the glory of them; and he said unto him, All these things will I give thee, if thou wilt fall down and worship me. Then saith Jesus unto him, Get thee hence, Satan: for it is written, Thou shalt worship the Lord thy God, and him only shalt thou serve. Then the devil leaveth him; and behold, angels came and ministered unto him.

and the glory of them: for it hath been delivered unto me; and to whomsoever I will I give it. If thou therefore wilt worship before me, it shall all be thine. And Jesus answered and said unto him, It is written, Thou shalt worship the Lord thy God, and him only shalt thou serve. And he led him to Jerusalem, and set him on the pinnacle of the temple, and said unto him, If thou art the Son of God, cast thyself down from hence: for it is written, He shall give his angels charge concerning thee, to guard thee: and, On their hands they shall bear thee up, lest haply thou dash thy foot against a stone. And Jesus answering said unto him, It is said, Thou shalt not tempt the Lord thy God. And when the devil had completed every temptation, he departed from him for a season.

This temptation is not only the counterpart of the temptation of our first parents in the garden of Eden; but it presents many contrasts with the temptation of Israel in the wilderness. The temptations of the devil all aim to induce Jesus to claim his Messianic dominion and exercise his Messianic authority at once. The devil assumes that Jesus is the Messiah and argues from it. Jesus seems, on this occasion, to ignore his Messiahship altogether. He declines to act as the prophet of Deuteronomy,[1] or the Son of Man of Daniel,[2] or as the Messianic king of Isaiah.[3] He acts as the pious man of the Law and the Psalter. He thus asserts, not indeed in words, but still more forcibly in deeds, a more fundamental

---

[1] Deut. xviii. 18–20.  [2] Dan. vii. 13, 14.  [3] Isa. xi.

Messiahship than any recognized by the devil, namely, that he was the second Adam, the ideal man, the seed of the woman, the conqueror of the serpent.

Why should he fast in the wilderness, is the suggestion of the devil, when he had authority to transform stones into bread. Even if he would be the Messianic prophet rather than the Messianic king, Moses gave the people of Israel, in the wilderness, manna from heaven, why should not the Messianic prophet, in the wilderness, provide himself with nourishment. Jesus declines the temptation. He thinks of the teaching of Moses rather than of his example. The Messiah's time for miracle-working has not come. He declines the nourishment of miraculous bread and prefers the spiritual nourishment afforded to every man by the word of God. He came into the wilderness, not to work miracles, but to prepare for his work on earth. He came there not to feast, but to fast; not to nourish his body, but to invigorate his spirit by communion with God.

If Jesus will not exercise his Messianic authority in miracle-working, suggests the devil, why not show his confidence in God by assuming that God will fulfil His promises; and so cast himself upon Him for support? As the Son of Man well-pleasing to God, he was assured of the support of angels. An ancient psalmist had sung that the pious man who is in communion with God will be delivered from all evil:

> For he will give his angels charge over thee,
> To keep thee in all thy ways;
> Upon their palms they will bear thee up,
> Lest thou dash thy foot against a stone.[1]

Why not put this promise to the test, descend from

---
[1] Ps. xci. Briggs' *Messianic Prophecy*, p. 460.

the pinnacle of the temple as if from the clouds of heaven, and so display his glory as the Son of Man, and receive the homage of the people as the Son of Man from heaven. Thus he would throw upon God the responsibility of his Messianic manifestation. Jesus, knowing that the Pharisees and the people expected just such a Son of Man from heaven in accordance with the prediction of Daniel,[1] declines to transfer his own Messianic responsibility, given him by God, back again to God. He refuses to tempt God. He has entire confidence in God. He is assured that he is the Messianic Son of Man, why then should he put it to the test? The time has not yet come for him to come on the clouds. He has other work to do prior to that time.[2]

If now Jesus declines to use his Messianic authority as the Messianic Prophet and the Messianic Son of Man, why not as the Messianic King receive the kingdom of the world from the prince of the world? This is the third and last temptation. The devil will renounce his dominion, give it all over to the Messiah, if he will do obeisance to him. Why battle for a throne when it may be received as a gift? This generous offer of the devil was at once declined. Jesus will be a pious man, and in accordance with the divine law will worship and serve God alone. He came to be well-pleasing to God in his life and character as a holy man. He has not come at present to reign, but to serve. He will live as a man well-pleasing to God and undergo all the hardships of human life. This decision meant conflict with the devil throughout his life. The devil offered him dominion and peace at the price of recognition. Jesus chose

---

[1] Dan. vii. See Briggs' *Messianic Prophecy*, p. 420.

[2] Luke inverts the order of the second and third temptations. The order matters little, but Matthew's seems to be preferable.

battle and suffering, and undertook the Messianic war.

### THE RIGHTEOUSNESS OF THE KINGDOM.

§ 32. *The heirs of the kingdom are the poor in spirit, the persecuted, those whose righteousness exceeds that of the Pharisees, those who do the least commands, and the godlike.*

Early in his ministry Jesus delivered a discourse, which is usually called the Sermon on the Mount, in which he set forth some of the features of the kingdom. The main stock of the discourse is found in Luke. Matthew, in accordance with his custom, gathers about it sayings of Jesus which are scattered in other passages in Luke.

This discourse begins with the Beatitudes. Luke seems to give the original form in which Jesus delivered them. Matthew adds other Beatitudes, and puts them all in the third person, with explanatory and generalizing additions.[1] We shall follow Luke in our efforts to find the original words of Jesus.

### *The Four Beatitudes.*

Blessed are ye poor;[2] for yours[3] is the kingdom of God.[4]
Blessed are ye that hunger[5]; [3] for ye[3] shall be filled.
Blessed are ye that weep; [5] for ye[3] shall laugh.

---

[1] See Wendt, *Lehre Jesu*, i. 535 *seq.*

Matthew adds τῷ πνεύματι. This is explanatory, and doubtless a true explanation. It is not probable that it was original.

[3] Matthew changes to the third person the original direct address in order to generalize and make all the Beatitudes harmonious in form.

[4] Matthew, as usual, changes kingdom of God into kingdom of heaven.

[5] Luke inserts "now" in several places. It is not given by Matthew. It merely intensifies the simple antithesis of the original. See Wendt, *Lehre Jesu*, i., s. 56.

[6] Matthew adds "and thirst after righteousness." This is explanatory and not original. It destroys the measure of the line.

Blessed are ye[1] when men shall hate you,
And when they shall separate you from their company,[2] and reproach you,
And cast out your name as evil.[3]
Rejoice in that day and leap for joy :[4]
For behold, your reward is great in heaven :
For in the same manner did their fathers unto the prophets.[5]

(Luke vi. 20–23.)

### The Four Woes.

Woe unto you rich ! for ye have received your consolation.[6]
Woe unto you that are full ![7] for ye shall hunger.
Woe, ye that laugh ![7] for ye shall mourn and weep.
Woe, when all men shall speak well of you,
For in the same manner did their fathers to the false prophets.

(Luke vi. 24–26.)

Matthew adds five other Beatitudes. These were either from other discourses in the Logia or from other sources than the Logia. Their gnomic form favors their original place in the Logia :

Blessed are the meek : for they shall inherit the land.[8]
Blessed are the merciful : for they shall obtain mercy.[9]
Blessed are the pure in heart : for they shall see God.[9]

---

[1] Here Matthew retains the original second person and agrees with Luke.

[2] Matthew omits "hate you" of previous line, and "separate you from their company" of this line.

[3] Matthew substitutes " say all manner of evil against you," and prefixes "persecute you." It also adds an explanatory "falsely, for my sake." Luke also explains here "for the Son of Man's sake."

[4] Matthew substitutes "be exceeding glad," which is less graphic.

[5] The two are, apart from slight variations, the same in these two lines, save that Matthew substitutes the more specific "persecuted" for the "did unto" of Luke.

[6] These antithetical woes are not given in Matthew. They seem to be original from the natural antithesis of the four Woes to the four Beatitudes.

[7] See note (5) on page 171.

[8] Ps. xxxvii. 11. It is probable that there is here, as in the psalm, a reference to the land of blessing, the holy land, rather than to the earth.

[9] Comp. Ps. xxiv. 4 ; lxxiii. 1.

Blessed are the peacemakers : for they shall be called sons of God.
Blessed are the persecuted : for theirs is the kingdom of God.[1]
(Matt. v. 5, 7–10.)

In this discourse Jesus is giving the character of those who will be members of the kingdom and enjoy its rewards. The rewards are suited to the characters. Both alike are spiritual and not carnal or temporal. Luke gives us the frame which Matthew fills up with material from other sources, and with qualifying words. The poor, the hungry, the weeping, and the hated disciples of Jesus, those who like their Master are in this condition because they have followed in the footsteps of the ancient prophets, will eventually rejoice when they receive their reward in the kingdom of God. It is reserved in heaven for them. They are not to expect it apart from the kingdom of God or from other than a heavenly source. Matthew adds to these four beatitudes other five which give qualifications of a more positive kind. The meek, the merciful, the pure in heart, the peacemakers and the persecuted imply qualifications, which, with the promises that accompany them, look more decidedly toward a kingdom, future to the disciples, to be entered after the attainment of meritorious character and a judgment of approval. The persecuted have a right to the kingdom. It is theirs because they suffer for it as a part of the kingdom of grace, and they will eventually enter into the kingdom of glory.

The peacemakers will be recognized as children of God in their work on earth, but more effectually by the Messiah at the gate of the kingdom of glory. The pure in heart will see God in the beatific vision of the reason,

---

[1] Matthew explains as usual " for righteousness' sake," and uses " kingdom of heaven " for the original " kingdom of God."

in this life, but face to face only in the kingdom of glory. The merciful will obtain mercy in the beginnings of their redemption in the kingdom of grace, but finally in the judgment when the doors of the kingdom of glory are opened. The meek cannot inherit the land, the land of promise, the holy land, the fruition of the land of Canaan, until the inheritance is bestowed in the kingdom of glory. Thus these beatitudes, in part may be referred to the kingdom of grace and its privileges; but they cannot be fully realized until the advent of the kingdom of glory.

These nine beatitudes are the beatitudes of the kingdom, and set forth the character of its citizens. It is evident therefore that Jesus had in view a very different kind of kingdom from that of temporal dominion and civil administration. And he had no thought of realizing such a kingdom in a very short time.

Besides the five additional beatitudes, Matthew gives, in a long discourse, other features of these citizens of the kingdom.

Whosoever therefore shall break one of these least commandments,
And shall teach men so,
He shall be called least in the kingdom of God:[1]
But whosoever shall do and teach them,
He shall be called great in the kingdom of God.[1]
For I say unto you,
That except your righteousness shall exceed that of the scribes and Pharisees,
Ye shall in no wise enter into the kingdom of God.[1]
(Matth. v. 19, 20.)

The kingdom of God as here conceived is a king-

---

[1] As usual, Matthew substitutes "kingdom of heaven" for an original "kingdom of God."

dom that is inherited by those who have a righteousness that exceeds that of the legal requirements of the Pharisee. Jesus explains this righteousness in expounding three of the ten commandments. He shows that Pharisaic obedience to the external requirements in conduct must be exceeded by conformity in speech and also in heart; that something more than justice is required; even the heathen are equal to that. The law of the kingdom requires self-sacrifice, love, mercy, and indeed, likeness to God. Such a righteousness cannot be gained in a moment. Greater devotion to the will of God and personal service are necessary. Jesus has not come to destroy the law and the prophets, but to fulfil them in a righteousness which is the higher, holier, and more godlike life of himself and his disciples. The preparation for the kingdom required by the Pharisees was exact conformity to legal righteousness. This is insufficient. The disciples of Jesus must be conformed to the personal righteousness of God. They must be godlike in order to be thought worthy of entrance into the kingdom of God. Those who do not exceed the Pharisees in righteousness will gain no entrance into it.

The righteousness which is to inherit the kingdom is not to be like that of the Pharisees, ostentatious in the presence of men, but likeness to God, and therefore before the eyes of God, having God only in view. Prayer, fasting, almsgiving, and all the exercises of practical religion are to be done in the eyes of God. Such righteousness will be rewarded in the kingdom of God.[1] The true disciple obeys the words of the Master, and in this way erects his building on the sure foundation of a rock that will abide the storms of judgment.[2]

---

[1] Matt. vi. 1-18.  [2] Matt. vii. 24-27.

In this discourse Jesus had in view a kingdom into which there is no entrance except after an act of judgment, and into which only the truly righteous and godlike can enter. This kingdom therefore is not the kingdom of grace which extends until the day of judgment, but the kingdom of glory which follows the day of judgment.

### THE MESSIAH'S CREDENTIALS.

§ 33. *His miracles of mercy and his preaching to the poor were evidences that Jesus was the Messianic servant of God.*

Jesus began his official life as the Messiah by miracles. His miracles accompanied his preaching and had the same character. They were both with wonderful authority, but they lacked the marvellous display of divine power which is so characteristic of the miracles of the Old Testament. They were not therefore such striking evidences of the Messiahship of Jesus as were expected. It would seem that even John the Baptist was somewhat disappointed. He did not falter in his faith in Jesus as a prophet of God, but he seems to have been in doubt whether Jesus was the expected Messiah or another herald of the Messiah like himself. Accordingly he sends to Jesus for information on this point. The reply of Jesus and his discourse on the occasion give us the best interpretation of the evidential character of his preaching and miracle-working.

| MATT. xi. 2–14. | LUKE vii. 18–28. |
|---|---|
| Now when John heard in the prison the works of the Messiah, he sent by his disciples, and said unto him, Art thou he that cometh, or look we for another? And Jesus answered and said | And the disciples of John told him of all these things. And John calling unto him two of his disciples sent them to the Lord, saying, Art thou he that cometh, or look we for another? |

unto them, Go your way and tell John the things which ye do hear and see: the blind receive their sight, and the lame walk, the lepers are cleansed, and the deaf hear, and the dead are raised up, and the poor have good tidings preached to them. And blessed is he whosoever shall find none occasion of stumbling in me. And as these went their way, Jesus began to say unto the multitudes concerning John, What went ye out into the wilderness to behold? a reed shaken with the wind? But what went ye out for to see? a man clothed in soft *raiment?* Behold, they that wear soft *raiment* are in kings' houses. But wherefore went ye out? to see a prophet? Yea, I say unto you, and much more than a prophet. This is he, of whom it is written, Behold, I send my messenger before thy face, who shall prepare thy way before thee. Verily I say unto you, Among them that are born of women, there hath not arisen a greater than John the Baptist: yet he that is but little in the kingdom of heaven is greater than he. And from the days of John the Baptist until now the kingdom of heaven suffereth violence, and men of violence take it by force. For all the prophets and the law prophesied until John. And if ye are willing to receive *it* this is Elijah, which is to come.

And when the men were come unto him, they said, John the Baptist hath sent us unto thee, saying Art thou he that cometh, or look we for another? In that hour he cured many of diseases and plagues and evil spirits; and on many that were blind he bestowed sight. And he answered and said unto them, Go your way, and tell John what things ye have seen and heard; the blind receive their sight, the lame walk, the lepers are cleansed, and the deaf hear, the dead are raised up, the poor have good tidings preached to them. And blessed is he, whosoever shall find none occasion of stumbling in me. And when the messengers of John were departed, he began to say unto the multitudes concerning John, What went ye out into the wilderness to behold? a reed shaken with the wind? But what went ye out to see? a man clothed in soft raiment? Behold, they which are gorgeously apparelled, and live delicately, are in kings' courts. But what went ye out to see? a prophet? Yea, I say unto you, and much more than a prophet. This is he of whom it is written, Behold, I send my messenger before thy face, who shall prepare thy way before thee. I say unto you, Among them that are born of women there is none greater than John: yet he that is but little in the kingdom of God is greater than he.

The evidences of his Messiahship given by Jesus to the messengers of the Baptist are not marvels of miracle-working, displaying power; but miracles of mercy—the healing of the sick, the lame, the blind, the lepers, the deaf, and the raising of the dead. A few such miracles of mercy are found in the Old Testament, but they are occasional and not characteristic of the Old Testament. Miracles of mercy are characteristic of the preaching of Jesus, and it is this characteristic that is the evidence of his Messiahship. For Jesus equally with Moses recognized that false prophets might work miracles, and warns his disciples not to be deceived. Miracles of power may excite the wonder and the credence of marvel-loving men. But miracles of mercy are the true credentials of the Messiah, for they express the redemptive love of his nature. Associated with the miracles of mercy is preaching to the poor. Preaching is a work of prophets as a class. But preaching to the poor is a special work of the Messiah. In this passage Jesus doubtless has in mind and refers John to the gentle preacher of the great prophecy of the exile.[1]

The inquiry of John affords Jesus an opportunity to give his testimony respecting John. Jesus declares that the Baptist was the herald predicted in the prophecies of Malachi and of the great prophet of the exile.[2] John was the greatest who had appeared in the old dispensation, a second Elijah, the herald of the Messiah. But the least in the kingdom of the Messiah will be greater than John, because he is in the kingdom of the Messiah, which is the culmination of the kingdom of God of the Old Covenant. John is the last of the entire dispensation of the prophets, but they all prepared for the Advent of the Messiah. The kingdom of God suffered violence during the time beginning with the Baptist. Bold, zealous men think that they can bring the kingdom by violence, by rebellion and deeds of arms. It is

---

[1] Isaiah xlii., lxi. See Briggs' *Messianic Prophecy*, pp. 343, 369.
[2] Isaiah xl. 1-11; Mal. iii. See Briggs' *Messianic Prophecy*, pp. 375, 473.

at hand, but it cannot be established in this way. The Messianic prophet is laying its foundations in peace, in quietness, in righteousness by his prophetic ministry, and by transformations of the life and character of men.

These words to the messengers of the Baptist show that Jesus regarded himself as the Messianic servant of the great prophet of the exile.

THE KINGDOM WHICH HAD COME UPON THEM.

§ 34. *The kingdom of God had come upon the Jews in the war of the Son of Man against the kingdom of Satan. In the Messianic age all other sins may be forgiven. But the blasphemy of the Spirit of God is an everlasting sin not to be forgiven in either age.*

| MATT. xii. 22-32. | MARK iii. 22-30. | LUKE xi. 14-23. |
|---|---|---|
| Then was brought unto him one possessed with a demon, blind and dumb: and he healed him, insomuch that the dumb man spake and saw. And all the multitudes were amazed, and said, Is this the son of David? But when the Pharisees heard it, they said, This man doth not cast out demons, but by Beelzebub the prince of the demons. And knowing their thoughts he said unto them, Every kingdom divided against itself is brought to desolation; and every city or house divided against itself shall | And the scribes which came down from Jerusalem said, He hath Beelzebub, and, By the prince of the demons casteth he out the demons. And he called them unto him, and said unto them in parables, How can Satan cast out Satan? And if a kingdom be divided against itself, that kingdom cannot stand. And if a house be divided against itself, that house will not be able to stand. And if Satan hath risen up against himself, and is divided, he cannot stand, but hath an end. But no one can enter into the house of the | And he was casting out a demon *which was* dumb. And it came to pass, when the demon was gone out, the dumb man spake; and the multitudes marvelled. But some of them said, By Beelzebub the prince of the demons casteth he out demons. And others, tempting *him*, sought of him a sign from heaven. But he, knowing their thoughts, said unto them, Every kingdom divided against itself is brought to desolation; and a house *divided* against a house falleth. And if Satan also is divided against himself, how |

not stand: and if Satan casteth out Satan, he is divided against himself; how then shall his kingdom stand? And if I by Beelzebub cast out demons, by whom do your sons cast them out? therefore shall they be your judges. But if I by the Spirit of God cast out demons, then is the kingdom of God come upon you. Or how can one enter into the house of the strong *man*, and spoil his goods, except he first bind the strong *man*? and then he will spoil his house. He that is not with me is against me; and he that gathereth not with me scattereth. Therefore I say unto you, Every sin and blasphemy shall be forgiven unto men; but the blasphemy against the Spirit shall not be forgiven. And whosoever shall speak a word against the Son of man, it shall be forgiven him; but whosoever shall speak against the Holy Spirit, it shall not be forgiven him, neither in this world, nor in that which is to come.

strong *man*, and spoil his goods, except he first bind the strong *man;* and then he will spoil his house. Verily I say unto you, All their sins shall be forgiven unto the sons of men, and their blasphemies wherewith soever they shall blaspheme: but whosoever shall blaspheme against the Holy Spirit hath never forgiveness, but is guilty of an eternal sin: because they said, He hath an unclean spirit.

shall his kingdom stand? because ye say that I cast out demons by Beelzebub. And if I by Beelzebub cast out demons, by whom do your sons cast them out? therefore shall they be your judges. But if I by the finger of God cast out demons, then is the kingdom of God come upon you. When the strong *man* fully armed guardeth his own court, his goods are in peace: but when a stronger than he shall come upon him, and overcome him, he taketh from him his whole armour wherein he trusted, and divideth his spoils. He that is not with me is against me; and he that gathereth not with me scattereth.

The kingdom of Satan and the kingdom of God are at

war. Satan will not war against himself and divide his own kingdom into warring factions. If war is carried on against the kingdom of Satan that war must be waged by the kingdom of God. The casting out of demons is an attack upon the kingdom of Satan. He who makes the attack represents the kingdom of God. His warfare is an evidence that the kingdom of God has come in him. The kingdom of God was therefore present with the Messiah in his war with Satan.

The Pharisees might be excused and forgiven for not recognizing Jesus as the Messiah and for speaking against him. But to attribute to the devil, what was really an attack on the devil by the power of the divine Spirit, was a more serious matter. It was a denial of the work of the Spirit, a blasphemy against God. Such a sin was unpardonable. It would not be forgiven either in this age of the world or in the age that was to come —it would have no forgiveness forever—for it was an everlasting sin, a sin going on forever. The antithesis between the two ages is a Messianic antithesis between the age prior to the Messianic reign and the age of his reign. In neither of these ages could the blasphemy against the divine Spirit be forgiven. Whether other sins might be forgiven in the coming age which are not forgiven in this, whether there is only one sin that is an everlasting sin, and so the only one unpardonable in the Messianic age, we are not told; but the antithesis between the one sin and all others is very suggestive of such possibilities.

### THE KINGDOM NIGH.

§ 35. *The twelve were commissioned to preach that the kingdom of heaven was nigh. The Messiah was to come ere they could complete the cities of Israel in their ministry.*

The Synoptists agree in a report of the commission of

the twelve. Mark does not attach it to the doctrine of the kingdom, and accordingly we have reserved it from his Messianic idea to treat it here. Matthew mingles with the commission of the twelve, sayings of Jesus given by Luke in the commission of the seventy and also on other occasions. We shall endeavor to separate them, giving first the parallel reports of Mark and Luke, and then the report of Matthew so far as it can be determined in the parallelism of the poetry of the Aramaic Logia.

The twelve are commissioned to preach the same doctrine as that of the Baptist and Jesus.

| MARK vi. 7–8a. | MATT. x. 1, 5. | LUKE ix. 1–3a. |
|---|---|---|
| And he called unto him the twelve, and began to send them forth by two and two; and he gave them authority over the unclean spirits; and he charged them— | And he called unto him his twelve disciples, and gave them authority over unclean spirits, to cast them out, and to heal all manner of disease and all manner of sickness. . . . . . These twelve Jesus sent forth, and charged them, saying, | And he called the twelve together, and gave them power and authority over all demons, and to cure diseases. And he sent them forth to preach the kingdom of God, and to heal the sick. And he said unto them, |

The words of Jesus commissioning the twelve are given in Luke, in a fragmentary form, from the Logia, and in Mark from his own independent source. The report of Matthew is fuller, and is really a series of sentences of the Wisdom of Jesus. We shall follow Matthew in the main; but shall use the other gospels in order to aid in the reconstruction of the original sentences of the Wisdom of Jesus.[1]

---

[1] It is evident that if we desire to know the original words of Jesus, the only way is to study the three reports of them, and from the three discern the original which underlies them all. The only way possible is the path of criticism.

Go not into [any] way of the Gentiles. (Matt. x. 5-8.)
And enter not into [any] city of the Samaritans:
But go rather to the sheep,
The lost of the house of Israel.
And as ye go, preach, saying,
The kingdom of God is at hand.
Heal the sick, raise the dead,
Cleanse the lepers, cast out demons:
Freely ye received, freely give.[1]
Take nothing for your journey[2] (Luke ix. 3b.)
Save a staff only.[3] (Mark vi. 8b.)
Get you no gold nor silver, (Matt. x. 9.)
Nor brass in your girdles,
No wallet for your journey, (Matt. x. 10a.)
Neither have two coats;[4] (Luke ix. 3d.)
But be shod with sandals:[5] (Mark vi 9a.)
For the laborer is worthy of his food. (Matt. x. 10d.)
And into whatsoever city ye enter,[6] (Matt. x. 11.)
Search out who in it is worthy;
And there abide till ye go forth.
And whosoever shall not receive you, (Matt. x. 14.)
Nor hear your words,

---

[1] These nine lines are given only in Matthew. Here as elsewhere he uses "kingdom of heaven" for an original "kingdom of God."

[2] This line is from Luke. It has been omitted by Matthew. In Mark it is in a clause with ἵνα which is clearly not so original as the imperative.

[3] This clause is doubtless original. Matthew, verse 10, gives a reverse statement that they were not to take a staff. Μηδὲ ῥάβδον, is appended to plurals, and is obscure. In Luke, verse 3, the staff is prohibited, and begins the list of prohibited objects, μήτε ῥάβδον. The statement of Mark comes from the original Mark; those of Matthew and Luke from the Logia, but in an incorrect form, because the words of Mark give a true line of poetry appropriate in this place—the words in Matthew and Luke mar the line of poetry to which they are attached.

[4] Mark has, verse 9b, μὴ ἐνδύσασθαι, Matthew only, μηδὲ (δύο χιτῶνας), verse 10b.

[5] Matthew, verse 10a, has only μηδὲ ὑποδήματα; it is absent altogether from Luke.

[6] Matthew, verse 11a, adds *village*, which is an enlargement by explanation; it did not belong to the original. The *house* of Mark and Luke is due to an abbreviation of the two lines of Matthew.

> As ye go forth out of that city [1]
> Shake off the dust of your feet,
> For a testimony against them. (Luke ix. 5*d*.)
> But when they persecute you in this city, (Matt. x. 23.)
> Flee unto the next:
> For verily I say unto you,
> Ye shall not have gone through the cities of Israel,
> Till the Son of Man be come.

These words of Jesus give the commission of the twelve for their first missionary journey in Palestine. The only one of these sayings which is not altogether harmonious, is Matthew x. 23. These words are so well suited to the words with which Matthew begins the commission, limiting their ministry to Israel, that it seems likely that they were spoken at this time rather than in connection with the words which immediately precede them in Matthew, but which are given elsewhere in Luke. Moreover, they disclose an early stage in the teaching of Jesus respecting the second Advent.

A study of this commission of the twelve makes it clear that the theme of their preaching was the same as that of the Master itself. The kingdom of God was at hand. This was to be proclaimed everywhere among the Jews. The nation of Israel was called to repent and to prepare for the kingdom by repentance. The preachers were endowed with miraculous energy to do the same miracles as Jesus himself did. They were assured that they must limit their labors to Israel, for the time would be insufficient to herald the glad tidings even to all Israel. The Messiah would come before they could complete the list of the cities of Israel in their ministry. This coming of the Son of Man is a coming, future to the

---

[1] Matthew prefixes *house* to *city*, but this is only an explanatory addition to the original *city* as given in Luke, verse 5*b*, and ἐκεῖθεν, Mark, verse 11*c*.

first coming. It is probably to be conceived as his coming to establish the kingdom of God, and not as his coming to judgment. To his hearers, at the time when it was spoken, it had an indefinite meaning which could only be cleared up through subsequent teachings of Jesus or by the events themselves. These two comings had not yet been distinguished. Two things are, however, clearly taught—(1) the speedy coming of the Son of Man, and (2) the nearness of the kingdom; however these events might be related to one another.

The words of Jesus which Matthew has inserted here, according to his custom, about the main stock of the commission of the twelve, are scattered in Luke and belong to several different occasions, as the parallels show.

(1) Matt. x. 12, 13 = Luke x. 5, 6.
" x. 15 = " x. 12.
" x. 16 = " x. 3.
" x. 40 = " x. 16.
" x. 41, 42.

These sayings are given their historical setting in the commission of the Seventy in Luke. They may be better understood in that connection. They are reserved for treatment there, although they were taken from the Logia.[1]

(2) Matt. x. 17–22 = Mark xiii. 9–13 = Luke xxi. 12–17. These were taken from the Apocalypse of Jesus and have already been considered.[2]

(3) Matt. x. 24, 25 = Luke vi. 40.
" x. 26-33 = Luke xii. 2-9.
" x. 34-36 = " xii. 51-53.
" x. 37, 38 = " xiv. 26, 27.

---

[1] See p. 238.   [2] See p. 143.

These sayings belong to several occasions in connection with the Perean ministry, and may be appropriately considered later.[1]

(4) Matt. x. 39 = Luke xvii. 33.

This sentence belongs to the lesser Apocalypse of Jesus as given in Luke, where it will be considered.[2]

### THE SIGN OF THE PROPHET JONAH.

§ 36. *The story of Jonah is the symbol of the Son of Man. His preaching, like that of Jonah, calls for repentance, and if rejected will receive severer condemnation. He is to remain three days in the grave.*

The time when Jesus began to predict his death and resurrection is not altogether certain. The transfiguration is the great event opening the second stage of his career. Luke reports in connection with that event that Moses and Elijah, who appeared in the Glory, spake of his decease, which he was to accomplish at Jerusalem.[3] But a week before, the confession of the apostles is followed by a prediction of his death and resurrection.[4] This confession is due to a crisis which follows the miracle of the loaves and fishes, the death of John the Baptist, and the return of the apostles. It is in connection with this crisis that we meet with the demand for a sign and the prediction of his death, in the gospel of John. The gospel of Mark gives at the same time a Pharisaic demand for a sign which appears in the parallels of Matthew and Luke, in different connections. Mark does not report the sign that was predicted, and therefore we have reserved the matter for consideration here. But a careful study of the whole subject makes it probable that this prediction of his death and resurrection is really based

---

[1] See p. 196.  [2] See p. 246.  [3] ix. 31. See p. 100.  [4] See p. 94.

upon a demand for a sign, and is presented for the first time, in the order of the Synoptists, in the sign of Jonah.

| MARK viii. 10–13. | MATT. xii. 38–42. | LUKE xi. 29–32. |
|---|---|---|
| And straightway he entered into the boat with his disciples, and came into the parts of Dalmanutha. And the Pharisees came forth, and began to question with him, seeking of him a sign from heaven, tempting him. And he sighed deeply in his spirit, and saith, Why doth this generation seek a sign? verily I say unto you, There shall no sign be given unto this generation. And he left them, and again entering into *the boat* departed to the other side. | Then certain of the scribes and Pharisees answered him, saying, Master, we would see a sign from thee. But he answered and said unto them, An evil and adulterous generation seeketh after a sign; and there shall no sign be given to it but the sign of Jonah the prophet: for as Jonah was three days and three nights in the belly of the whale; so shall the Son of Man be three days and three nights in the heart of the earth. The men of Nineveh shall stand up in the judgment with this generation, and shall condemn it: for they repented at the preaching of Jonah; and behold, a greater than Jonah is here. The queen of the south shall rise up in the judgment with this generation, and shall condemn it: for she came from the ends of the earth to hear the wisdom of Solomon; and behold, a greater than Solomon is here. | And when the multitudes were gathering together unto him, he began to say, This generation is an evil generation: it seeketh after a sign; and there shall no sign be given to it but the sign of Jonah. For even as Jonah became a sign unto the Ninevites, so shall also the Son of Man be to this generation. The queen of the south shall rise up in the judgment with the men of this generation, and shall condemn them: for she came from the ends of the earth to hear the wisdom of Solomon; and behold, a greater than Solomon is here. The men of Nineveh shall stand up in the judgment with this generation, and shall condemn it: for they repented at the preaching of Jonah; and behold, a greater than Jonah is here. |

The Pharisees were not convinced by the miracles of mercy which Jesus wrought, or the gospel to the poor that Jesus preached. They demanded a Messianic sign. There was some propriety in this request when the Messianic idea was conceived in the lines of the king and the kingdom, or of the Son of Man of the Apocalypse of Daniel. But Jesus was at present fulfilling rather the ideal of the Messianic servant, which, to the Jews of the time, was in the background and not understood. He was indeed the Son of Man, but engaged in a work prior to the advent in the clouds. Jesus refuses to give them a sign at present. But at the same time he refers them to the future, when a sign would be given. The story of Jonah is the symbol of the sign, both in his abode in the belly of the fish and in his preaching, only the order of the story is reversed. The preacher is now in their presence, he is calling them to repentance. Nineveh repented at the preaching of Jonah. The queen of the south came to learn from the wisdom of Solomon. Jesus is a greater preacher and offers them surpassing wisdom. Those who do not repent will be more severely condemned in the judgment.

But Jonah is especially the symbol of the sign of the Son of Man in his abiding in the belly of the fish. The Son of Man is also to spend three days in the grave. It is not said here that he will be put to death, but it is implied that he will die. It is not said that he will rise again; but the limit of three days implies it. This brief form of the prediction is an evidence that it is prior to all others relating to his death. It not only gives a sign, but interprets it in part by predicting the abode in the grave and the serious consequences of rejecting the gospel. Thus Jesus points to his death and resurrection as the sign of the Son of Man, the sign which is to give to men the divine testimony of his Messiahship. But that sign could not be given until the event itself. It could only be given in the form of prediction prior to the event.¹

### THE ROCK PETER.

§ 37. *Peter is the rock upon which the Church will be built. He will have the keys of the kingdom, and his discipline will be ratified in heaven. Jesus will be present in the assembly of his disciples during their exercise of discipline.*

The four evangelists unite in giving the confession of Peter in the region of Cæsarea Philippi and his recognition of Jesus as the Messiah;² but Matthew alone gives the prediction respecting Peter as the rock.³ This pre-

---

¹ The story of Jonah as here used by Jesus is not thereby accredited as history. Jesus uses fiction of his own composition in his beautiful parables. Why should he not use, for purposes of illustration, fiction from the Old Testament likewise? Paul uses the story of Jannes and Jambres (2 Tim. iii. 8), and Jude (verse 9) the story of the contest of Michael with the devil over the body of Moses, both from legends of Jewish Haggada. If the modern critical theory of Jonah be correct, that the story of Jonah was designedly written as historic fiction to set forth in a symbol the resurrection of Israel in order to renew his prophetic calling to minister salvation to the Gentiles, then the use which Jesus makes of it is not only appropriate in itself, but closely allied to its original meaning.

² See p. 94.

³ This passage was originally in Aramaic and in the measures of poetry, the parallelism of which appears in the Greek; but the present mode of expression in the Greek shows a later stage of reflection than the discourses of the Logia. If this passage had been in the Logia, it would not have been omitted by Luke; for though of the school of Paul, it is not probable that Luke would have omitted a passage so highly honorable to Peter and so important for Peter's position and authority in the Church, all the more that Luke ascribes to Peter a prominence in the founding of the Church which seems to be a fulfilment of the prediction of this passage. Matthew must have derived this saying of Jesus from a traditional source, which had moulded the words of Jesus into a cast of language suited to a later stage of the history of the apostolic church. The history of the earlier chapters of the book of Acts seems to be behind the present form of this word of Jesus.

diction has been the theme of much discussion, especially in the controversy between the Roman Catholics and the Protestants. But a scientific exegesis finds a meaning which is above the strife of sects, and which gives an important development of the Messianic idea.

> And Jesus answered and said unto him,
> Blessed art thou, Simon bar-Jonah:
> For flesh and blood hath not revealed it unto thee,
> But my Father which is in heaven.
> And I also say unto thee, that thou art Peter,
> And upon this rock I will build my church;
> And the gates of Hades shall not prevail against it.
> I will give unto thee the keys of the kingdom of God.[1]
> And whatsoever thou shalt bind on earth,
> Shall be bound in heaven:
> And whatsoever thou shalt loose on earth,
> Shall be loosed in heaven.           (Matt. xvi. 17–19.)

It is clear that Peter is the rock upon which the Church is built, as the Roman Catholics and the best modern Protestant interpreters, following the ancient church, teach.[2] The efforts of the older Protestant interpreters to overcome this by making the confession of Peter, or the person to whom he confesses, the Messiah, the rock of the Church, are shattered on the plain statements of the text. There are two parallel figures of speech. In the one the Church[3] is compared to a great building

---

[1] The original was doubtless kingdom of God. See p. 79.

[2] See Weiss, *Matthäusevangelium*, s. 393; Holtzmann, *Die Synoptiker*, s. 193. As Weiss says, the Aramaic original used כֵּיפָא in the place rendered in the Greek πέτρος, as well as in that rendered πέτρα. The gospel of John briefly refers to this meaning when Jesus said, "Thou art Simon, the son of John: thou shalt be called Cephas, [which is by interpretation, Peter]" (John i. 42). There is a word-play which in Aramaic was made by the use of the one word, but which had to be given in the Greek idiom by two words.

[3] It is probable that in the original Aramaic words of this saying, kingdom was used, and that ἐκκλησία was unconsciously substituted for it in the tradition, in

erected on a rock; in the other the kingdom is a city with gates of which Peter has the keys. The figure of a church built on a rock is similar to the kingdom of God in the Old Testament, which is built on the rock Yahweh, whose corner-stone is laid in Zion,[1] and whose corner-stone and cap-stone are the Messiah.[2] We should doubtless expect that God or the Messiah would be the rock of the kingdom (church) here, as He is elsewhere in the New Testament, the foundation;[3] but Christ is here the builder, and therefore cannot be at the same time the rock of the kingdom (the church). The prediction that Peter will be the rock does not contradict the more important doctrine that God and his Messiah are the rock of the Church. But there is a propriety in the prediction that Peter will be the rock, for here, as elsewhere, the kingdom (the church) is made up of persons, and not of doctrines and laws.[4] Peter is the rock upon

---

accordance with the usage of the early Christians as reflected in the Epistles. They interpreted the kingdom of grace of the gospels as the Church, and for the most part limited the use of the kingdom of God to the kingdom of glory of the second Advent. Jesus uses kingdom for both of these stages of his kingdom. The only exception to his usage in the gospels is here. In the corresponding passage, also peculiar to Matthew and also from a traditional source, Matthew xviii. 15-20, ἐκκλησία is used. But in that passage church is used for a congregation, as we shall see—here, however, for the whole body of Christians. The Aramaic קְהָלָא is used in the Targums for Israel as a whole, and this usage is justified by the use of קהל in the Old Testament. There is no reason to doubt that Jesus was familiar with the expression. But why did he avoid it in every passage but this? Is it probable that he would use it here alone? The answer to this question does not in any way modify our interpretation of the kingdom. The question is simply whether this use of the term קְהָלָא, ἐκκλησία, Church, began with Jesus or with his apostles. There can be no doubt that kingdom and Church are identified in this passage. See Weiss, *Matthäusevangelium*, s. 394.

[1] Isaiah xxviii. 16. See Briggs' *Messianic Prophecy*, p. 208 *seq*.
[2] Zechariah iii. 9.
[3] 1 Cor. iii. 10, 11.
[4] 1 Peter ii. 4 *seq*.; Eph. ii. 19-22; 1 Cor. iii. 12-15.

which all the other members of the kingdom rest, because he was the first to enter the kingdom, by first confessing the Messiah and by first speaking at Pentecost the word of the Holy Spirit, constituting the Church. All others are his successors, built upon him, upon his teaching and his example. So afterwards he and other apostles are the pillars of the Church,[1] and the twelve foundations of the temple and city of God.[2] But Peter is also the porter of the city of God. Elsewhere the Messiah himself keeps the gate and has the keys.[3] Here he gives them to Peter. In other places they are given to the apostles and to an assembly of Christians.[4] They are here given to Peter first because he was first, the spokesman of the apostolic body and of the kingdom (church) in its recognition of the Messiah. He has the keys to admit into the kingdom and to exclude from the kingdom. This government is not an arbitrary government of Peter, but it is a government that is ratified in heaven and is therefore in accordance with instruction from heaven, for Peter acts as the representative and mouthpiece of the Messiah himself. The connection of the kingdom with Peter is of great importance in the development of the Messianic idea.

The kingdom and the Church are synonymous expressions. The figures of speech employed in their explication give two other parallel and synonymous expressions which recur in the epistles, namely, the temple of God and the city of God. These four phases of the same thing, these synonymous conceptions of the kingdom of

---

[1] Gal. ii. 9.
[2] Eph. ii. 20; Rev. xxi. 14.
[3] Rev. iii. 7.
[4] Matt. xviii. 15-20; xxviii. 19, 20; Mark xvi. 15.

God, are all to come into existence in connection with the ministry of Peter. The doctrine that the kingdom was near and that it would be established during the ministry of the disciples is now made more definite by the prediction that it would be established during the ministry of Peter. Peter was to be the foremost in establishing it. It was to be built on him and he was to open its gates to those who followed him. The kingdom of God was thus to be a considerable time prior to the death of Peter, for Peter was to be the chief agent among the apostles in establishing it.

The authority of the keys, given into the hands of Peter in the passage just considered, was in another passage given to the church.

And if thy brother sin against thee,
Go, shew him his fault between thee and him alone:
If he hear thee, thou hast gained thy brother.
But if he hear *thee* not, take with thee one or two more,
That at the mouth of two witnesses or three every word may be established.
And if he refuse to hear them, tell it unto the church;
And if he refuse to hear the church also,
Let him be unto thee as the Gentile and the publican.
Verily I say unto you,
What things soever ye shall bind on earth
Shall be bound in heaven:
And what things soever ye shall loose on earth
Shall be loosed in heaven.
Again I say unto you,
That if two of you shall agree on earth
As touching anything that they shall ask,
It shall be done for them of my Father which is in heaven.
For where two or three are gathered together in my name,
There am I in the midst of them. (Matthew xviii. 15-20.)

The church, as here used, is the assembly of brethren,

the congregation of disciples.¹ The one, the two or three, the brotherhood represent the three steps for the recovery of the sinner. This is doubtless the earliest law of discipline for the Church. It directs the three stages of process—(1) the private, the fraternal visit; (2) the fraternal admonition in the presence of witnesses; (3) the appeal to the congregation. The decision is made by the voice of the congregation, which is really the voice of the Messiah who is with them in spiritual invisible presence. They act in his authority as Peter did and their discipline will be ratified in heaven as his was.

There is, however, a difference in conception between the discipline of Peter and that of the congregation. The discipline of Peter is a discipline at the gates of the kingdom to admit or exclude those who would enter the Church. He is the porter to keep the door and decide finally who may enter the Church. The discipline of the congregation is an internal discipline of those already within the church, and has to do with the recovery of sinning Christians or the exclusion of the unworthy from the kingdom.

---

¹ Ἐκκλησία is used twice in this passage, which like the previous one bears traces of the gnomic style of the sayings of Jesus and yet was probably not derived from the Logia, at least in its present form. Ἐκκλησία here alone in the gospels is used apparently of a local congregation, as frequently in the epistles, and yet there is nothing to suggest a plurality of congregations such as we find in the epistles. The congregation is here conceived of as one assembly. There is nothing to suggest official members of the congregation. The congregation seem to act as a whole. All this favors the primitive origin of this saying. Ἐκκλησία is a familiar word in the LXX. It is there used 56 times for the Hebrew קהל, which is thus translated everywhere in the Old Testament apart from the Pentateuch, and in Deuteronomy with the exception of v. 22. The other Pentateuchal examples are rendered συναγωγή. As Hatch says: "It is reasonable to infer a close similarity of meaning between συναγωγή and ἐκκλησία" (*Essays on Biblical Greek*, p. 21).

It is not certain whether the last of these sayings of Jesus is in its original place. It is in some respects more important than those which precede it. It promises a real but spiritual presence of the Messiah with his assembled disciples even when they were no more than two or three in number. This promise of the presence of the Messiah is the guarantee of the granting of their petitions. But they must agree in their asking. No promise of ratification is given to a disagreeing or a divided congregation.

The doctrine of the kingdom receives an important advance in this discourse. As the previous passage has shown that the Church and the kingdom are synonymous terms, and there the Church was compared to a city with gates, and a building erected on a rock, so here the Church is a congregation assembled together in the name of Jesus, in the midst of which he himself is ever present to preside and to direct its discipline and government. The promise of the presence of Jesus is here so comprehensive that it is impossible to think of a bodily or visible presence. He promises his spiritual presence, real though unseen, powerful though insensible. This doctrine of the spiritual presence of the Messiah with the congregation of his Church or kingdom is to be carefully distinguished from his advent to establish his kingdom on the one side, and his Advent to judge the kingdom on the other.

### THE DISCIPLE LIKE THE MASTER.

§ 38. *Jesus came to cast fire and sword upon the earth. There will be divisions among the most intimate relatives. Jesus has a baptism of suffering to undergo, and the disciples will be treated as their Master. When called they should separate themselves from all other ties, abstain from marriage, hate all relatives who interpose between them and the Messiah, bear his cross and follow him in a homeless life, to a shameful death. They have nothing to fear; God values them so highly that they will be carefully guarded. Whosoever confesses Jesus before men will be confessed before the Father in heaven. Those who deny the Messiah will be denied before the Father in heaven. He is to be feared who may destroy soul and body in Gehenna.*

Matthew, as we have seen, inserts some sentences of Jesus in the commission of the twelve which are given by Luke very properly in connection with the Perean ministry.[1] There are two sets of these. We shall try to give the original sentences from a comparative study of the two evangelists. Luke begins with the historical introduction,

In the meantime, when the many thousands of the multitude were gathered together, insomuch that they trode one upon another, he began to say unto his disciples first of all,

Beware ye of the leaven of the Pharisees,[2]   (Luke xii. 1.)
A disciple is not above his master,   (Matth. x. 24-26.)
Nor a servant above his lord.
It is enough for the disciple that he be as his master,
And the servant as his lord.
If they have called the master of the house Beelzebub,
How much more them of his household!
Fear them not therefore:[3]
For there is nothing covered,[4] that shall not be revealed;
And hid, that shall not be known.

---

[1] See p. 186.
[2] "Which is hypocrisy," is an explanatory addition of Luke.
[3] These lines of Matthew are prefixed to the same lines as those which follow in Luke, and they seem appropriate in this setting.
[4] Matthew's κεκαλυμμένον = Luke's συγκεκαλυμμένον.

Wherefore¹ whatsoever ye have said in the darkness    (Luke xii. 3.)
Shall be heard in the light;
And what in the ear in the inner chambers
Shall be proclaimed upon the housetops.²
And I say unto you my friends,³    (Luke xii. 4a, b.)
Be not afraid of them which kill the body,
But are not able to kill the soul:⁴    (Matt. x. 28b.)
But I will warn you whom ye shall fear:    (Luke xii. 5a.)
Fear him, who after he hath killed, is able
To destroy both soul and body in Gehenna.⁵    (Matt. x. 28d.)
Are not two sparrows sold for a penny    (Matt. x. 29–31.)
And not one of them shall fall on the ground
Without your Father:
But the very hairs of your head,
All are numbered,
Fear not therefore;
Ye are of more value than many sparrows.⁶
And I say unto you,⁷    (Luke xii. 8a.)
Every one who shall confess me before men.    (Matt. x. 32, 33.)

---

¹ Matthew's ὃ λέγω ὑμῖν is a modification of Luke's ἀνθ' ὧν ὅσα εἴπατε to suit the use of the saying in the commission.

² The ἐλαλήσατε of Luke is unnecessary and it makes the line too long. The antithesis of inner chambers to housetops is in its favor. Ear is common to Matthew and Luke. Matthew inserts ἀκούετε for the reason given above. The change of κηρυχθήσεται into κηρύξατε had the same motive.

³ This line is given only in Luke.

⁴ This of Matthew is simpler than Luke "after that have no more that they can do," which seems more comprehensive and a later enlargement of the thought.

⁵ The original lies back of both Matthew and Luke, each having made modifications; Luke's τὸν ἔχοντα ἐξουσίαν being a different translation of the original from Matthew's τὸν δυνάμενον, which latter is given above. Matthew omits μετὰ τὸ ἀποκτεῖναι, because of his retaining of "soul and body" in the next line. The antithesis of soul and body is important as it appears above. Luke generalizes when he substitutes "cast into Gehenna."

⁶ Matthew is to be preferred throughout to Luke xii. 6, 7. Luke has abbreviated and generalized, and injured the measurement of the lines.

⁷ This line introducing another saying is given only by Luke. Because of its omission Matthew uses the particle οὖν.

> Him will I confess before my Father.[1]
> But whosoever shall deny me before men,
> Him will I also deny before my Father.

The disciples are warned to beware of the leaven of the Pharisees, which is defined by Luke as hypocrisy, and to keep in view the final clearing up of all things. They are to have no fear of men, but to fear God alone, who pronounces the final doom of the judgment day, and who will deal with men with the greatest interest and paternal care. The most important thing to do is to confess the Messiah. Upon this everything depends. Those who confess him before men will be confessed by him before the Father. But those who deny him before men will be denied by him before the Messiah's Father. In other words, the life of the disciple and his preaching of the gospel are to be conducted in view of the presence of God, before whom he will ultimately stand for judgment. That judgment is either a confession and recognition, or a denial and rejection which results in the destruction of soul and body in Gehenna.

On a later occasion the following sentences were spoken by Jesus:

> I came to cast fire upon the earth; (Luke xii. 49, 50.)
> And what do I desire, if it is already kindled?
> But I have a baptism to be baptized with;
> And how am I straitened till it be accomplished!
> Think not that I came  (Matthew x. 34.)
> To cast peace upon the earth;[2]

---

[1] The "angels of God" of Luke, instead of "Father who is in heaven" in Matthew, seems to be a later and less simple conception, not so natural in the discourse of Jesus. It is also probable that "who is in heaven" is an amplification of Matthew. The verses which follow in Luke xii. 10 = Matthew xii. 31, 32; and Luke xii. 11, 12 = Matthew x. 19, 20 seem to belong elsewhere (see pp. 180, 144). They seem not quite in harmony with the sayings given above.

[2] Matt., ver. 34a, is closer to Luke xii. 49, and is simpler and more graphic than Luke xii. 51a.

Not to cast peace, but a sword.¹
For there shall be from henceforth divided,   (Luke xii. 52, 53.)
Five in one house;
Three against two, and two against three;
Father against son, and son against father;²
Mother against daughter, and daughter against her mother;
Mother-in-law against her daughter-in-law, and daughter-in-law against her mother-in-law,³
And a man's foes shall be they of his own household.⁴   (Matt. x. 36.)

The results of the first advent of Jesus are not peace and the kingdom of glory, but strife, warfare, and suffering. The Messiah is hastening on to the climax of his sufferings, and these will be followed by the sufferings of his disciples. Families will be divided and intimate relationships broken up.

We may appropriately consider here another lesson of discipleship spoken on a different and probably a later occasion.

> If any man cometh to me
> And hateth not his own father, and his mother,⁵
> And his wife, and his son and his daughter,⁶
> And his brothers and his sisters,

---

¹ Both Matt., ver. 34*b*, and Luke, ver. 51*b*, have changed the original to make it clearer. The sword of Matthew is doubtless original. Luke changed it to suit the subsequent context.

² Matt., vers. 35, 36, is greatly abbreviated. Luke, ver. 53, inserts the verb for explication.

³ These lines vary in length because of the English words. In Hebrew or Aramaic they would be tetrameters or four separate words each.

⁴ This line is given only by Matthew.

⁵ Matt. x. 37-39 softens the "*hateth*" of the original into a comparative "love." This is of the nature of interpretation. He also softens "cannot be my disciple" into "is not worthy of me."

⁶ It is probable that "son or daughter" of Matthew is nearer the original than the compressed "children" of Luke. It is most probable that the original words were as given above.

> Yea, and his own self also,[1]
> He cannot be my disciple.
> Whosoever doth not bear his own cross,
> And come after me,
> Cannot be my disciple.[2]   (Luke xiv. 26, 27.)

The disciples of Jesus are required to follow him with the renunciation of every other tie that will hinder the claims of discipleship. Even the most sacred claims of father and mother, wife and children, which no one exalts higher than Jesus, must not restrain the disciple. He is not only to love the Messiah above his parents, but he is so to love him as to hate whatever relatives obstruct this love. The disciple is to hazard his life for the Master, and to hate himself in order to love the Master supremely. Only by entire self-renunciation and cross-bearing can he attain the prize of his own higher self.

There are two other sayings of Jesus which were probably taken from the Logia relating to this subject, the one reported by Matthew, the other by Luke. Their historical occasion is doubtful. Luke reports the one saying just before the sending forth of the seventy. He attaches it to the words reported also by Matthew which are cognate. It is improbable that Matthew would have omitted it, if it was connected in the original. These sayings are loosely attached.

| MATTHEW viii. 19, 20. | LUKE ix. 57, 58. |
|---|---|
| A certain man said unto him, I will follow thee whithersoever thou goest. And Jesus said unto him: | And there came a scribe, and said unto him, Master, I will follow thee whithersoever thou goest. And Jesus saith unto him: |

---

[1] ψυχή is *self* here and not *life*, see p. 97.

[2] The cross-bearing of the disciple is involved in the cross-bearing of Jesus. Matt., ver. 39, adds a word suggested by ver. 38 from an earlier connection, Mark viii. 34, 35 = Matt. xvi. 24, 25 = Luke ix. 23, 24.  See p. 98.

> The foxes have holes,
> And the birds of the heaven nests;
> But the Son of Man hath not where to lay his head.[1]

No greater contrast is conceivable than that between the Son of Man enthroned in the clouds, of Daniel, and the homeless Son of Man, of the Logia. This was a preexistence on earth not thought of in the Apocalypses of Daniel and of Enoch. Such a homeless life does the prophet Jesus hold out to the man who would follow him in his mission in Palestine.

| MATTHEW viii. 21, 22. | LUKE ix. 59, 60. |
|---|---|
| And another of the disciples said unto him, Lord, suffer me first to go and bury my father. But Jesus saith unto him, | And he said unto another, Follow me. But he said, Lord, suffer me first to go and bury my father. But he said unto him, |

> Leave the dead to bury their own dead;
> But go thou and publish abroad the kingdom of God.[2]

The proclamation of the kingdom of God was so important that even the most sacred duty of burial of the dead must not impede it.

Luke now gives a third incident:

And another also said, I will follow thee, Lord; but first suffer me to bid farewell to them that are at my house. But Jesus said unto him,

> No man, having put his hand to the plough,
> And looking back,
> Is fit for the kingdom of God. (Luke ix. 61, 62).

The service of the kingdom demands a faithful disciple who will go straight forward without regrets and

---

[1] Matthew and Luke are exactly the same in these three lines.

[2] Matthew transposes the lines and reduces the last to the simple "Follow me," which was suggested by the previous context. It destroys the measure of the line as preserved by Luke.

without leave-takings, in spite of every difficulty, in the work of the kingdom.

Matthew appends a saying of Jesus, doubtless from the Logia, to a discourse of Jesus respecting divorce. This was probably not its original place; as it is not in the gospel of Mark, or in the corresponding passage of Luke.

> All men cannot receive this saying, but they to whom it is given.
> For there are eunuchs, which were so born from their mother's womb:
> And there are eunuchs, which were made eunuchs by men:
> And there are eunuchs, which made themselves eunuchs for the sake of the kingdom of God.
> He that is able to receive it, let him receive it.
> (Matthew xix. 11, 12.)

This passage clearly teaches that there are some men who are to abstain from marriage for the sake of the kingdom of God; that is, in order that they may do the work of the kingdom without hindrances from the state of matrimony with its wife and children. It is not a universal precept; but it is a counsel of perfection to those who are able to receive it and to do it. It is of the same nature as the advice given above, that the disciple must give up all earthly ties of family, or property, or self-indulgence, in order to consecrate himself absolutely and entirely to the work of the kingdom.[1]

## THE KINGDOM THE SUPREME QUEST.

§ 39. *The kingdom is the supreme object of the disciples' pursuit. It is the great pleasure of God to give it to them. They are to strive to enter its gates, for it is guarded by an act of judgment. Many will be excluded who have enjoyed great privileges; but multitudes from all parts of*

---

[1] See p. 104.

*the earth will sit down with the patriarchs and prophets in the kingdom of God. The kingdom is one of the objects of prayer.*

Matthew in his report of the Sermon on the Mount has given portions of two discourses which are in a more appropriate connection in the gospel of Luke. The first of these is as follows:

Be not therefore anxious, saying,[1]  (Matt. vi. 31, 32.)
What shall we eat? or, What shall we drink? or, Wherewithal shall we be clothed?[2]
For after all these things do the nations[3] seek,
And your Father knoweth that ye have need[4] of these things.
                                      (Luke xii. 30*b*-32.)
But seek ye first his kingdom,[5]
And these things[6] shall be added unto you.
Fear not, little flock,[7]
For it is your Father's good pleasure to give you the kingdom.

There is a great contrast between the things of this life about which we are not to be anxious, and the kingdom about which we are to be so anxious that we are to make it our supreme quest. The kingdom has as its parallel in Matthew righteousness. This righteousness is the righteousness of God, the righteousness of the kingdom. The kingdom to be thus sought is not the kingdom of grace as it exists in this world, which is not

---

[1] Luke xii. 29 transposes this line with the following, and modifies it.

[2] Luke xii. 29 prefixes "seek not ye," and therefore changes the first person of Matthew to the second person. He also omits the reference to clothing. That makes the line long in English, but in Aramaic it would not be too long.

[3] Luke adds "of the world" to the nations.

[4] Luke xii. 30 preserves the original line which has been enlarged by Matthew, who adds "heavenly" to Father, and "all" to these things.

[5] Matthew adds "righteousness," in accordance with the leading idea of the Sermon on the Mount. Luke weakens πρῶτον to πλήν.

[6] Matthew adds πάντα.

[7] This saying is given by Luke alone.

guarded by an act of judgment, and which requires simply faith and repentance for entrance. It is the kingdom of glory that Jesus has in view. This kingdom may well excite anxiety on the part of man for its attainment. Accordingly Luke gives a word of encouragement on the part of Jesus. The seeking disciples are assured that God is willing to bestow it upon them even though they be a little flock.

This encouragement is followed by several parables exhorting to watchfulness, some of which are given by Matthew in another connection. They seem appropriate in their connection in Luke. But as it is probable that both of the evangelists use them apart from their historical connection, we shall use them under another head.

The second of these passages exhorts to earnest striving to enter into the kingdom.

LUKE xiii. 23-30.

And one said unto him, Lord, are they few that be saved? And he said unto them, Strive to enter in by the narrow door: for many, I say unto you, shall seek to enter in, and shall not be able. When once the master of the house is risen up, and hath shut to the door, and ye begin to stand without, and to knock at the door, saying, Lord, open to us; and he shall answer and say to you, I know you not whence ye are; then shall ye begin to say, We did eat and drink in thy presence, and thou didst teach in our streets; and he shall say, I tell you, I know not whence ye are; depart from me, all ye workers of iniquity. There shall be the

MATT. vii. 13-14, 21-23.

Enter ye in by the narrow gate: for wide is the gate, and broad is the way, that leadeth to destruction, and many be they that enter in thereby. For narrow is the gate, and straitened the way, that leadeth unto life, and few be they that find it.

. . . . .

Not every one that saith unto me, Lord, Lord, shall enter into the kingdom of heaven; but he that doeth the will of my Father which is in heaven. Many will say to me in that day, Lord, Lord, did we not prophesy by thy name, and by thy name cast out demons, and by thy name do many mighty works? And then will I profess unto them, I never weeping and gnashing of teeth, when ye shall see Abraham, and Isaac, and Jacob, and all the prophets, in the kingdom of God, and yourselves cast forth without. And they shall come from the east and west, and from the north and south, and shall sit down in the kingdom of God. And behold, there are last which shall be first, and there are first which shall be last.

knew you: depart from me, ye that work iniquity

The narrow door of Luke is the door of the kingdom of glory at the advent of the Messiah. But the meaning of the narrow gate of Matthew is not plain. Meyer, Bengel, Schaff, Vincent, and others, take it as the gate at the beginning of the Christian life, the gate of regeneration, or repentance; but De Wette, Tholuck, Stier, and others, think of the gate at the end of the way. If it is parallel with Luke it is certainly the latter.[1]

Holtzmann and others think that the way is not before the gate or behind the gate, but between the posts of the gate. The parallels favor this interpretation. There would then be a broad way leading to Apoleia, and many entering Apoleia by means of it; and a narrow gateway leading unto life and few finding it. The way to Apoleia would be the way to the Middle State of the lost; the gate to life would be the gate into the kingdom of glory, which few find because they know not the righteousness which is required to sustain the judgment at the gate.

---

[1] The $εἰς τὴν ἀπώλειαν$ of Matthew seems to refer to a place and not a condition. It is the Apoleia of the Hellenistic Apocrypha and Pseudepigrapha (see p 27) and the Abaddon of the Old Testament, the place of ruin in the state immediately after death. If that be so, then the way of Matthew would seem to be a way through which the multitudes go when entering the Middle State, whereas the door of Luke, which conceives of a Messianic judgment closing the door, is the door into the ultimate state.

This discourse teaches us the difficulty of access to the kingdom of God and the necessity of striving in order to enter it. The kingdom is here conceived as a kingdom whose entrance is guarded by the Lord, and an act of judgment decides the entrance. It is therefore the kingdom of glory. The title to entrance is not conditioned upon earthly knowledge of Jesus, is not limited to those who met him in Palestine, is not determined by professions or by public ministry or miracle-working; but entirely by good works in a good life. Many will be excluded who offer claims of birth, or of knowledge, or of service. All workers of iniquity will be cast forth, no matter how great their privileges have been. The patriarchs and prophets will be there, and many from all parts of the earth, for it is a universal kingdom for which we pray: "*Thy Kingdom come.*" (Matt. vi. 10.)

### THE JUDGMENT OF THE KINGDOM.

§ 40. *The kingdom of God is the most precious treasure, worth all things else. In its growth it is entangled with evil men and evil influences. These cannot be separated from it until the judgment at the End of the Age, when the angels will gather out the wicked from the kingdom and cast them into the furnace of fire. Then will the righteous shine forth in the kingdom of glory.*

Matthew gives a group of Parables of the Kingdom which he appends to the Parable of the Sower which we have already studied in the Gospel of Mark.[1]

Another parable set he before them, saying, The kingdom of heaven is likened unto a man that sowed good seed in his field; but while men slept, his enemy came and sowed tares also among the wheat, and went away. But when the blade sprang up, and

---

[1] See p. 88.

brought forth fruit, then appeared the tares also. And the servants of the householder came and said unto him, Sir, didst thou not sow good seed in thy field? whence then hath it tares? And he said unto them, An enemy hath done this. And the servants say unto him, Wilt thou then that we go and gather them up? But he saith, Nay; lest haply while ye gather up the tares, ye root up the wheat with them. Let both grow together until the harvest: and in the time of the harvest I will say to the reapers, Gather up first the tares, and bind them in bundles to burn them: but gather the wheat into my barn. (Matt. xiii. 24–30.)

This parable describes several difficulties in the growth of the kingdom of God. In the parable of the sower, the evil one [Satan, the Devil] overcame the good in the hearts of the superficial hearers. But in this parable the enemy takes a more aggressive part. He sows tares or bad seed in the midst of the wheat. These tares are not noticed when planted, for the enemy has worked in secret. They do not disclose themselves when first they appear above the ground. It is not until the third stage when the ear begins to form into fruit, that the difference appears. It is now too late to remove the tares. The separation must wait until the harvest. This parable teaches that it is impossible to prevent evil men from entering into the kingdom of grace and mingling with its true members. The difference between counterfeit Christians and real Christians will appear only in the kind of fruit they produce. The kingdom in its external form, as it appears to men, will be mixed. This doctrine seems to contradict the doctrine of the kingdom that we have learned from other discourses. But the contradiction is only apparent. The kingdom of those sections is the kingdom of God in its purity and integrity in the eyes of God. Into that kingdom none but the childlike and the godlike can enter. That is the kingdom of glory. But the kingdom of our parables is the kingdom as it appears in the field of the world, where the gospel is preached, and where the good and the bad mingle. Into this kingdom not only the true members enter, but there are several other classes, including not only the three unfruitful classes of the parable of the sower, but also the class producing evil fruit of the parable of the tares. All these are counterfeit Christians and not worldlings. The harvest alone will separate them completely. Jesus accordingly explains this parable:

And he answered and said, He that soweth the good seed is the Son of Man; and the field is the world; and the good seed, these are the sons of the kingdom; and the tares are the sons of the evil *one;* and the enemy that sowed them is the devil: and the harvest is the End of the Age; and the reapers are angels. As therefore the tares are gathered up and burned with fire; so shall it be in the End of the Age. The Son of Man shall send forth his angels, and they shall gather out of his kingdom all things that cause stumbling, and them that do iniquity, and shall cast them into the furnace of fire: there shall be the weeping and gnashing of teeth. Then shall the righteous shine forth as the sun in the kingdom of their Father. He that hath ears, let him hear. (Matt. xiii. 37-43.)

The parable of the tares lays stress upon the consummation of the kingdom, the κρίσις; as the parable of the sower laid stress upon its origin, and the parable of the growing seed upon its gradual growth.[1] The Son of Man and the Evil One are contrasted, the one the sower of the good seed, the other of the evil seed. The good seed are the sons of the kingdom, those who really belong to it, have a right in it, and are destined to possess it. The evil seed are the sons of the Evil One, who have intruded into the kingdom, have no rights in it, and are destined to be excluded from it.

---

[1] See p. 90.

But during the entire course of the development of the kingdom they cannot be excluded. The separation comes first at the harvest at the End of the Age. Then the Son of Man will employ his angels in the judgment and the kingdom will be purified. The evil will be cast into the furnace of fire, the Gehenna of weeping and wailing. The righteous, no longer hindered by the presence of the wicked and conflict with them, will shine as the sun in the kingdom.

This parable teaches us to distinguish (1) the kingdom as established, (2) the kingdom in its growth and struggles with evil, or the kingdom of grace, and (3) the kingdom of glory. In the growing kingdom we distinguish between the real kingdom composed only of the children of the kingdom, and the apparent kingdom in which several classes are mingled.

Matthew associates with these parables five others that have their propriety here.

The kingdom of heaven is like unto leaven, which a woman took and hid in three measures of meal, till it was all leavened. (Matt. xiii. 33.)

The kingdom of heaven is like unto a treasure hidden in the field; which a man found, and hid; and in his joy he goeth and selleth all that he hath, and buyeth that field.

Again, the kingdom of heaven is like unto a man that is a merchant seeking goodly pearls: and having found one pearl of great price, he went and sold all that he had, and bought it.

Again, the kingdom of heaven is like unto a net, that was cast into the sea, and gathered of every kind: which, when it was filled, they drew up on the beach; and they sat down, and gathered the good into vessels, but the bad they cast away. So shall it be in the End of the Age: the angels shall come forth, and sever the wicked from among the righteous, and shall cast them into the furnace of fire: there shall be the weeping and gnashing of teeth.

Have ye understood all these things? They say unto him,

Yea. And he said unto them, Therefore every scribe who hath been made a disciple to the kingdom of heaven is like unto a man that is a householder, who bringeth forth out of his treasure things new and old. (Matt. xiii. 44–52.)

Two of these parables set forth the preciousness of the kingdom as the supreme object of human pursuit. They take up the thought of the wonderful virtue wrapt up in the mustard seed and in the leaven, in order to make the kingdom the most valuable possession that man can have. A treasure worth all other possessions, a pearl priceless and alone above the sum of all other values—such is the worth of the kingdom of God and as such men are to seek it. These parables recall the exhortation, "Seek ye first his kingdom."[1] We return by these parables to the origin of the kingdom as set forth in the parable of the sower.[2] There it was good seed planted, to grow in grace unto glory as its final aim. Here it is a priceless treasure sought by man as the supreme and final object of his ambition. There it was the kingdom of grace, here it is the kingdom of glory. It is the Father's good pleasure to give it; men will not seek in vain. They must learn the word and through it become godlike.

The third parable returns to the theme of the parable of the tares, the fruition of the kingdom. There the End of the Age was a harvest field and the angels were reapers. Here it is a drag-net full of fishes and the angels are fishermen. There the harvest field was covered with bundles of grain and tares. Here the net is full of fishes good and bad. The separation in both is made by the angels, who alone can make the discrimination under the eyes of the judge. The fish cannot be distinguished whether they are good or bad till they

---

[1] See p. 203.    [2] See p. 88.

are landed on the shore, as the wheat and tares could not be separated till they were ripe. In the parable of the tares the stress is laid upon the blessedness of the righteous, but in this parable of the drag-net only the fate of the wicked is brought into view.

Matthew concludes this series with the parable of the householder, which returns to the doctrine of the development of the kingdom. The sons of the kingdom were fruitful grain; here they are in possession of varied treasures. The hidden treasure has been taken possession of, the choice pearl has been won. The disciple of the kingdom has untold wealth, and he bringeth from his treasure things new and old as he may need them in the work of the kingdom.

Taking these nine parables together, great light is cast upon the doctrine of the kingdom. The kingdom that was nigh was the kingdom in its modest, secret, and insignificant origin, composed of a few men who had received the word and taken it into their hearts and lives, who had become poor and childlike. Such was the kingdom in its origin. When it comes into manifestation in the world as a kingdom of grace it will be mingled with forces of evil, and the good and bad will remain in its visible forms until the End of the Age, when the kingdom of glory appears.

### THE OBSTRUCTIONS TO THE KINGDOM.

§ 41. *The Pharisees will not enter the kingdom themselves, nor suffer those who are entering to enter. All the guilt of the historic rejection of the prophets will come upon the generation of Jesus. The temple will be left desolate, but eventually Jesus will be welcomed as the Messiah.*

Matthew gives a collection of seven woes pronounced by Jesus upon the Pharisees, the most of which are given by Luke on an earlier occasion. There is also a prologue and an epilogue made up of sayings gathered from different places:

Prologue.
- Matt. xxiii. 1–3.
- "      "    4=Luke xi. 45–46.
- "      "    5–7=Mark xii. 38–40; Luke xi. 43; xx. 45–47.
- "      "    8–12. Parenetic words of evangelist.

Woes.
- 1. Matt. xxiii. 13=Luke xi. 52.
- "      "    14. Not in best MSS., omitted by R. V., assimilated from Mark xii. 40; Luke xx. 47.
- 2. "      "    15.
- 3. "      "    16–22.
- 4. "      "    23–24=Luke xi. 42.
- 5. "      "    25–26=   "    37–41.
- 6. "      "    27–28=   "    44.
- 7. "      "    29–33=   "    47–48.

Epilogue.
- Matt. xxiii. 34–36=Luke xi. 49–51.
- "      "    37–39=   " xiii. 31–35.

The Messianic material is limited to the Epilogue and the first Woe, which in Luke is interposed between the two parts of the Epilogue of Matthew. We follow the order of Luke.

| LUKE xi. 49–51. | MATT. xxiii. 34–36. |
|---|---|
| Therefore also said the Wisdom of God, I will send unto them prophets and apostles; and *some* of them they shall kill and persecute; that the blood of all the prophets, which was shed from the foundation of the world, may be required of this generation; from the blood of Abel unto the blood of | Therefore, behold, I send unto you prophets, and wise men, and scribes: some of them shall ye kill and crucify; and some of them shall ye scourge in your synagogues, and persecute from city to city: that upon you may come all the righteous blood shed on the earth, from the blood of Abel the righteous |

Zachariah, who perished between the altar and the sanctuary. Yea, I say unto you, it shall be required of this generation.

unto the blood of Zachariah son of Barachiah, whom ye slew between the sanctuary and the altar. Verily I say unto you, All these things shall come upon this generation.

LUKE xi. 52.

Woe unto you lawyers! for ye took away the key of knowledge: ye entered not in yourselves, and them that were entering in ye hindered.

MATT. xxiii. 13.

But woe unto you, scribes and Pharisees, hypocrites! because ye shut the kingdom of heaven against men: for ye enter not in yourselves, neither suffer ye them that are entering in to enter.

The first part of the Epilogue of Matthew, which is really in Luke a part of the woe upon the Pharisee lawyers, is connected by Luke with a feast at which Jesus was invited, and where the Pharisees sought to entrap him. He charges them with a guilt greater than that of their fathers, who rejected and slew the prophets. This rejection of the prophets is enforced by a citation which Jesus makes from a lost writing entitled "The Wisdom of God," which was probably another example of the Wisdom Literature of the Pseudepigrapha. This rejection was a blood-red record of guilt from Abel to Zechariah. All has come down as an inheritance of woe to the generation that has rejected the Baptist and is about to reject the Messiah and put him to death. But the full measure of iniquity has been reached. It will all be required of this generation in the judgment that is impending over them. The general character of this warning of impending judgment favors its earlier date.

The first woe of Matthew, which is the last woe of Luke, represents the Pharisees as interposing themselves between the entrance to the kingdom, and those who have accepted the Messiah's invitation and are entering it. Luke represents them as lawyers. They themselves will not enter, and they will not permit others to enter. The kingdom is here again conceived as present, with gates open to those who accept the invitation of the gospel.

The second part of the Epilogue of Matthew is given at a later date in Luke, who connects it with a warning against Herod given by the Pharisees while he was on his way to Jerusalem.

| LUKE xiii. 31–35. | MATT. xxiii. 37–39. |
|---|---|
| In that very hour there came certain Pharisees, saying to him, Get thee out, and go hence: for Herod would fain kill thee. And he said unto them, Go and say to that fox, Behold, I cast out demons and perform cures to-day and to-morrow, and the third *day* I am perfected. Howbeit I must go on my way to-day and to-morrow and the *day* following: for it cannot be that a prophet perish out of Jerusalem. O Jerusalem, Jerusalem, that killeth the prophets, and stoneth them that are sent unto her! how often would I have gathered thy children together, even as a hen *gathereth* her own brood under her wings, and ye would not! Behold, your house is left unto you *desolate:* and I say unto you, Ye shall not see me, until ye shall say, Blessed *is* he that cometh in the name of the Lord. | O Jerusalem, Jerusalem, that killeth the prophets, and stoneth them that are sent unto her! how often would I have gathered thy children together, even as a hen gathereth her chickens under her wings, and ye would not! Behold, your house is left unto you desolate. For I say unto you, Ye shall not see me henceforth, till ye shall say, Blessed *is* he that cometh in the name of the Lord. |

Jesus in enigmatic language predicts that he has three days to work, and on the third day he will be perfected, and his work will be accomplished. It cannot be that he thinks of three actual days of labor to be followed by his departure, but of a brief period which was to close with his passion in Jerusalem.¹ He had nothing to fear from Herod in Galilee either as to time or place; for his time was not yet complete, and he was not in the place where he was to die. This thought occasions the lament over Jerusalem. The Messiah would gladly have taken the children of his people under the wings of his protection, but they refused to come to him. The time is well-nigh elapsed. Their doom is sure. Their home, their temple, the symbol and pledge of the divine protection, is to be destroyed; and they will no more see Jesus until he comes with such evidence of glory and power that they will pronounce him blessed. It is evident that this passage, even in Luke, cannot refer to his subsequent entry into Jerusalem: for the context has in mind the death of Jesus and the desolation of the temple; and this advent must be subsequent to these events. It is the Messiah's Advent in judgment and in glory, which we have seen in so many passages.²

## THE HEAD OF THE CORNER.

§ 42. *The Pharisees reject the Messiah, the corner-stone of the kingdom, and refuse the invitation to the marriage feast. The kingdom will be taken from them and given to others. Publicans and sinners accept the Messiah's invitation, enter the kingdom, and are welcomed and honored guests. The corner-stone will destroy all who come in collision with it, and will marvellously become the head of the corner.*

Matthew gives two parables of Jesus and attaches them to his ministry in Jerusalem, in the closing week. It

---

¹ Three days was the time of the abode in the grave. See p. 95.
² See pp. 99, 127, 153.

matters little whether they were uttered at this time or not. They have no parallel in the Synoptists, and may have been derived from another source than the Logia. The first of these is the parable of the marriage feast; the second, the parable of the two sons. It is sufficient to refer to the Messianic elements in these parables.

In the parable of the marriage feast,[1] those who have been invited to the marriage of the king's son, reject and slay the messengers. The king sends his armies, destroys the murderers and burns their city. This parable sets forth the guilt of the Pharisees and their predecessors in rejecting and slaying the prophets, and predicts their ruin in the burning of Jerusalem. But the marriage will not lack guests. The servants, the disciples of Jesus, go out into the highways and hedges, to the poor, the suffering, the outcast, the publicans and sinners; and bring them in, and the wedding is filled with guests. The wedding will not lack decorum and dignity even with these guests. They are provided with appropriate garments, and only the churl will refuse to put them on. There are some among these who will share the fate of the Pharisees; but the larger proportion of them will not only come to the feast, but will be so provided for that they will be the most suitable guests. This parable clearly teaches the rejection of the Pharisees and the ruin of Jerusalem, but also the preaching of the gospel and the gathering in of a multitude who will abide the judgment.

The parable of the two sons presents the other side of the case.[2] The Pharisees promise to enter the kingdom, but enter it not. They profess to prepare for the kingdom by legal righteousness, and to be eager for the

---

[1] xxii. 1–14.   [2] xxi. 28–32.

coming of the kingdom and for entrance into it. But when the kingdom comes and the Messiah invites them, they decline his invitation. The publicans and sinners, on the other hand, refuse to enter the kingdom, but subsequently repent and enter. They refuse the invitation because they refuse to prepare themselves for the kingdom by righteousness; they persist in evil lives, they give no promise of repentance. But when the Messiah's invitation comes to them, they repent and precede the Pharisees into the kingdom. This teaches that the kingdom is present, and that its gates are open to those who will accept the invitation of the gospel of the kingdom.

Between these two parables Matthew inserts the parable of the wicked husbandmen which we have already seen and studied in the gospel of Mark.[1] It is probable that this parable was in both sources, all the more that Matthew and Luke give additional material to that of Mark. It is doubtful whether this material comes from the Logia. At all events it is in the poetic form which is usual in the Logia. Matthew gives it more completely:

Did ye never read in the Scriptures,[2]
The stone which the builders rejected,
The same was made the head of the corner:
This was from the Lord,
And it is marvelous in our eyes?
Therefore say I unto you,[3]
The kingdom of God shall be taken away from you,
And shall be given to a nation bringing forth the fruits thereof.
Every one that falleth on that stone will be broken to pieces:
But on whomsoever it shall fall, it will scatter him as dust.

(Matthew xxi. 42–44; Luke xx. 17, 18.)

---

[1] See p. 116.  [2] Luke substitutes " What then is this that is written."
[3] Luke omits lines 4–8.
[4] Matthew gives " And he that falleth on this stone." But these two lines are bracketed by Westcott and Hort.

Jesus, the corner-stone of the kingdom, is to be rejected by the rulers of Israel; but the kingdom will be taken from them and given to other rulers, who will be fruitful in good works. The corner-stone will then be made the head of the corner. But, as a living stone, it will fall on the enemies and scatter them as dust; or it will break in pieces all who stumble and fall on it. All the enemies of the kingdom of God will eventually be destroyed.

### WATCHING.

§ 43. *The Son of Man may delay his coming. It may not be for a long time. Great patience and watchfulness will be required. When he comes he will reward the faithful.*

Matthew appends to the great apocalypse of Jesus[1] several parables and a judgment scene, some of which we have already considered in another connection.[2] Some of these parables are given by Luke at an earlier period and in better connections. But the topical arrangement of Matthew is more suited to our present purpose.

It is doubtful whether Luke xii. 35–38 is another form of the parable of the virgins in Matthew xxv. 1–13. Critics differ in their opinion. Whatever the case may be, there are so many differences that it seems best not to place them in parallelism, but to let the richer parable of Matthew follow the simpler parable of Luke. There can be no doubt, however, that Matthew xxiv. 45–51 is parallel with Luke xii. 41–46, and that the order of topics in Luke is preferable. Luke's parable is as follows:

---

[1] See Chap. IV.     [2] See p. 164.

Let your loins be girded about, and your lamps burning; and be ye yourselves like unto men looking for their lord, when he shall return from the marriage feast; that, when he cometh and knocketh, they may straightway open unto him. Blessed are those servants whom the lord when he cometh shall find watching: verily I say unto you, that he shall gird himself, and make them sit down to meat, and shall come and serve them. And if he shall come in the second watch, and if in the third, and find *them* so, blessed are those *servants*. (Luke xii. 35-38.)

This parable teaches the duty of waiting and watching for the Advent, without any hint as to the time. It also sets forth the great rewards that will be given to those servants who are ready when the Lord returns. Matthew's parable is much fuller.

Then shall the kingdom of heaven be likened unto ten virgins, which took their lamps, and went forth to meet the bridegroom. And five of them were foolish, and five were wise. For the foolish, when they took their lamps, took no oil with them: but the wise took oil in their vessels with their lamps. Now while the bridegroom tarried, they all slumbered and slept. But at midnight there is a cry, Behold, the bridegroom! Come ye forth to meet him. Then all those virgins arose, and trimmed their lamps. And the foolish said unto the wise, Give us of your oil; for our lamps are going out. But the wise answered, saying, Peradventure there will not be enough for us and you: go ye rather to them that sell, and buy for yourselves. And while they went away to buy, the bridegroom came; and they that were ready went in with him to the marriage feast: and the door was shut. Afterward come also the other virgins, saying, Lord, Lord, open to us. But he answered and said, Verily I say unto you, I know you not. Watch therefore, for ye know not the day nor the hour. (Matthew xxv. 1-13.)

This parable has the same essential idea as the one just considered, but it distinguishes two classes of virgins, the one waiting and watching, ready for the bridegroom, the other unready. The element of time is introduced into this parable. The advent tarries, is delayed, it is not till midnight. The parable concludes with the rewards of the wise virgins, but lays great stress upon the exclusion of the foolish virgins from the marriage feast. It enforces the exhortation to watchfulness; for the day and the hour of the Advent of the Messiah are altogether unknown.

These two parables are exceedingly appropriate to emphasize the duty of being watchful and ready to meet the Messiah on his return. They serve to introduce the stronger lessons of the parable that follows:

> But know this, that if the master of the house had known in what watch[1] the thief was coming, he would have watched, and would not have suffered[2] his house to be broken through. Therefore[3] be ye also ready; for in an hour that ye think not the Son of Man cometh. (Matt. xxiv. 43, 44.)

The teaching of these parables and their introduction, is that the kingdom of God is to be the supreme object of pursuit. The hearts of men are to be fixed upon it, and they are to seek it. Their lamps are to be burning and their loins girded as men waiting for the marriage procession of the bridegroom, and as the householder expecting the thief. The Lord will come unexpectedly and reward the faithful servant. The Advent is sure, but the time of it uncertain. He may not come in the first watch, and his servants may think he delays his coming. He may not come in the second watch. He may wait until the third watch and so try the faith of his servants, and test the unfaithful. Blessed are they who are faithful till the Advent of the Messiah.

---

[1] Luke xii. 39 has "hour" for "watch" of Matthew.
[2] Luke xii. 39 has "left" for "suffered" of Matthew.
[3] "Therefore" is omitted by Luke xii. 40.

## THE ROYAL JUDGMENT.

§ 44. *The Messiah may be long absent. During his absence his servants have sacred trusts, and will be dealt with on his return in accordance with their fidelity to their trusts and their mercy to the suffering, with whom the Messiah identifies himself. The Messiah comes on his throne of glory with attending angels. All nations are assembled for judgment and are separated into two great classes. On the right hand are the blessed. These have been faithful and merciful. They inherit the kingdom and everlasting life. On the left hand are the accursed. They have been unfaithful and unmerciful. They are doomed to outer darkness, the everlasting fire of Gehenna and torment. But there are degrees of guilt. The careless and unthinking are beaten with few stripes, the wilful transgressor with many stripes. The unmerciful receive no mercy.*

Matthew gives the final scene of the royal judgment in connection with the Apocalypse of Jesus, and combines them by parables teaching the lessons of watchfulness and the principles of the judgment.

We have already considered some of these as appropriate to the previous topics, but others now come into view. We shall first consider the parable of the waiting servants, which makes the transition.[1]

And Peter said, Lord, speakest thou this parable unto us, or even unto all?[2] And the Lord said, Who then is the faithful and wise steward,[3] whom his lord hath set[4] over his house-

---

[1] Matt. xxiv. 45-51; Luke xii. 41-46.

[2] Luke, only, has this historical occasion of the parable.

[3] It is probable that "steward" was the original reading rather than "servant" of Matthew.

[4] The aorist of Matthew seems more original than the future of Luke.

hold, to give them their portion [1] of food in due season? Blessed is that servant whom his lord when he cometh shall find so doing. Verily [2] I say unto you, that he will set him over all that he hath. But if that servant [3] shall say in his heart, my lord tarrieth; [4] and shall begin to beat the men servants and the maid servants, [5] and shall eat and drink, with the drunken; [6] the lord of that servant shall come in a day when he expecteth not, and in an hour when he knoweth not, and shall cut him asunder, and appoint his portion with the unfaithful.[7] (Luke xii. 41-46.)

Luke's version is fuller and richer and more original than Matthew's. Little is said of the wise and faithful steward. He is approved and exalted to a high rank in the household. The parable deals with the foolish and unfaithful steward. He prefers evil conduct to the good pleasure of his lord. He presumes upon his long absence. He becomes an unmerciful tyrant to his fellow servants. At the sudden and unexpected advent he is doomed, is cut asunder, and is given his portion with the unfaithful.

Luke appends to this parable a saying of Jesus which seems appropriate here, but which may have been uttered on another occasion, as Wendt supposes.[8] It mat-

---

[1] οἰκετεία of Matthew and θεραπεία of Luke may be due to difference in translation of the original Aramaic word of Jesus, as also τροφή of Matthew and σιτομέτριον of Luke.

[2] The ἀμὴν of Matthew is to be preferred to the ἀληθῶς of Luke.

[3] Matthew inserts "evil" before "servant," which is merely explanatory.

[4] Luke inserts "his coming" after "delayeth" for explanation.

[5] Matthew condenses into "his fellow servants."

[6] Matthew's phrase is better here than the three infinitives of Luke.

[7] Matthew gives "hypocrites" instead of "unfaithful," which is not so suited to the context and involves a covert application to the Pharisees. The addition of "there shall be the weeping and gnashing of teeth" is not original, but an explanation of the portion of the unfaithful.

[8] *Lehre Jesu*, i., s. 148. Wendt attaches it to Luke xvi. 10-12 in his reconstruction of the Logia.

ters little for our purpose. We shall use it here where Luke uses it for lack of a better place :

> And that servant, who knew his lord's will, and made not ready, nor did according to his will, shall be beaten with many *stripes ;* but he that knew not, and did things worthy of stripes, shall be beaten with few *stripes.* And to whomsoever much is given, of him shall much be required: and to whom they commit much, of him will they ask the more. (Luke xii. 47, 48.)

In Luke it is conceived that there may be two classes of unfaithful stewards—one who did not know his lord's will and another who did know. They both sin in the same way and do things worthy of stripes. The wilful transgressor receives many stripes, the ignorant transgressor few stripes. Of each one is exacted punishment in accordance with the trust committed to him. The significance of the passage lies in this. The parable has in view the Messianic judgment at the End of the Age. This difference of punishment, involved between many stripes and few, is not a difference of punishment in the Middle State after death : it is a difference of degree of punishment in the Day of judgment, and in the age that follows that judgment in the Final State. How are we to conceive these few stripes as compared with the many? In Gehenna, are the stripes few in character, or of less degree of punishment, everlasting in duration but less intensive in degree of suffering : or less in the number of the blows, so that the punishment of the less guilty comes to an end before the punishment of the more guilty? This opens up a field for speculation where we can only say that all everlasting duration is subject to such limitations as God in his sovereign reserved right may deem best to put upon it.

The parable of the talents[1] enlarges upon the rewards and punishments of the servants. It represents that the lord is absent *a long time.* During his absence the servants are engaged with their talents, each according to his several ability, having difference of trusts. There are the same three classes as in the parable of the pounds, in Luke.[2] There the trusts are the same; here the trusts are different. There the grades of service in the use of the same trust were different. Here the difference in grade is in the ability, and in the amount of the trusts, but the proportion is the same and the reward seems to be the same. The unfaithful servant is very much alike in both parables. He is deprived of his trust and is punished.

The parable of the talents represents that he is cast into the outer darkness and the weeping and gnashing of teeth in Gehenna. This parable is an appropriate introduction to the judgment scene that closes the chapter. But before considering this, it will be best to bring into view two other parables of Matthew setting forth the principles of the royal judgment. These are the parable of the debtors[3] and the parable of the laborers in the vineyard.[4] It is doubtful whether they are given in their proper historical connection by Matthew. We follow his example and use them where they are appropriate to the topic in hand.

The first of these parables represents the king reckoning with his servants. There are several scenes. The first represents the mercy of the king to his unprofitable servant. Thus the king deals with the penitent when he admits them into his kingdom of grace. He assigns a term of grace and service. The next scene shows the

---

[1] Matt. xxv. 14–30.
[2] Luke xix. 11–27. See p. 249.
[3] Matt. xviii. 21–35.
[4] Matt. xx. 1–16.

miserable man unmerciful to his creditors. The third scene gives the complaint of his fellow servants. The last scene gives the judgment of the unmerciful man by the just monarch. We are taught that the king is merciful in his judgment, but only to those who have learned from him the law of mercy. The law of mercy requires forgiveness to an indefinite extent, even beyond the fiftieth time. It is the same doctrine as that taught in one of the petitions of the Lord's prayer and in the Beatitude of the merciful. The term of grace is to be used in becoming godlike.

The second of these parables sets forth the doctrine that the householder gives every one beyond his deserts, and that no one should complain at the extent of his kindness to others even if it exceed his apparent kindness to him. It seems unjust to give one servant as much for short service as another for much longer service; but when the whole service is a matter not of debt but of favour, the measurement is not by the scales of justice, but by the breadths of mercy. And it is in accordance with the nature of mercy that it should expand to greater breadths when it has to do with greater need. The same doctrine is taught in the parable of the prodigal.[1]

These four parables are the most suitable introduction to the judgment scene.

But when the Son of Man shall come in his glory, and all the angels with him, then shall he sit on the throne of his glory: and before him shall be gathered all the nations: and he shall separate them one from another, as the shepherd separateth the sheep from the goats: and he shall set the sheep on his right hand, but the goats on the left. Then shall the King say unto

---

[1] Luke xv. 11–32.

them on his right hand, Come, ye blessed of my Father, inherit the kingdom prepared for you from the foundation of the world: for I was an hungered, and ye gave me meat: I was thirsty, and ye gave me drink: I was a stranger, and ye took me in; naked, and ye clothed me: I was sick, and ye visited me: I was in prison, and ye came unto me. Then shall the righteous answer him, saying, Lord, when saw we thee an hungered, and fed thee? or athirst, and gave thee drink? And when saw we thee a stranger, and took thee in? or naked, and clothed thee? And when saw we thee sick, or in prison, and came unto thee? And the King shall answer and say unto them, Verily I say unto you, Inasmuch as ye did it unto one of these my brethren, *even* these least, ye did it unto me. Then shall he say also unto them on the left hand, Depart from me, ye cursed, into the eternal fire which is prepared for the devil and his angels: for I was an hungered, and ye gave me no meat: I was thirsty, and ye gave me no drink: I was a stranger, and ye took me not in; naked, and ye clothed me not; sick, and in prison, and ye visited me not. Then shall they also answer, saying, Lord, when saw we thee an hungered, or athirst, or a stranger, or naked, or sick, or in prison, and did not minister unto thee? Then shall he answer them, saying, Verily I say unto you, Inasmuch as ye did it not unto one of these least, ye did it not unto me. And these shall go away into eternal punishment: but the righteous into eternal life. (Matthew xxv. 31-46.)

This is the royal judgment scene. The Messiah is enthroned on his glorious throne with the angels ministering about him. First, he rewards his sheep. They receive their inheritance in the kingdom of glory and enter into everlasting life. Then he condemns the goats and assigns them to everlasting punishment, in the everlasting fires of Gehenna. The rule of judgment is the same that we have found in the parable of the debtors. The merciful are rewarded with the inheritance of the kingdom, but the unmerciful are cast into Gehenna. The judgment is in accordance with works.

## THE REWARDS OF THE KINGDOM.

*§ 45. The rewards of the kingdom will be in proportion to service. The greatest rewards will be seats at the table of the Messiah and enthronement with him.*

Matthew and Luke report a sentence of Jesus promising rewards to his faithful disciples. Luke gives it its historical place in the midst of the discourses at the last Passover:

And there arose also a contention among them, which of them is accounted to be greatest. And he said unto them, The kings of the Gentiles have lordship over them; and they that have authority over them are called Benefactors. But ye *shall* not *be* so: but he that is the greater among you, let him become as the younger; and he that is chief, as he that doth serve. For whether is greater, he that sitteth at meat, or he that serveth? is not he that sitteth at meat? but I am in the midst of you as he that serveth. (Luke xxii. 24-27.)

This is introductory to the word that is common to the two evangelists.

| LUKE xxii. 28-30. | MATT. xix. 28. |
|---|---|
| But ye are they that have continued with me in my trials; and I appoint unto you a kingdom, even as my Father appointed unto me, that ye may eat and drink at my table in my kingdom: and ye shall sit on thrones judging the twelve tribes of Israel. | And Jesus said unto them, Verily I say unto you that ye who have followed me, in the regeneration when the Son of Man shall sit on the throne of his glory, ye also shall sit upon twelve thrones, judging the twelve tribes of Israel. |

Jesus here teaches his disciples that rewards in the kingdom will be proportionate to the magnitude of service. These rewards will be surely gained. Luke reports the reward of eating and drinking at the table of the Messiah. This was appropriate to the occasion of the Lord's Supper. They would have the privilege of the royal table in the kingdom. This reward was omitted by Matthew as not appropriate to the context of the passage in which he used this word of Jesus. Both evangelists report the second reward, enthronement. Luke's report gives no statement of the time except as the time of reward after a period of service in the kingdom, and accordingly he gives "appoint unto you a kingdom." But Matthew gives two very important statements as to the time when the apostles would attain these rewards. It would be when the Son of Man should sit on the throne of his glory. It was not, therefore, to be at the foundation of the kingdom of grace in this world, or at any time during their ministry in the kingdom of grace in its period of development and persecution. It was to be at the time of the culmination of the kingdom of grace in the kingdom of glory. This general statement is introduced by the term [1] regeneration, which is a second indication as to time. The regeneration here is a general regeneration which concerns not merely the individual, but the whole body of the redeemed. It is that regeneration of the world that introduces the kingdom of glory. It is the period of transition to the new age of the world in which the Messiah will reign on his throne of glory over all things. This passage enlarges the scope of the doctrine of the kingdom, as it opens our eyes to see beyond the judgment into the glory of the kingdom that follows the judgment, in which the apostles share with their Lord in a glorious reign.

### THE GREAT COMMISSION.

*§ 46. Jesus rose from the dead and manifested himself unto his disciples, giving them the commission to preach the gospel to the world and to baptize believers, and prom-*

---

[1] ἐν τῇ παλινγενεσίᾳ.

*ising them his presence with them until the End of the Age.*

The gospel of Matthew reports two manifestations of Jesus after his resurrection. (1) He appears to the two Marys in the morning at the tomb. They recognize him and worship him. He commands them to tell the brethren to meet him in Galilee.[1] (2) The eleven disciples meet the risen Lord at the aforesaid place on a mountain in Galilee and he there gave them their commission.[2] There is great difficulty in dealing with this commission, for it is apparently assigned by the supplement to Mark[3] and by Luke[4] to Jerusalem. On the whole it is best to deal with Matthew and Mark together, and with Luke in a separate section.

MATT. xxviii. 16-20.

But the eleven disciples went into Galilee, unto the mountain where Jesus had appointed them. And when they saw him, they worshipped *him*: but some doubted. And Jesus came to them and spake unto them, saying, All authority hath been given unto me in heaven and on earth. Go ye therefore, and make disciples of all the nations, baptizing them into the name of the Father and of the Son and of the Holy Spirit: teaching them to observe all things whatsoever I commanded you: and lo, I am with you alway, even unto the End of the Age.

MARK xvi. 15-18.

And he said unto them, Go ye into all the world, and preach the gospel to the whole creation. He that believeth and is baptized shall be saved; but he that disbelieveth shall be condemned. And these signs shall follow them that believe: in my name shall they cast out demons; they shall speak with new tongues; they shall take up serpents, and if they drink any deadly thing, it shall in no wise hurt them; they shall lay hands on the sick, and they shall recover.

The commission given by Mark does not belong to

---

[1] Matthew xxviii. 1-10 = Mark xvi. 1-8.
[3] Mark xvi. 14-18.
[2] Matthew xxviii. 16-20.
[4] Luke xxiv. 36-49.

the original Mark, but is a later appendix to the gospel. However, it is a report that comes from an early date. It is simpler than the report of Matthew. It gives the command to preach the gospel to the whole world, the whole creation. This takes a most complete view of the universality of the gospel message. It is true that the apostles did not understand the extent of their commission until a long time afterwards; but this does not show that the commission itself, as given by Jesus, was limited to their understanding of it, still less to the land of Palestine as Russel argues.[1] The preaching of the gospel divides the hearers into two classes, the believing and the disbelieving. The former will be saved, the latter will be condemned; for the gospel has judgment in itself. We are not to suppose that the condemnation here refers to the final condemnation of the day of judgment, as the "damned" of the A. V. might seem to suggest; any more than that the salvation, spoken of here, is postponed till doomsday; but the antithesis is between a salvation which is received by believing and being baptized—that is, the salvation which is enjoyed in the kingdom of grace; and a condemnation which comes whenever and wherever the gospel is rejected, namely, a condemnation which abides in this life upon all who do not believe, are not baptized, and do not by faith and baptism become incorporated into the kingdom of grace. The commission in Mark lays stress upon the miracle-working that would attend the ministry of the apostles.

The report of Matthew enlarges the commission. (1) They are to make disciples of all nations. This implies their organization into a body of disciples, a

---

[1] *Parousia*, p. 121.

kingdom, or Church. (2) They are to baptize them into the name of the Father, the Son, and the Holy Spirit. This baptism into the name of the Son, the Messiah, as well as into the name of God the Father and of the Spirit of God, implies the organization of a separate body of the baptized as the kingdom of the Messiah. (3) They are to teach all the commands of the Messiah. The new kingdom is to be an organized body, and is therefore to have its rules and laws.

In place of the promise of miracle-working given by Mark, a more important promise is given by Matthew; namely, the abiding presence of the Messiah himself, with the apostles, in the exercise of their ministry. We have already studied this abiding presence as promised by Jesus to those who assemble in his name and agree in supplication.[1] This presence of Jesus is the spiritual, dynamic presence of the Messiah. It is to be distinguished from the presence for the forty days subsequent to the resurrection enjoyed by the apostles, as well as from the presence to establish the kingdom in the world, and also from the presence at the Advent for judgment at the End of the Age. This latter is not explicitly referred to in the commission, but it is implied in the term "End of the Age," which is elsewhere connected with the Advent to judgment.[2] The spiritual presence of the Messiah is to abide with the apostles in their ministry until the Age has been completed and the Advent for judgment has arrived. This commission was given to the eleven apostles, but it was given them for a world-wide ministry and a world-long ministry. The commission does not in itself contemplate a ministry other than apostolic. It could not do so without transcending the

---

[1] See p. 195.   [2] See p. 138.

sphere of prophecy and entering into the field of history, If in the development of the world-wide and world-long ministry it would appear that the apostles must have successors to carry on their ministry and complete it, the Messiah, whose presence was promised to them, would provide for whatever emergency might arise.

# CHAPTER VI.

### THE MESSIAH OF LUKE.

WE have already considered in the previous chapters the larger portion of the material that we would treat under this head, if we had to discuss the Messiah of Luke alone. We have found that Luke has used the Messianic material of Mark as his principal source. This material is not original with Luke, it does not belong to him. He merely used it and edited it for the purposes of his narrative. All of this material was therefore considered in Chapters III. and IV. under the Messiah of Mark. We have also seen that Luke used the Messianic idea of the Aramaic Logia of Matthew. He used the material and put it in a different form from that in which it appears in Matthew. He used it for the purpose of his narrative. But the material was not original to Luke. It was Matthew's. Accordingly we have treated it in Chapter V. in the Messiah of Matthew. We have left, therefore, only that portion of the Messianic idea of Luke which he derived from other sources than Mark and the Aramaic Matthew. This is not great in amount, but it is of considerable importance.

### THE SON OF GOD.

§ 47. *Jesus in boyhood was conscious of his Messianic calling as the Son of God, and he made it his a*͏͏͏͏͏*ing his Father's will. As he grew in years, he gre*

*5, seq.*

*prehension of his Messianic calling and in devotion to it.*

The story of the boyhood of Jesus reported by Luke alone, is of great importance for the development of the Messianic consciousness of Jesus.

And the child grew, and waxed strong, filled with wisdom: and the grace of God was upon him. And his parents went every year to Jerusalem at the feast of the passover. And when he was twelve years old, they went up after the custom of the feast; and when they had fulfilled the days, as they were returning, the boy Jesus tarried behind in Jerusalem; and his parents knew it not; but supposing him to be in the company, they went a day's journey; and they sought for him among their kinsfolk and acquaintance: and when they found him not, they returned to Jerusalem, seeking for him. And it came to pass, after three days they found him in the temple, sitting in the midst of the doctors, both hearing them, and asking them questions: and all that heard him were amazed at his understanding and his answers. And when they saw him, they were astonished: and his mother said unto him, Son, why hast thou thus dealt with us? behold, thy father and I sought thee sorrowing. And he said unto them, How is it that ye sought me? knew ye not that I must be about my Father's business? And they understood not the saying which he spake unto them. And he went down with them, and came to Nazareth; and he was subject unto them: and his mother kept all *these* sayings in her heart. And Jesus advanced in wisdom and stature, and in favor with God and men. (Luke ii. 40–52.)

There is some difference of opinion as to the rendering and interpretation of the words of Jesus in this story. The A. V. renders "*about my Father's business,*" which then is to be interpreted as follows. Jesus claims that he is the son of God, and that he must be about the work of his Father. This cannot mean that he was God in the sense that every true Christian is God; because that doctrine was revealed for the first time by Jesus himself subsequent to this event, and it is based on the doctrine of his Messiahship. It could hardly mean that he was the son of God in the theological sense as the second person of the Trinity; for that doctrine was not yet revealed, and there is nothing in the context to suggest it. It means that Jesus was the Son of God as the Messiah, for the term Son of God is a well-known name of the Messiah alternating with the son of David.¹ Jesus here at twelve years of age makes it known to his parents that he is assured of his Messianic calling. They knew it, according to the stories of the infancy of Jesus reported by Luke, through the testimonies they had received.² At the legal age for his appearance in the temple according to the traditional Jewish custom, he likewise was conscious of his Messiahship. As the Messiah he had the Father's work to do, and what should his parents find him doing but that work. It was for the present learning from the teachers of Israel what they had to give him.

The R. V., however, renders "*in my Father's house.*" This rendering does not change the interpretation so far as his Messiahship is concerned. In either case he is the Messianic Son of God. But it modifies the interpretation as to the work. According to this translation he points to the place of his activity rather than to his work. What place was so appropriate to the Messiah as the temple of God, where the ministry of Israel centred? This rendering is not suited to the context or the circumstances. For Jesus asks his parents why they sought him, and not why they did not seek him there. It was not a question of place, but a question of seeking

---

¹ See pp. 46, 76.   ² See pp. 45, *seq.*

him at all, when they ought to have had confidence in him that he was about his Father's work, wherever he might be. Furthermore, the temple was the centre of the priestly ministry. It was also the centre of the Rabbinical education. But it was not on that account the place where a prophet or the Messiah would necessarily carry on his ministry. In fact the ministry of the prophets was usually apart from the temple. The subsequent ministry of John the forerunner was in the wilderness of Judæa and in the valley of the Jordan. The ministry of Jesus was, according to Luke, chiefly in Galilee and Perea. Why then such a stress on the temple here, so different from the method of Jesus elsewhere in Luke? The work of the Father in heaven, the business the Messiah had to do for the Father: that was the ideal that was now pressing upon the mind of the boy Jesus and making him such a wonderful pupil of the doctors of the law.

### THE REJECTED PROPHET.

§ 48. *Jesus declares himself to be the prophet of the great prophecy of the exile and is rejected by his townsmen of Nazareth.*

Jesus early in his ministry delivers a discourse in the synagogue at Nazareth, which is preserved only in the gospel of Luke. In this he definitely claims to be the gentle preacher described in the great prophecy of the exile.[1]

And he came to Nazareth, where he had been brought up: and he entered, as his custom was, into the synagogue on the

---

[1] Isa. lxi.

Sabbath day, and stood up to read. And there was delivered unto him the book of the prophet Isaiah. And he opened the book, and found the place where it was written, The Spirit of the Lord is upon me, because he anointed me to preach good tidings to the poor: he hath sent me to proclaim release to the captives, and recovering of sight to the blind, to set at liberty them that are bruised, to proclaim the acceptable year of the Lord.[1] And he closed the book, and gave it back to the attendant, and sat down: and the eyes of all in the synagogue were fastened on him. And he began to say unto them, To-day hath this scripture been fulfilled in your ears. And all bare him witness, and wondered at the words of grace which proceeded out of his mouth. (Luke iv. 16-22.)

This passage from the great prophet of the exile[2] graphically describes the work of Jesus. He had been anointed at his baptism for his public ministry when the divine Spirit came upon him in the form of a dove to abide with him.[3] His ministry was the preaching of the gospel of the kingdom to the poor, and the doing miracles of mercy. Thus Jesus describes his own ministry, and these he gave as his credentials to the messenger of John the Baptist.[4] The acceptable year of the Lord which he proclaimed, was the year of the Advent, the establishment of the kingdom of God by the Messiah. Rightly, therefore, Jesus tells the men of Nazareth, "*To-day hath this Scripture been fulfilled in your ears.*"

---

[1] Isa. lxi. 1-2. See Briggs' *Messianic Prothecy*, p. 370 *seq*. The text has important variations from the LXX. as well as from the Hebrew, due doubtless to an Aramaic Targum used by Jesus in the synagogue. The people could not understand the original Hebrew. The passage was first read in Hebrew and then translated into Aramaic. There was a common traditional rendering which was followed and which is translated into Greek here.

[2] Isa. lxi. 1-3.

[3] See p. 75.

[4] See p. 176.

## THE GUILT OF REJECTING THE GOSPEL.

*§ 49. The seventy were commissioned to preach the nearness of the kingdom. It will be more tolerable for Sodom and the ancient cities than for those who reject the gospel. The Holy Spirit will guide the disciples in their ministry, and they will be successful notwithstanding persecution. Even Satan will fall as lightning from heaven. All things have been given by the Father into the hands of the Messiah who will reveal the Father to babes. The Messiah will acknowledge in the judgment all who confess him, and will deny those who reject him.*

The commission of the seventy and their return, with its mingled success and failure, give occasion for the discourse of Jesus in which he sets forth the ministry of the gospel and the great guilt of rejecting it.

The report of the mission of the seventy is given only by Luke. But Matthew gives so much of it in connection with the mission of the Twelve and in the subsequent discourses that it is necessary to compare the two reports and, so far as possible, ascertain the original sayings of Jesus.

Now after these things the Lord appointed seventy others, and sent them two and two before his face into every city and place, whither he himself was about to come. And he said unto them,
(Luke x. 1.)

> The harvest is plenteous, (Luke x. 2, 3.)
> But the laborers are few:
> Pray ye therefore the Lord of the harvest,
> That he send forth laborers into his harvest.[1]
> Go your ways: behold, I send you forth [2]

---

[1] These four lines are given by Luke here. Matt. ix. 37, 38, gives them as a prelude to the call of the Twelve.

[2] Matt. x. 16a, abbreviates by leaving off ὑπάγετε of Luke: it is graphic and doubtless original.

As lambs in the midst of wolves:[1]
Be ye therefore wise as serpents, (Matt. x. 16 c, d.)
And harmless as doves.[2]
Carry no purse, no wallet, no shoes; (Luke x. 4.)
And salute no man on the way.[3]
And into whatsoever house ye shall enter,
         (Luke x. 5, 6.)
First say, Peace to this house.[4]
And if a son of peace be there,[5]
Your peace shall rest upon him:[6]
But if it be not worthy, (Matt. x. 13 c, d.)
Your peace shall turn to you again.[7]
And in that same house remain, (Luke x. 7-11.)
Eating and drinking such things as they give:
For the labourer is worthy of his hire.
Go not from house to house.[8]
And into whatsoever city ye enter,
And they receive you,
Eat such things as are set before you:
And heal the sick that are therein,
And say unto them,
The kingdom of God is come nigh unto you.
But into whatsoever city ye shall enter,
And they receive you not,
Go out into the streets thereof and say,
Even the dust which cleaveth on us from your city,

---

[1] In Luke, verse 3b, "lambs" is preferable to the "sheep" of Matt., verse 16a.

[2] These two lines only in Matthew.

[3] These two lines in Luke. But see Matt. x. 9, 10, p. 183.

[4] These two lines of Luke have been contracted in Matt., verse 12.

[5] This orientalism of Luke has been weakened into ἡ οἰκία ἀξία in Matthew 13a, possibly in antithesis to verse 13c.

[6] Matthew, verse 13b, gives ἐλθάτω for ἐπαναπαήσεται of Luke.

[7] Luke, verse 6c, is evidently a contraction of two lines in antithesis to the previous couplet. We use Matthew's couplet for lack of a better, save that for consistency we use the ἀνακάμψει of Luke in preference to the ἐπιστραφήτω of Matthew.

[8] These four lines are given only by Luke.

That which cleaveth to our feet we do wipe off against
    you:[1]
Howbeit know this,
That the kingdom of God is come nigh.
Verily I say unto you,[2]  (Matt. x. 15.)
It will be more tolerable in that day
For the land of Sodom and Gomorrah than for that city.[3]
Woe unto thee, Chorazin![4]  (Luke x. 13.)
Woe unto thee, Bethsaida!
For if in Tyre and Sidon had been done,
The mighty works which were done in you,
Long ago would they have repented,
Sitting in sackcloth and ashes.
Howbeit I say unto you,[5]  (Matt. xi. 22a.)
It will be more tolerable in the judgment,[6]

                                (Luke x. 14, 15.)

For Tyre and Sidon than for you.[7]
And thou, Capernaum,
Shalt thou be exalted unto heaven?
Thou shalt be brought down unto Hades.[8]

---

[1] The best MSS. followed by the R. V. give εἰς τοὺς πόδας before the verb. It is impossible to attach this to the previous line. It makes it too long. It is needed with the verb to make up the couplet. I render it as I think it stood originally in the Aramaic. The translation into Greek has here, and not unfrequently elsewhere, obscured the poetry and made a single sentence out of the two of the original poetry.

[2] Matthew's complete line, verse 15a, is preferable to the shortened phrase of Luke, verse 12a.

[3] The fuller "land of Sodom and Gomorrah" of Matthew is preferable to the shortened "Sodom" of Luke, verse 12b. The arrangement of words differs in the evangelists. I arrange them as the parallelism of the poetry would probably be in the original. It is doubtful whether "that day" of Luke, referring to the day of the kingdom, is to be preferred to "day of judgment" of Matthew.

[4] Matthew gives an explanatory statement here.
"Then began he to upbraid the cities wherein most of his mighty works were done because they repented not." (xi. 20.)

[5] Matthew gives a complete line; Luke, verse 14a, only πλήν.

[6] It is probable that "judgment" of Luke, verse 14b, is to be preferred to "day of judgment" of Matthew. See above note ([3]).

[7] There is a remarkable closeness in agreement between the evangelists in these nine lines.

[8] Matthew, verse 23, is the same in these three lines.

For if in Sodom had been done, (Matt. xi. 23*d*, 24.)
The mighty works which were done in thee,
It would have remained until this day.
Howbeit I say unto you,
It will be more tolerable in the judgment,[1]
For the land of Sodom than for thee.[2]
He that receiveth you receiveth me,[3] (Matt. x. 40*a*.)
And he that rejecteth you rejecteth me; (Luke x. 16*b*.)
And he that receiveth me receiveth him that sent me,
            (Matt. x. 40*b*.)
And he that rejecteth me rejecteth him that sent me.[4]
            (Luke x. 16*c*.)
He that receiveth a prophet in the name of a prophet
Shall receive a prophet's reward; (Matt. x. 41, 42.)
And he that receiveth a righteous man in the name of a
 righteous man
Shall receive a righteous man's reward.
And whosoever shall give to drink unto one of these
 little ones
A cup of cold water only, in the name of a disciple,
Verily I say unto you,
He shall in no wise lose his reward.[5]

It is uncertain whether the sentences peculiar to Matthew have not been added because of the similarity of topic from a different occasion. But if this be so we have no means of determining the occasion when they were delivered. The evangelist gives them an appropriate topical place and we may consider them here.

This section of the discourse pronounces woes upon Chorazin, Bethsaida, and Capernaum, the favoured cities of Palestine, for their rejection of the Messiah, and de-

---

[1] Luke has not this line, but consistency requires that "judgment" should be here for the "day of judgment" which Matthew uses throughout.

[2] These six lines are given only by Matthew.

[3] The "receiveth" of Matthew is more suited to the context than the "heareth" of Luke, verse 16*c*.

[4] Luke, verse 16*b*, *c*, has lines 2 and 4; Matthew x. 40, lines 1 and 3.

[5] These eight lines are given only by Matthew.

clares that it will be more tolerable for Tyre, Sidon, and Sodom in the judgment day than for them. There are degrees of guilt and of condemnation even in the final Messianic judgment. The worst guilt is the guilt of rejecting the gospel.

The Seventy go forth with this commission, knowing that they bear with them the presence of the Messiah and the power of God. Those who reject them reject the Messiah and also reject the God of Israel.

Luke alone gives an account of the return of the Seventy and their joy in their victory over the demons. This rejoices the heart of Jesus, and he sees before him his great enemy Satan, the prince of the demons, no longer in his authority over the host of evil, but falling like a thunderbolt from heaven.

And the seventy returned with joy, saying, Lord, even the demons are subject unto us in thy name. And he said unto them, I beheld Satan fallen as lightning from heaven. Behold, I have given you authority to tread upon serpents and scorpions, and over all the power of the enemy: and nothing shall in any wise hurt you. Howbeit in this rejoice not, that the spirits are subject unto you; but rejoice that your names are written in heaven.
(Luke x. 17–20.)

Jesus here thinks of Satan as having access to heaven;[1] but that privilege is about to be taken from him. He is to be defeated and cast down from heaven. The success of his ministers rejoices the Messiah. Luke and Matthew give essentially the same additional sayings of Jesus in this connection.[2]

In that same hour Jesus said,[3]
I thank thee, O Father,

---

[1] So Job i.-ii.                   [2] Matthew xi. 25-27; Luke x. 21, 22.
[3] Luke inserts, according to his conception of the Holy Spirit abiding with Jesus, "he rejoiced in the Holy Spirit and" before "said" Matthew prefixes "answered." Matthew uses "season" for the more graphic "hour" of the original as given in Luke.

> Lord of heaven and earth,
> That thou didst hide these things from the wise and understanding,
> And didst reveal them unto babes:
> Yea, Father,
> For so it was well pleasing in thy sight.
> All things have been delivered unto me of my Father:
> And no one knoweth the Son,[1] save the Father;
> Neither doth any know the Father, save the Son,
> And he to whomsoever the Son willeth to reveal *him*.

In this passage the Messiah tells his disciples that the Father had given all things into his hands. The Father can only be known through the revelation made of him by the Son. The Son is the revealer of the Father. The wise and understanding, the scribes and Pharisees, do not understand this. But the babes, who desire to learn, receive the revelation of the Father through the Son.

Jesus is here thinking of his sonship as the Messianic king; but he advances in his consciousness of sonship far beyond anything given in the Old Testament prophecy as to the Son of God, the king. He conceives of an intimacy with God which is unique, and which has to do not only with the dominion of the king and the revelation by the prophet, but also with a personal acquaintance with God in this relation of sonship, which is the synthesis of prophecy and royalty in a more fundamental personal relation.[2]

The day long waited for by the prophets and kings of the Old Testament has come. The Messiah has ap-

---

[1] The reading of Matthew is simpler and to be preferred. Luke's τίς ἐστιν ὁ υἱός; τίς ἐστιν ὁ πατήρ—limits and explains the meaning of Jesus here.

[2] Wendt, *Lehre Jesu*, ii., s. 429; Beyschlag, *Neutestamentliche Theologie*, i., s. 75.

peared, to be rejected by the sages of Israel, but to be received by the babes.

And turning to the disciples, he said privately,
Blessed *are* the eyes which see the things that ye see:
For I say unto you, that many prophets and kings desired,
To see the things which ye see, and saw them not;
And to hear the things which ye hear, and heard them not.[1]
(Luke x. 23, 24.)

Luke has used this saying here because it was appropriate to his topic, and we may do the same. It is a brief but strong statement of the exceeding great privileges of the Messianic age and of the presence of the Messiah. The humblest hearers of the Messiah were to be envied by prophets and kings of the old dispensation.

### THE INVISIBLE KINGDOM.

§ 50. *The kingdom came without being observed. It was already among the people of Israel in the times of Jesus, in the Messiah and his disciples.*

The gospel of Luke gives a discourse of Jesus that emphasizes the inner spiritual nature of the kingdom with more plainness than any we have found in Mark or Matthew, and distinguishes a kingdom as actually present during the ministry of the Lord himself.

And being asked by the Pharisees, when the kingdom of God cometh, he answered them and said, The kingdom of God cometh not with observation: neither shall they say, Lo, here! or There! for lo, the kingdom of God is in the midst of you.
(Luke xvii. 20, 21.)

This passage teaches the Pharisees that the kingdom

---

[1] Matt. xiii. 16-17 gives essentially these words on another occasion in connection with the parable of the sower.

of God comes without those external, visible, and extraordinary signs which they were expecting and craving. It was not a kingdom to be seen or to be detected by the closest external watching and scrutiny. In its origin and in its progress it would be invisible. The invisibility of the kingdom is brought out in the contrast of the words "in the midst of you." It is thought by many that this teaches that the kingdom of God is "within you"; that is, in your hearts, in the secret recesses of your spiritual nature. This is in accord with the teaching of Jesus as to the spiritual nature of his kingdom in the parables of the kingdom. But it does not seem appropriate to the context. Jesus would hardly say to his Pharisaic questioners and tempters, "The kingdom of God is within you." Pfleiderer and Weiffenbach, who accept that explanation, think that he was speaking to his disciples and not to the Pharisees; but there is no evidence of a change of address. It is better therefore to follow the margin of the R. V. and think of the kingdom of God as "in the midst of you"; that is, in the unrecognized Messianic king and in his believing disciples who have entered the kingdom by their childlike faith in him.[1] The kingdom was already among them in the land of Israel; in an unorganized condition, it is true, because the Messiah had not yet ascended his throne, and his apostles had not yet been installed in their offices; but the essential elements of the kingdom were there in its Messianic king and in the foundations, the apostles, upon which it was soon to be built.

---

[1] See Vincent, *Word Studies*, I., p. 401, who cites with approval Trench after Meyer, "The whole language of the kingdom of heaven being within men, rather than men being within the kingdom, is modern." Also Weiss, *Bib. Theologie N. T.*, s. 49; Wendt, *Lehre Jesu*, ii. 295; Beyschlag, *Neutest. Theologie*, i., s. 48; Adeney, *Theology of New Test.*, p. 23.

## THE LESSER APOCALYPSE OF JESUS.

§ 51. *The Advent of the Messiah for judgment will be like a flash of lightning, as unexpected as the deluge and the destruction of Sodom, when there will be a separation of the closest relatives.*

The gospel of Matthew[1] combines material which is separated by Luke and assigned to two different occasions. It is evident that Luke is correct, for the separation makes the discourses much more intelligible, and the one becomes a preparation for the other. Mark gives only a little bit of the first discourse of Luke and agrees with Matthew in combining it with the second. The separation enables us to distinguish two apocalypses of Jesus, the lesser and the greater. In both of these Jesus builds on the discourses already considered and on the Apocalypses of the Old Testament.

| (*a*) MARK xiii. 21–23. | MATT. xxiv. 23–25. |
|---|---|
| And then if any man shall say unto you, Lo, here is the Messiah; or Lo, there; believe *it* not: for there shall arise false Messiahs and false prophets, and shall shew signs and wonders, that they may lead astray, if possible, the elect. But take ye heed: behold, I have told you all things beforehand.[2] | Then if any man shall say unto you, Lo, here is the Messiah, or Here; believe *it* not. For there shall arise false Messiahs, and false prophets, and shall shew great signs and wonders; so as to lead astray, if possible, even the elect. Behold, I have told you beforehand. |

| (*b*) LUKE xvii. 22–25. | MATT. xxiv. 26, 27. |
|---|---|
| And he said unto the disciples, The days will come, when ye shall desire to see one of the | If therefore they shall say unto you, Behold, he is in the wilderness; go not forth: Be- |

---

[1] xxiv.

[2] It would appear that *a* is only a variation of *b*. Mark has attached it to the Apocalypse of Jesus. Luke derived his version from the Logia of Matthew. Our Matthew then using both sources combines the two versions and uses them both.

days of the Son of Man, and ye shall not see it. And they shall say to you, Lo, there! Lo, here! go not away, nor follow after *them*: for as the lightning, when it lighteneth out of the one part under the heaven, shineth unto the other part under heaven; so shall the Son of Man be in his day. But first must he suffer many things and be rejected of this generation.

hold, he is in the inner chambers; believe *it* not. For as the lightning cometh forth from the east, and is seen even unto the west; so shall be the coming of the Son of Man.

LUKE xvii. 26-37.

And as it came to pass in the days of Noah, even so shall it be also in the days of the Son of Man. They ate, they drank, they married, they were given in marriage, until the day that Noah entered into the ark, and the flood came, and destroyed them all. Likewise even as it came to pass in the days of Lot; they ate, they drank, they bought, they sold, they planted, they builded; but in the day that Lot went out from Sodom it rained fire and brimstone from heaven, and destroyed them all: after the same manner shall it be in the day that the Son of Man is revealed.

In that day, he who shall be on the housetop, and his goods in the house, let him not go down to take them away: and let him that is in the field likewise not return back. Remember Lot's wife. Whosoever shall seek to gain his life shall lose it: but whosoever shall lose *his life* shall preserve it. I say unto you, In that night there shall be two men on one bed; the one shall be taken, and the other shall be left.

MATT. xxiv. 37-39.

And as *were* the days of Noah, so shall be the coming of the Son of Man. For as in those days which were before the flood they were eating and drinking, marrying and giving in marriage, until the day that Noah entered into the ark, and they knew not until the flood came, and took them all away; so shall be the coming of the Son of Man.

MATT. xxiv. 40, 41.

Then shall two men be in the field; one is taken, and one is left: two women *shall be* grind-

| | |
|---|---|
| There shall be two women grinding together; the one shall be taken, and the other shall be left. | ing at the mill; one is taken and one is left. |
| And they answering say unto him, Where, Lord? And he said unto them, Where the body *is*, thither will the vultures also be gathered together. | MATT. xxiv. 28.<br><br>Wheresoever the carcass is, there will the vultures be gathered together. |

The introduction to the discourse, given by Luke only, is an appropriate one. It would be omitted from necessity in the combination of this apocalypse with the other in Matthew and Mark. The Son of Man is soon to leave his disciples and remain absent from them for a season. In the time of his absence and his expected return there will be grave peril from false Messiahs. These will, as the false prophets predicted in Deuteronomy,[1] work miracles, so as to deceive even the elect. They will appear in the wilderness as Moses and Elias, with the claim that they will, in the same manner, lead Israel to the conquest of the land. They will appear in a secret place in the house as a sort of sanctum sanctorum. The Messiah is not to appear in any such fashion. His first advent was in secret, and the kingdom came without observation; but the second Advent is to be of an entirely different character. It is to be with observation, so that all may see it. It will be like a flash of lightning, lighting up the whole face of the heaven. In view of such an advent as this the disciples need never be deceived.

The first advent is to end with the sufferings and rejection of the Messiah by the generation to which he came. The second Advent is to be an advent in judgment like the deluge and the destruction of Sodom; in which there will be a selection of the elect and a separa-

---

[1] Deut. xiii. 1-5.

tion of the most intimate relatives. And this will be in the most open and visible manner, in a blaze of lightning.

## THE SHINING FORTH OF THE KINGDOM.

§ 52. *The kingdom is not immediately to shine forth. The king is to go into a far country to take the kingdom to himself and to return. Then he will reward the faithful in accordance with the measure of their fidelity, and destroy the unfaithful.*

Luke gives the historical occasion for the prophecy respecting the departure and return of Jesus. He illustrates it by a parable. The parable of the Pounds[1] resembles the parable of the Talents given by Matthew,[2] in many respects, so that some critics think they are two versions of the same parable. But there are also striking differences, which seem to require that they should receive different treatment.

And as they heard these things, he added and spake a parable, because he was nigh to Jerusalem, and *because* they supposed that the kingdom of God was immediately to appear. He said therefore, A certain nobleman went into a far country, to receive for himself a kingdom, and to return. And he called ten servants of his, and gave them ten pounds, and said unto them, Trade ye *here with* till I come. But his citizens hated him, and sent an ambassage after him, saying, We will not that this man reign over us. And it came to pass, when he was come back again, having received the kingdom, that he commanded these servants, unto whom he had given the money, to be called to him, that he might know what they had gained by trading. And the first came before him, saying, Lord, thy pound hath made ten pounds more. And he said unto him, Well done, thou good servant: because thou wast found faithful in a very little, have

---

[1] xix. 11–27.  [2] xxv., see p. 224.

thou authority over ten cities. And the second came, saying, Thy pound, Lord, hath made five pounds. And he said unto him also, Be thou also over five cities. And another came, saying, Lord, behold, *here is* thy pound, which I kept laid up in a napkin : for I feared thee, because thou art an austere man : thou takest up that thou layedst not down, and reapest that thou didst not sow. He saith unto him, Out of thine own mouth will I judge thee, thou wicked servant. Thou knewest that I am an austere man, taking up that I laid not down, and reaping that I did not sow ; then wherefore gavest thou not my money into the bank, and I at my coming should have required it with interest ? And he said unto them that stood by, Take away from him the pound, and give it unto him that hath the ten pounds. And they said unto him, Lord, he hath ten pounds. I say unto you, that unto every one that hath shall be given ; but from him that hath not, even that which he hath shall be taken away from him. Howbeit these mine enemies, which would not that I should reign over them, bring hither, and slay them before me. (Luke xix. 11-27.)

In this parable Jesus corrects his disciples who had the opinion, based on several of his discourses, that the kingdom of God was immediately to shine forth. The manifestation, or shining forth of the kingdom of glory, was not at hand, as they supposed. The kingdom that was at hand, that was among them, was a kingdom of grace, a kingdom without external marks of observation. This distinction the disciples had not yet learned. The kingdom of glory was the culmination and resultant of the kingdom of grace, as was taught in the parables of the kingdom. Jesus here points to the distant future for the realization of the kingdom of glory. The king is not yet enthroned. He is to go into a far country to take to himself the kingdom. There he is to be enthroned. This far country, as the subsequent events show, is heaven, the presence of the Father, who is to enthrone the Messiah at his right hand. But the Messiah is to return for judgment. During his absence his servants, in his kingdom of grace, have their respective trusts. They will be judged at his advent in accordance with their fidelity to these trusts. There are two classes of subjects that are brought out by the tests of the judgment, the faithful and the unfaithful. There are also two classes of the faithful who receive their rewards in proportion to their fidelity and gains. The one unfaithful and rebellious man represents the rebellious citizens who are deprived of all their trusts and slain.

### THE WOES OF JERUSALEM.

*§ 53. Jerusalem will be besieged and utterly destroyed, because she did not know the time of her visitation by the Messiah. Then will woes come upon women and children so dreadful that they will long for convulsions of nature to destroy them.*

Luke gives us a brief saying of Jesus which was spoken in connection with his Messianic entry into Jerusalem, when with deep sorrow of heart he utters this touching prediction:

And when he drew nigh, he saw the city and wept over it, saying, If thou hadst known in this day, even thou, the things which belong unto peace! but now they are hid from thine eyes. For the days shall come upon thee, when thine enemies shall cast up a bank about thee, and compass thee round, and keep thee in on every side, and shall dash thee to the ground, and thy children within thee; and they shall not leave in thee one stone upon another; because thou knewest not the time of thy visitation. (Luke xix. 41-44.)

Looking down upon the temple and the city in all its beauty and magnificence from the ridge of Olivet, before descending into the valley of the Kedron, Jesus saw, in prophetic vision, the city besieged by the Romans, its inhabitants shut in on every side, the city captured, the people slain, and the city so utterly destroyed that not one stone was left in its place. The people had not recognized their great opportunity. The Messiah visited them to redeem them, and they rejected him and were about to put him to death. The crucifixion of the rejected Messiah involved, in a few brief years, the utter ruin of Jerusalem.

A similar lament was made on the way to the crucifixion.

And there followed him a great multitude of the people, and of women who bewailed and lamented him. But Jesus turning unto them said, Daughters of Jerusalem, weep not for me, but weep for yourselves, and for your children. For behold, the days are coming, in which they shall say, Blessed are the barren, and the wombs that never bare, and the breasts that never gave suck. Then shall they begin to say to the mountains, Fall on us; and to the hills, Cover us. For if they do these things in the green tree, what shall be done in the dry? (Luke xxiii. 27–31.)

The lamentations of the women of Jerusalem over the sorrow of the Messiah are heralds of still greater lamentations of these women over their children, their city and themselves. All these passages set forth the impending woes of Jerusalem, when the penalties of the rejection of the Messiah would come upon the generation that rejected him, so far as this world and this life are concerned.

### THE RISEN MESSIAH.

§ 54. *The Christophanies of the resurrection and ascension fulfil the predictions of Jesus and prove him to be the ever-living Messiah.*

Once during his life, on the Mount of Transfiguration,

Jesus let the light of his glory shine forth in Christophany to three chosen disciples. In his resurrection Christophanies were multiplied. Several of these are reported by Luke.

(1) Jesus manifested himself to two disciples at Emmaus.[1] They did not recognize him until he manifested himself to them in the breaking of bread. Then he vanished from their sight.

(2) Jesus also manifested himself to Peter,[2] but no details are given with reference to this event.

(3) Jesus appeared in the evening to the assembled disciples, including ten apostles, the two from Emmaus and others with them.[3] From the parallel passages it would appear that Jesus suddenly manifested himself and then suddenly vanished without regard to the obstructions of doors and walls. It is also stated that he showed them his flesh and bones, the wounds in his hands and feet, and that he ate fish with them, showing that it was the same Jesus with the same body that was crucified and buried.

(4) Jesus manifested himself to his disciples over against Bethany. Here, having blessed them, he was parted from them and carried up into heaven.[4] The Appendix to Mark tells us that he was received up into heaven and sat down on the right hand of God.[5] Luke in the Book of Acts[6] reports that "He was taken up and a cloud received him out of their sight." These four manifestations of the risen Messiah are only specimens of many more such manifestations. There are ten

---

[1] Luke xxiv. 13-35 = Mark xvi. 12, 13.
[2] Luke xxiv. 34 = 1 Cor. xv. 5.
[3] Luke xxiv. 33-43 = Mark xvi. 14-18 = John xx. 19-24.
[4] Luke xxiv. 50-53.
[5] Mark xvi. 19, 20.
[6] Acts i. 9.

manifestations recorded in the gospels and epistles. But we have no reason to suppose that these exhaust the number. For, as Luke tells us, he "shewed himself alive after his passion by many proofs, appearing unto them by the space of forty days, and speaking the things concerning the kingdom of God."[1] These manifestations are all Christophanies or shinings forth of Messianic glory. In them the Messiah gave the sign and evidence of his Messiahship, a more wonderful sign than the descent from heaven in a cloud, or descent from the cross that the Pharisees and people demanded of him. To this sign he had referred them in the symbol of Jonah,[2] and in his predictions of his death and resurrection.[3] The rising from the grave and from Hades, the living for forty days in the world, manifesting himself to his disciples so that they might testify of his resurrection, and then ascending to heaven on the clouds—these were Christophanies which transcended all the predictions of the Old Testament prophets, and even the predictions of Jesus himself.

### THE POWER FROM ON HIGH.

§ 55. *Jesus explained to his disciples that his life, death, resurrection, and ascension were in fulfilment of the Messianic ideals of the Old Testament. He referred to the advent of the divine Spirit as the time for the inauguration of the kingdom in the world; but warned them that the times of the kingdom are exclusively in the authority of the Father.*

Jesus before departing from his disciples gave them a commission to preach the gospel to all nations. This is

---

[1] Acts i. 3.     [2] See p. 186.     [3] See p. 94.

more general than that given in Matthew, and it is set in the midst of an exposition of the predictions of the Old Testament. It gives a final prediction of the power that was to come upon them in the advent of the Spirit.

And he said unto them, These are my words which I spake unto you, while I was yet with you, how that all things must needs be fulfilled, which are written in the law of Moses, and the prophets, and the psalms, concerning me. Then opened he their mind, that they might understand the scriptures; and he said unto them, Thus it is written, that the Messiah should suffer, and rise again from the dead the third day; and that repentance and remission of sins should be preached in his name unto all the nations, beginning from Jerusalem. Ye are witnesses of these things. And behold, I send forth the promise of my Father upon you: but tarry ye in the city, until ye be clothed with power from on high. (Luke xxiv. 44-49.)

The interpretation of the prophecies of the Old Testament by the life of Jesus we shall consider later on. We confine ourselves here to the commission and the prediction. The commission is to all nations, but it is added that the ministry must begin at Jerusalem. Jerusalem is the beginning, but it is only the beginning of a world-wide ministry. The gospel call is summed up in the two words, repentance and remission of sins. The preaching has as its parallel, witnessing, namely, to the Messiah and his instruction. Luke adds a very important statement, which sheds light upon the commission and also upon other predictions of Jesus. The apostles were not to begin their ministry at once, but they were to wait until they had been clothed with power from on high, to enable them to minister. This power is the promise of the heavenly Father unto them, and they are to wait in Jerusalem for its bestowal. This advent of power from on high, to enable them to exercise their ministry, is therefore connected with a spiritual advent of Jesus himself, who had promised to be with them in the exercise of their ministry from the beginning of it until the end of the gospel age.[1]

In accordance with the promises of Jesus, the apostles anticipate that the kingdom will be established in a very short time. After the resurrection of Jesus and immediately before his ascension,

> They therefore, when they were come together, asked him, saying, Lord, dost thou at this time restore the kingdom to Israel? And he said unto them, It is not for you to know times and seasons, which the Father hath set within his own authority. But ye shall receive power, when the Holy Spirit is come upon you: and ye shall be my witnesses both in Jerusalem, and in all Judaea and Samaria, and unto the uttermost part of the earth. (Acts i. 6-8.)

The apostles did not yet understand the doctrine of the kingdom or the time of its establishment. They could not understand these things until they received the endowment of the Holy Spirit, who alone could interpret the predictions by the events. For this they were to wait in Jerusalem, and then, when they had been endowed with the Spirit, they would understand the doctrine of the Messiah and his kingdom; at least so far as to begin their apostolic ministry. Thus the establishment of the kingdom of God is finally referred by Jesus definitely to the Pentecostal gift of the Holy Spirit.

---

[1] See p. 229.

# CHAPTER VII.

### THE MESSIAH OF JOHN.

THE Gospel of John gives us a Messianic ideal that is beyond the conceptions of the synoptic evangelists, and which may be summed up under the title, the *Messiah from heaven*. We have already studied those few Messianic passages of John which are parallel with the synoptists. But the great body of the Gospel of John stands apart by itself as unique.[1] The conception of the Messiah from heaven is more speculative and theological than any of the conceptions given in the synoptists. There is little preparation for it in them or in the prophecy of the Old Testament. There are indeed more parallels with it in the pseudepigrapha.

### THE MESSIAH IN GLORY.

§ 56. *Jesus accepts the recognition of his Messiahship by his disciples, but declines to exercise his royal authority during his earthly ministry. He predicts a second Advent when he will be seen surrounded by angels and enthroned in glory.*

Jesus was recognized as the Messianic king by his

---

[1] This chapter abstains from using the Prologue of the Gospel of John and also several other portions which clearly give the Messianic idea of John rather than of Jesus. These passages will be considered in the volume, *The Messiah of the Apostles*, now in press and soon to be published.

disciples, according to the synoptists, on many occasions during the progress of his ministry. The transfiguration, however, is the occasion on which that recognition first becomes clear and definite. The Gospel of John represents the earlier groups of the apostles as hearing the testimony of the Baptist, and following that testimony in the recognition of Jesus as the Messiah. Jesus accepts their testimony and their recognition. From the beginning, therefore, in the most intimate circle of the apostles, according to John, there was the understanding between the Master and his disciples that he was the Messianic king.

One of the two that heard John *speak*, and followed him, was Andrew, Simon Peter's brother. He findeth first his own brother Simon, and saith unto him, We have found the Messiah (which is, being interpreted, Christ). He brought him unto Jesus. Jesus looked upon him, and said, Thou art Simon the son of John: thou shalt be called Cephas (which is, by interpretation, Peter). On the morrow he was minded to go forth into Galilee, and he findeth Philip: and Jesus saith unto him, Follow me. Now Philip was from Bethsaida, of the city of Andrew and Peter. Philip findeth Nathanael, and saith unto him, We have found him, of whom Moses in the law, and the prophets, did write, Jesus of Nazareth, the son of Joseph. And Nathanael said unto him, Can any good thing come out of Nazareth? Philip saith unto him, Come and see. Jesus saw Nathanael coming to him, and saith of him, Behold, an Israelite indeed, in whom is no guile! Nathanael saith unto him, Whence knowest thou me? Jesus answered and said unto him, Before Philip called thee, when thou wast under the fig tree, I saw thee. Nathanael answered him, Rabbi, thou art the Son of God; thou art King of Israel. Jesus answered and said unto him, Because I said unto thee, I saw thee underneath the fig tree, believest thou? thou shalt see greater things than these. And he saith unto him, Verily, verily, I say unto you, Ye shall see the heaven opened, and the angels of God ascending and descending upon the Son of Man. (John i. 40–51.)

In the last verse Jesus gives a prediction to Nathanael. He accepts his recognition that he is the Messianic king, the Son of God, of the Davidic promise. But he points him to the future for the enthronement. The Messiah has come, not as an enthroned king, but as a king whose enthronement is in prospect. As David was anointed and solemnly set apart to a kingdom whose throne he was to obtain only after a period full of uncertainties, perils, and sufferings, so was it to be with his son the Messiah. The enthronement, however, is not conceived after the manner of the kingdoms of the world, or even after the model of the kingdom of David, of the history and prophecy of the Old Testament. The ministers of the Messiah's throne are the angels who ascend and descend from heaven to wait upon him. Thus, at the outset, in the first of his predictions, according to John, the Messiah's throne is a heavenly throne encompassed by ministering angels.

### THE SIGN OF THE NEW TEMPLE.

§ 57. *Jesus predicts that the temple will be destroyed and that he will raise it up on the third day.*

Jesus, according to the Gospel of John, begins his public ministry in Jerusalem at the passover feast by a sublime act of cleansing the temple from the traders who were defiling its courts. This event is given also by the synoptists, but is placed by them at the last passover of Jesus. They know of only this one passover feast of Jesus during his ministry, and it is thought by Weiss, Beyschlag and others, that they, therefore, all depending on the original Mark, give it there; but that it really belongs where John has placed it, at the beginning of the ministry. And yet it is so appropriate to the course of events in its place in the synoptists that many critics suppose that John has given it in the wrong place. It is improbable that Jesus would have repeated the act. But we may leave this question undecided, for the evangelist John alone gives the prophetic words which concern us here. The importance of this act of Jesus, whenever precisely it occurred, is clear from the fact that these prophetic words were cited against him in a perverted form by false witnesses at his trial before the Sanhedrin. The simplicity of the sign, the lack of explanation at the time, and the fact that neither his disciples nor the Pharisees could possibly have understood its meaning at its utterance, favor the opinion that this is the first of the signs that set forth the death and resurrection of Jesus.

> The Jews therefore answered and said unto him, What sign shewest thou unto us, seeing that thou doest these things? Jesus answered and said unto them, Destroy this temple, and in three days I will raise it up. The Jews therefore said, Forty and six years was this temple in building, and wilt thou raise it up in three days? But he spake of the temple of his body. When therefore he was raised from the dead, his disciples remembered that he spake this; and they believed the scripture, and the word which Jesus had said. (John ii. 18-22.)

In this grand scene in which Jesus displays the wrath of the Messiah against the spoilers of the temple, the disciples aptly see the zealous servant of the Psalter.[1] The Jews demand of him a sign of his Messianic authority. What they want is some sign from heaven. But he declines to give them such a sign at present. He points them forward to his resurrection as the true Messianic sign. He veils it in a symbol which they could not understand until the event itself had transpired. He

---

[1] Psalm lxix. 9. See Briggs, *Mess. Proph.*, p. 330 *seq.*

represents himself as the temple of God, and challenges them to destroy the temple, predicting that in three days he will raise it up. The people thought that he referred to the temple buildings of Jerusalem, and it was not until his resurrection that the apostles understood that he spake of himself. In this symbol of the temple we have veiled one of the most important phases of the Messianic idea of the Old Testament.[1] Jesus was the true temple of God, of which the temple at Jerusalem was a shadow. The true temple would be rejected by those who glorified the shadow. But it would be raised up again with the resurrection of Jesus and ever after remain the temple of God.

### THE KINGDOM OF THE HEAVEN-BORN.

§ 58. *The kingdom of God is not to be seen or entered except by those who have been born from heaven by the divine Spirit and by baptism with water.*

In his discourse with Nicodemus Jesus gave a profound utterance with reference to the doctrine of the kingdom of God.

Jesus answered and said unto him, Verily, verily, I say unto thee, Except a man be born from above, he cannot see the kingdom of God. Nicodemus saith unto him, How can a man be born when he is old? Can he enter a second time into his mother's womb, and be born? Jesus answered, Verily, verily, I say unto thee, Except a man be born of water and the Spirit, he cannot enter into the kingdom of God. (John iii. 3-5.)

In our study of the Messianic idea of the synoptists, we have seen that the kingdom of God is, in its initiation, an invisible kingdom, and that it only gradually comes into manifestation.[2] We have seen that in the

---

[1] See Briggs, *Mess. Proph.*, p. 479 *seq.*   [2] See p. 244.

visible kingdom, as it appears in this world, there are tares mingled with the wheat, and bad fish mixed in the same net with the good; and that the separation cannot take place until the judgment divides the kingdom of grace from the kingdom of glory.[1] We have also seen that into the invisible kingdom, the spiritual kingdom, only those who become poor and childlike can enter.[2]

The words of Jesus to Nicodemus set forth this doctrine with still greater profundity. The kingdom of God here is a present kingdom. It is therefore the kingdom of grace that Jesus has in mind. But this kingdom of grace is invisible to the eye of man. It cannot be entered by any human instrumentality. A birth is necessary because it is the entrance upon a new, a higher, a spiritual, a heavenly, an eternal life. Such a life comes from heaven and from God. It is imparted by the divine Spirit. Born of God through the quickening of the Spirit of God, the eye is opened to see the kingdom and the ability is given to enter its gates. The regeneration here would then be only a parallel expression to becoming poor and childlike, in the synoptists.

The difficulty in this passage is in the word "*born of water.*" It is disputed whether this refers to the water of baptism, or whether water is anything more than the Old Testament symbol of the pouring out of the divine Spirit.[3] The oldest and most natural interpretation is to refer the water to the water of baptism. John the Baptist had made this institution the means of preparation for the kingdom of God. Jesus himself and his apostles had all been baptized with water. Jesus in the apostolic commission gives baptism and faith as requirements for salvation.[4]

---

[1] See p. 206.   [2] See p. 101.
[3] See Briggs, *Mess. Proph.*, p. 488; Weiss, *Bib. Theo.*, s. 681.   [4] See p. 229.

As faith and baptism go together in the preaching of the gospel of the kingdom, we would expect that, from the divine side of the initiation into the kingdom, the work of the Holy Spirit and baptism would be associated.[1]

The regeneration of this passage is a double one, by water and by Spirit.[2] Both are necessary in order to enter the kingdom of God, just as faith and baptism are necessary to salvation in accordance with the great commission. Water alone does not regenerate or admit to the kingdom. Such a baptism may admit to the visible kingdom as an external organization, but no more. Bad fish may pass through the waters of baptism as well as good fish. Tares may enjoy the watering of the ministry as well as the wheat. If there be such an identification of baptism by water with baptism by the Spirit, that the water conveys magical grace and works *ex opere operato*, then it may be held that the admission into the kingdom of the Church is made when the ceremony of baptism by water is celebrated, and that the regeneration by the Spirit then takes place. But such an identification is certainly not taught in our passage.

The teaching of Jesus here admits of a doctrine of

---

[1] It is true that this interpretation finds the doctrine of baptismal regeneration in this passage, a doctrine which has become unpopular in British and American theology since the rise of Methodism in the 18th century. On the other hand baptismal regeneration is a doctrine common to all the great Churches of the Reformation as well as to the ancient Churches of Rome and of Greece. It was held by the Puritan divines of the 17th century no less than by the Anglicans. The great Awakening called Methodism with its emphasis upon regeneration in connection with religious Revivals and Awakenings, brought baptismal regeneration into discredit with a large section of Protestants in Great Britain and America. (See Briggs' *American Presbyterianism*, p. 260, and *Whither*, p. 124 *seq*). The doctrine of baptismal regeneration may be held in a variety of forms. Our purpose is not irenic or polemic, but simply and alone to learn the lesson Jesus teaches and to state that form in which the Master taught it.

[2] Holtzmann, *Handcommentar*, iv., s. 52. Wendt (*Lehre Jesu*, ii., s. 402) thinks that the reference to Baptism is an addition of the evangelist.

baptismal regeneration without such an identification. The birth from heaven by the Spirit is necessary in order to enter the kingdom, and no one can enter the kingdom without that. If there can be baptism by water without baptism by the Spirit, then the entrance into the kingdom cannot take place through baptism by water alone. Baptism by the Spirit is essential. But on the other hand baptism by the Spirit is insufficient. Baptism by water is required by Jesus in order to enter the kingdom of God. If the two baptisms may be separated in time and place, then the two baptisms are required at these different times and places. Jesus does not tell us here whether they may be separated or not. That we must learn from other teachings of Holy Scripture or from Christian experience. Theological difficulties arise here which are not contemplated in the passage and are not solved by these words of Jesus. There are many theological speculations possible on the basis of his words, and there is a peril of falling into error on the right and on the left. But the peril from these speculations should not deter us from following Jesus in his teaching that regeneration by baptism is necessary, as well as regeneration by the divine Spirit. We have seen that it has been necessary to distinguish between the invisible and essential kingdom into which only the true disciple and real Christian can enter, and the visible and larger kingdom which is mixed in this world. Regeneration by water admits to the external organization of the visible kingdom. Regeneration by the Spirit admits to the spiritual kingdom itself. It certainly is not in the mind of Jesus here that any one should be a member of the inner kingdom who shall not be a member of the outer kingdom likewise.[1] The members of

---

[1] Vincent, *Word Studies*, ii., pp. 91, 92.

the inner kingdom from the very nature of the case become members of the outer kingdom. Hence regeneration by water ought not to be omitted by them, however unimportant it may be in comparison with regeneration by the Spirit. For baptism by water is necessary for their entrance into the kingdom of God in this world. This sacrament is the one appointed by Jesus for that purpose. It is in his mind here. There is no other lawful mode of entrance into the organization of the kingdom as it exists in this world.[1]

It is not to be doubted that Nicodemus was a godly man of the Old Testament type when Jesus gave him this lesson. He stood on the highest plain of preparation for the Messiah's kingdom ; but he no less than others needed the regeneration both of water and of Spirit, in order to enter the kingdom of the Messiah. It was not the question of salvation in its elementary sense that was raised, but the question of the Messianic kingdom. Though Nicodemus were the best of the Old Testament saints and might enter into salvation in the Old Testament way, he could not enter into the Mes-

---

[1] The introduction of larger questions raises theological difficulties. The question of the redemption of little children, of the heathen, and of others, who for various reasons have not been baptized, must be candidly considered on the basis of these words of Jesus. So far as these classes are concerned, we should bear in mind that Jesus is speaking of his kingdom of grace in this world as an organization of redemption. He is not dealing with the heathen who have had no opportunity for entrance into this kingdom ; or with little children who have died too soon to be baptized ; or with those who for various reasons, partly innocent and partly guilty, have been induced to discredit the use of baptism for children or for adults. According to the teaching of Jesus here, all such have not availed themselves of the regeneration by water and so have not entered into the organization of his kingdom. But this by no means implies that they are beyond the pale of salvation. We should not forget that the Old Testament prophets were saved in the kingdom of God of the Old Testament without the regeneration here spoken of by our Lord. They had neither the baptism by the Holy Spirit which was not given by Jesus until Pentecost, nor the baptism by water which was a sacrament of the New Testament (cf. Acts xix. 1-7).

sianic kingdom and enjoy the Messianic redemption without regeneration by water and Spirit.[1]

### THE EXALTED MESSIAH.

§ 59. *The Son of Man descended from heaven to do the will of the Father in this world. He will be lifted up that he may attract all to him and that they may believe in him. The world will be judged and its prince cast out.*

At the climax of his dialogue with Nicodemus, Jesus said:

---

[1] So it is not a just inference from these words of Jesus that all are excluded from the grace of God who do not have this birth from water. They are excluded from the Messianic kingdom of grace as set up in this world. But the salvation of men in its elementary form is carried on by the grace of God outside the kingdom of the Church. Doubtless all men who enter into the discipline of redemption outside the Church, in wider circles than those of the kingdom of the Messiah set up in this world, eventually enter into the kingdom of the Messiah in order that their redemption may be perfected and that they may abide the Messianic judgment at the close of the gospel age. But all these are left to the rich grace of God and the mercy of the Redeemer, which work even outside the kingdom of grace in constant efforts to bring men into it, and whose activities are not confined to the brief period of human life in this world, but continue in the Middle State between the hour of death and the day of judgment. Those who have begun a life of salvation in this world in its pre-christian sense, as enjoyed by the antediluvians, or the families of the patriarchs, or the devout heathen, or the children of Israel at the different stages of their religious growth prior to the advent of the Messiah, and by those in our times who are in similar stages of advancement, but who have not yet been brought to the Messiah— all therefore outside the kingdom of the baptized, will doubtless be brought to the feet of the Messiah in the Middle State and be there received into his kingdom. The great majority of mankind pass centuries and some live millenniums in the Middle State prior to the judgment of the day of doom. There they will have the opportunities denied them in this life. But all these deductions from the words of Jesus are speculative. The author has stated his own opinion in order to overcome difficulties in the minds of some of his readers, but especially in order to eliminate the teachings of Jesus himself from the many theological speculations which have been founded thereon. The doctrine of regeneration as a dogma of modern Evangelicalism has been extended so as to embrace all who have entered the gateway of redemption, including all infants dying in infancy and unbaptized. This is a doctrine which has truth in it, but it is not the doctrine taught by Jesus in his discourse with Nicodemus.

If I told you earthly things, and ye believe not, how shall ye believe, if I tell you heavenly things? And no man hath ascended into heaven, but he that descended out of heaven, *even* the Son of Man. And as Moses lifted up the serpent in the wilderness, even so must the Son of Man be lifted up: that whosoever believeth may in him have eternal life. (iii. 12-15.)

Jesus here teaches that he descended from a life of pre-existence in heaven with the Father into the world. But he is not to remain in the world. He is to be lifted up, or exalted.[1] This exaltation is in order that he may become an object of faith to men and that they may thereby find in him a Saviour. The manner of this lifting up is described here by the simile of the lifting up of the brazen serpent in the wilderness. It is usually supposed that this refers to the elevation of Jesus on the cross, and that it is faith in the Messiah hanging on the cross that is here taught. This is a mistaken interpretation, for there is nothing in the context to indicate any reference whatever to the crucifixion. The only thing in the story of the brazen serpent to suggest the crucifixion, is the pole upon which the serpent was lifted; but it is noteworthy that this pole is not mentioned at all here in the words of Jesus, showing that he was not thinking of the pole of the cross. The reference to the brazen serpent brings into prominence two things: (1) the elevation or exaltation of the Messiah as Saviour, and (2) the faith of those who would be saved. The exaltation that Jesus had in mind was rather his exaltation as the Messianic servant in accordance with the prediction of the great prophet of the exile.

> Behold, my servant will prosper,
> He will be lifted up and be exalted and be very high.[2]
> (Is. lii. 13-15.)

---

[1] ὑψωθῆναι.    [2] See Briggs, *Mess. Proph.*, p. 357 *seq.*

The exaltation of the servant implied his previous humiliation, but the humiliation was not the exaltation. By the current interpretation of these words of Jesus, the humiliation of Jesus on the cross is substituted for his exaltation after the endurance of the cross and the shame.[1]

Jesus was thinking in the previous context of his descent from heaven and accordingly here of his exaltation thither after the accomplishment of his earthly work, in accordance with the constant representations of the Gospel of John. As the exalted and living Messiah, he is the Saviour, who having accomplished his earthly work in the redemption of men, undertakes his heavenly work of mediation, and imparts life and righteousness to all who believe in him.[2]

This thought of the exaltation of the Messiah appears again in the words of Jesus at a later period:

He said therefore again unto them, I go away, and ye shall seek me, and shall die in your sin: whither I go, ye cannot come. The Jews therefore said, Will he kill himself, that he saith, Whither I go, ye cannot come? And he said unto them, Ye are from beneath; I am from above: ye are of this world; I am not of this world. I said therefore unto you, that ye shall die in your sins: for except ye believe that I am *he*, ye shall die in your sins. They said therefore unto him, Who art thou? Jesus said unto them, Even that which I have also spoken unto you from the beginning. I have many things to speak and to judge concerning you: howbeit he that sent me is true; and the things

---

[1] It is true that faith in the crucified Saviour is saving faith according to Christian doctrine; but it is not faith in the Messiah hanging dead on the cross that redeems us, it is faith in the living Christ who was once crucified, but who is now enthroned; the Lamb that was slain, but now liveth forevermore; the Messiah who once descended the path of humiliation as servant to the cross and to the abode of the dead, but who was exalted by his resurrection, ascension, and enthronement at God's right hand.

[2] See Beyschlag, *Neutest. Theologie*, i., s. 271; Wendt, *Lehre Jesu*, s. 596.

which I heard from him, these speak I unto the world. They perceived not that he spake to them of the Father. Jesus therefore said, When ye have lifted up the Son of Man, then shall ye know that I am *he* and *that* I do nothing of myself, but as the Father taught me, I speak these things. (John viii. 21–28.)

This passage also teaches the descent of the Messiah from heaven and his departure again from this world. This departure, the Jews who heard him understood to be by his death. Jesus also teaches the same, and in this respect this passage is in advance of the one we have just considered. But the death is here only conceived as the transition to that which is beyond death. His death is really an exaltation, because it brings on the exaltation that follows, in the resurrection, ascension, enthronement, and the Messianic judgment. His hearers, the Jews, will have a hand in this exaltation. They will put him to death; but when they think they are degrading him and humiliating him to the last degree, they are really bringing on that crisis which results in his enthronement. As in the previous passage the exaltation of the Messiah was in order that he might be the Saviour of all who believed on him, so in this passage the exaltation is in order that it may convince the Jews of his Messiahship.

There is a third passage in which this prediction of his exaltation is still further advanced:

Jesus answered and said, This voice hath not come for my sake, but for your sakes. Now is the judgment of this world: now shall the prince of this world be cast out. And I, if I be lifted up from the earth, will draw all men unto myself. But this he said, signifying by what manner of death he should die. The multitude therefore answered him, We have heard out of the law that the Messiah abideth forever: and how sayest thou, The Son of Man must be lifted up? who is this Son of Man?

Jesus therefore said unto them, Yet a little while is the light among you. Walk while ye have the light, that darkness overtake you not: and he that walketh in the darkness knoweth not whither he goeth. While ye have the light, believe on the light, that ye may become sons of light. (John xii. 30-36.)

Jesus, contemplating his glory as announced from heaven by the theophanic voice, also sees the judgment that is connected therewith. This is a judgment of the world and of Satan the prince of the world. Jesus sees Satan cast out, as, in his discourse in Luke, he had seen him hurled like a thunderbolt from heaven.[1] This is the one side of his Messianic glory, his victory over the world and the devil. But the other side is still more important. The Messiah will become an attracting power, drawing men unto himself. This attraction is to be exerted after he has been lifted up. The lifting up is usually explained as his lifting up on the cross. This interpretation is apparently justified by the comment of the evangelist, that he thus indicated the manner of his death; and it is urged that the attracting power is that of the cross. But this superficial interpretation is not the real one. The apostle by "manner of death" does not mean merely the way in which he would die, but he thus briefly states what was the theme of Jesus, his death and departure thereby to heaven. The context lays stress upon the glorification of the Messiah and not upon his humiliation. The lifting up is here, as in the two previous passages, to the heavenly throne.[2] From his throne in heaven the Messiah will send forth waves of centripetal force which will draw all men to Himself as the centre of all dominion, all redemption, and all judgment.

---

[1] See p. 242.
[2] See Stevens, *Johannine Theology*, p. 181.

There is a progress in these three predictions of the exaltation of the Messiah. In all three the final end of the exaltation is his heavenly throne. In the first there is no hint of the mode of the departure; in the second, death is suggested; and in the third, crucifixion is hinted. The object of the exaltation in the first passage is to be the Saviour of all who believe; in the second, to prove his Messiahship to those who would not believe in him otherwise; in the third, to draw all men to himself, and to judge and cast out the devil.

### UNIVERSAL WORSHIP.

§ 60. *Jesus teaches the Samaritans that he is the Messianic prophet, and that the hour has come in which worship at local sanctuaries will give place to a universal spiritual worship of the Father.*

Jesus, in his discourse with the woman of Samaria, does not, it is true, bring out his heavenly origin and destiny, but he teaches the kindred thought that worship in his dispensation is to be heavenly and universal over against the earthly, local and national worship of the old dispensation.

The woman saith unto him, Sir, I perceive that thou art a prophet. Our fathers worshipped in this mountain; and ye say, that in Jerusalem is the place where men ought to worship. Jesus saith unto her, Woman, believe me, the hour cometh, when neither in this mountain, nor in Jerusalem, shall ye worship the Father. Ye worship that which ye know not: we worship that which we know: for the salvation[1] is from the Jews. But the hour cometh, and now is, when the true worshippers shall wor-

---

[1] ἡ σωτηρία, the salvation, the Messianic salvation predicted in the Old Testament.

ship the Father in spirit and truth: for such doth the Father seek to be his worshippers. God is Spirit: and they that worship him must worship in spirit and truth. The woman saith unto him, I know that Messiah cometh (who is called Christ): when he is come, he will declare unto us all things. Jesus saith unto her, I that speak unto thee am *he*. And upon this came his disciples; and they marvelled that he was speaking with a woman; yet no man said, What seekest thou? or, Why speakest thou with her? So the woman left her waterpot, and went away into the city, and saith to the men, Come, see a man, who told me all things that *ever* I did: can this be the Messiah? (John iv. 19-29.)

The term Messiah is here used by the Samaritan woman and also by Jesus. But it is evident that the conception of the Messianic prophet is in their minds and not that of the king. The Samaritans built their hopes of a Messiah upon the prediction of the prophet greater than Moses.[1] Accordingly they expected that this Messianic prophet would teach them all things. Jesus is the prophet and teacher. And he predicts that the Samaritans will have a share in the worship of the new dispensation. The local worship of Jerusalem, as well as that of Gerizim, will pass away, and a universal worship will take their place, in which Jew and Samaritan and all nations will alike share. This prediction was in the line of the teaching that the prophet greater than Moses was expected to give. At the same time even here Jesus advances the prediction of the great prophet of the exile. The "house of prayer for all nations"[2] has expanded in his mind to a universal worship in spirit and truth.

---

[1] Deut. xviii. 18-22; Briggs, *Mess. Proph.*, p. 110 *seq.*
[2] Isa. lvi. 7; Briggs, *Mess. Proph.*, p. 391.

## THE FATHER'S OWN SON.

*§ 61. Jesus declares that he is the Father's own son, making himself equal with God. He has authority over life and judgment. All who believe in him pass from death into everlasting life. Some will soon hear his quickening voice and rise from the dead. All will rise from the dead when the Son of Man summons them to the universal judgment.*

But Jesus answered them, My Father worketh even until now, and I work. For this cause therefore the Jews sought the more to kill him, because he not only brake the sabbath, but also called God his own Father, making himself equal with God. Jesus therefore answered and said unto them, Verily, verily, I say unto you, The Son can do nothing of himself, but what he seeth the Father doing: for what things soever he doeth, these the Son also doeth in like manner. For the Father loveth the Son, and sheweth him all things that himself doeth: and greater works than these will he shew him, that ye may marvel. For as the Father raiseth the dead and quickeneth them, even so the Son also quickeneth whom he will. For neither doth the Father judge any man, but he hath given all judgment unto the Son; that all may honour the Son, even as they honour the Father. He that honoureth not the Son honoureth not the Father which sent him. Verily, verily, I say unto you, He that heareth my word, and believeth him that sent me, hath eternal life, and cometh not into judgment, but hath passed out of death into life. Verily, verily, I say unto you, The hour cometh, and now is, when the dead shall hear the voice of the Son of God; and they that hear shall live. For as the Father hath life in himself, even so gave he to the Son also to have life in himself: and he gave him authority to execute judgment, because he is a son of man. Marvel not at this: for the hour cometh, in which all that are in the tombs shall hear his voice, and shall come forth; they that have done good, unto the resurrection of life; and they that have done ill, unto the resurrection of judgment. (John v. 17–29.)

The expression "his own Father," implying that

Jesus was the Father's "own son" or that he was "equal with God," was in the eyes of the Pharisees blasphemy and guilt worthy of death.¹ No mere man could use such an expression, or make such a claim of relationship to God. It was something more than saying that he was the Messiah, the son of David, and so the son of God. To say that he was the Messiah was not making himself equal with God; for the Messianic king of the Old Testament has no such prerogatives. Jesus was now saying that there was God the Father and God the Son, and that he as God the Son was equal with God the Father. It is the representation of the evangelist that Jesus claims to be the Son of God in the theological sense, that he is divine, and that the Pharisees regarded him as blasphemous on that account. Only such a divine person could have the attributes

---

¹ Apart from the Prologue, the Gospel of John uses Father, of God as the Father of the Messianic Son from heaven; and only in a single passage, of God as the Father of men. In this latter passage, xx. 17, Jesus says to the woman, "I ascend unto my Father and your Father." Westcott, *Epistles of John*, p. 31, claims iv. 21, 23; v. 45; vi. 45, 46, 65; x. 29, 32; xii. 26; xiv. 6. 8; xv. 16; xvi. 23, 26, 27, for the Fatherhood of men. But there is nothing in the context of any of these passages to constrain us to think of the Fatherhood of men. In several of them the reference to the Son, in the context, suggests the prevailing usage. In others, while it is possible to think of the Fatherhood of men, that mere possibility cannot resist the overwhelming usage of this gospel. ὁ πατήρ is used 79 times of God; ὁ πατήρ μου, 25 times; πάτερ, 9 times; ὁ πατήρ σου, viii. 19; ὁ ζῶν πατήρ, vi. 57; πατὴρ ἴδιος, v. 18. In the synoptic gospels, God's Fatherhood of men seems to come from the Logia chiefly if not entirely. In Mark it is found only in xi. 25, 26, where the use of ὁ ἐν τοῖς οὐρανοῖς suggests the derivation of this passage from Matthew. It is found in Luke, apart from passages parallel with Matthew, only xii. 32, which is also probably from the Logia. But God's Fatherhood of the Messiah is in all the gospels: Mark viii. 38 = Matth. xvi. 27 = Luke ix. 26; Mark xvi. 36; xxvi. 39 = Luke xxii. 42; Matth. xi. 25–27 = Luke x. 21–22; besides in Luke iii. 8, xxii. 29; xxix. 49, and in Matthew with ὁ οὐράνιος xv. 13. xviii. 35; with ὁ ἐν (τοῖς) οὐρανοῖς 7 times and without 7 times. It is evident that the use of "heavenly" and "who (is) in heaven" comes from Matthew and not from Jesus himself; just as Matthew uses kingdom of heaven for the original kingdom of God. See p. 79.

that Jesus now ascribes to himself. He has within him the energy of God. He worketh as the Father worketh. He doeth whatsoever the Father doeth, for the Father hath shown him all things. The Son quickeneth whom he will. He giveth life to men at his discretion. The Father hath given all judgment unto the Son, the Son is to be honored as the Father.[1] This preliminary statement as to the attributes of Jesus as the Son of God is in order to the prediction that follows.

This prediction is in the line of life, resurrection, and judgment. It moves in three sections. The first section predicts the impartation of everlasting life to all who hear the word of the Messiah and believe in God. All such have passed out of death into life. They will no more die. They will not come into judgment. This is a spiritual resurrection imparted by the word of the Messiah to all believers during their physical life in this world. This spiritual resurrection is a parallel to the spiritual regeneration of the discourse with Nicodemus.[2]

The second section predicts that an hour is coming and now is, when the dead will hear the quickening voice of the Son of God and live. The hour coming points to the future and therefore indicates a different resurrection from the spiritual resurrection of the previous section, which was already enjoyed by all who heard the Messiah's word and believed. The additional word "and

---

[1] Some, as Beyschlag and Adeney, claim that Jesus meant to deny equality with God and to assert his subordination to God, when he said: "The Son can do nothing of himself, but what he seeth the Father doing"; but this is rather an explanation of his sonship and of his equality with God. As Holtzmann says, the subordination is only in order to an assertion of equality. He does nothing but what he seeth the Father doing, not simply because he is subordinate to the Father, but because he is in unity with the Father. "The Father loveth the Son and sheweth him all things that himself doeth," and so out of this relation of love and unity all that the Father doeth the Son doeth likewise.

[2] See p. 261.

now is" does not so qualify the previous sentence as to indicate that the coming hour is already a present hour, and so the spiritual resurrection, which is enjoyed in the hour that now is, will be enjoyed also in the coming hour.  That would be rather an insipid repetition of the previous section, which was indeed so plain that it needed no explication.  The "now is" implies the speedy coming of that hour,—indicates that it is at hand.  The voice of the Son of God here is something other than his word of the previous section; it is a voice that is heard, whereas the word is not only heard but excites faith. The voice here is the same as the voice in the next section; it is the voice of command, the authoritative voice calling the dead into life.  Accordingly the dead here are not the spiritually dead, but those who are physically dead.  Those who hear will live, that is a limited number as compared with the "all that are in the tombs" of the next section.  This then is a prediction of a speedy resurrection from the dead, in the near future, of a limited number of persons who are to be favored with hearing the quickening voice of the Messiah.  The meaning of this prediction could not be clear at that time.  But it was a prediction of a resurrection from the dead of certain ones hearing the Messiah's voice before the universal resurrection of the last section.[1]

The third section predicts a universal resurrection of the dead at the ultimate judgment, in which some will rise to life and others to condemnation.  The hour of that resurrection is coming.  It cannot be said of it that it "now is," or that it is at hand.

We have thus a prediction of three resurrections, the

---

[1] It was doubtless the resurrection from Hades at the resurrection of the Messiah.  See Matth. xxvii. 52–53.

first spiritual, the last universal;[1] the intermediate one, distinct from the first and last, and impending, being connected with the resurrection of the Messiah himself.

## THE BREAD FROM HEAVEN.

§ 62. *Jesus came down from the Father as the true bread from heaven. He will give his flesh and blood for the life of the world. He will then ascend where he was before.*

The Gospel of John gives us in Capernaum the same demand for a sign as we have met before in Jerusalem.[2] The time was immediately after the miracle of the Loaves and Fishes, and it is replied to by a discourse based upon that event.

They said therefore unto him, What then doest thou for a sign, that we may see, and believe thee? What workest thou? Our fathers ate the manna in the wilderness; as it is written, He gave them bread out of heaven to eat. (John vi. 30, 31.)

The people were not satisfied with the miracle of the Loaves and Fishes. That was a sign indeed, but it was not a sign equal to the miracles of Moses. They saw in the miracles of Jesus no such great sign as the Messiah ought to present for their acceptance of him. They had been warned by Moses against the miracles of false prophets.[3] Why should they believe that Jesus was the Messiah unless he gave them evidence by signs equal to those of Moses? Jesus takes the story of the giving of the manna here, as he took the symbol of the temple, in Jerusalem, to set before them a sign, which they could

---

[1] This is the first prediction of a universal resurrection in the canonical Scriptures. We have seen it, however, in the Book of Enoch. See p. 28.
[2] See p. 186.
[3] Deut. xiii. 1-5.

not have at present, but which they would see in the near future.[1]

Jesus said unto them, I am the bread of life: he that cometh to me shall not hunger, and he that believeth on me shall never thirst. But I said unto you, that ye have seen me, and yet believe not. All that which the Father giveth me shall come unto me; and him that cometh to me I will in no wise cast out. For I am come down from heaven, not to do mine own will, but the will of him that sent me. And this is the will of him that sent me, that of all that which he hath given me I should lose nothing, but should raise it up at the last day. For this is the will of my Father, that every one that beholdeth the Son, and believeth on him, should have eternal life; and I will raise him up at the last day. The Jews therefore murmured concerning him, because he said, I am the bread which came down out of heaven. And they said, Is not this Jesus, the son of Joseph, whose father and mother we know? how doth he now say, I am come down out of heaven? Jesus answered and said unto them, Murmur not among yourselves. No man can come to me, except the Father which sent me draw him: and I will raise him up in the last day. It is written in the prophets, And they shall all be taught of God. Every one that hath heard from the Father, and hath learned, cometh unto me. Not that any man hath seen the Father, save he which is from God, he hath seen the Father. Verily, verily, I say unto you, He that believeth hath eternal life. I am the bread of life. Your fathers did eat the manna in the wilderness, and they died. This is the bread which cometh down out of heaven, that a man may eat thereof, and not die. I am the living bread which came down out of heaven: if any man eat of this bread, he shall live forever: yea and the bread which I will give is my flesh, for the life of the world. The Jews therefore strove one with another, saying, How can this man give us his flesh to eat? Jesus therefore said unto them, Verily, verily, I say unto you, Except ye eat the flesh of the Son of Man and drink his blood, ye have not life in yourselves. He that eateth my flesh and drinketh my blood hath eternal life; and I will raise him up at the last day. For my flesh is meat indeed, and

---

[1] See p. 259.

my blood is drink indeed. He that eateth my flesh and drinketh my blood abideth in me, and I in him. As the living Father sent me, and I live because of the Father; so he that eateth me, he also shall live because of me. This is the bread which came down out of heaven: not as the fathers did eat, and died: he that eateth this bread shall live forever. These things said he in the synagogue, as he taught in Capernaum. Many therefore of his disciples, when they heard *this*, said, This is a hard saying; who can hear it? But Jesus knowing in himself that his disciples murmured at this, said unto them, Doth this cause you to stumble? *What* then if ye should behold the Son of Man ascending where he was before? It is the spirit that quickeneth; the flesh profiteth nothing: the words that I have spoken unto you are spirit, and are life. (John vi. 35-63.)

In the previous discourse Jesus said that his voice had the power to quicken and raise from the dead. Here he presents himself at first under the form of bread and afterwards under the form of flesh and blood. He imparts life to all who feed upon him. His word is spirit and is life, because it emanates from him who is the source of spirit and life. There is no other spiritual life than that which is imparted by the Messiah from heaven. The life that he imparts is everlasting life, and it involves the resurrection unto life of the day of judgment. The nourishment that he imparts is everlasting nourishment; for it removes the pangs of hunger once for all and forever, and leaves only an appetite which it everlastingly feeds. The Messiah came from heaven to the earth, but he is not to remain on the earth. He is going to ascend to heaven where he was before.[1] His

---

[1] Beyschlag (*Neutestament. Theologie*, i. s. 348) claims that this passage does not teach the pre-existence of the Messiah in any other sense than in the line of the development we have met in the Apocalypses of Daniel and Enoch (see pp. 26 *seq.*), "the everlasting archetypal man of God" (s. 249), who "returns to the heart of God" (s. 255). But this does not afford a proper antithesis. The Son of Man ascends where he was before. If he was before merely the archetypal

earthly mission is bounded by this coming and this going. It is a mission from his heavenly life; it is an episode in his heavenly ministry, a work which he undertook to complete in a brief period of earthly life.

We notice here the same brief and veiled reference to the death of the Messiah that we have seen in the passages already considered.[1] The representation of the Messiah as the heavenly bread passes over into the symbol that he is the victim slain for sacrifice. His flesh is the meat that gives life. To this Jesus adds a statement which must have shocked his Jewish hearers to the utmost, namely: that his blood would be the drink of life. It was forbidden to the Jews to eat or drink the blood even of a sacrificial victim,[2] and yet Jesus does not hesitate to tell the Jews that they must drink his blood. It was simply impossible at that time for them to understand him, and he certainly did not mean that they should understand him. How could they reconcile themselves to such a flagrant violation of the Levitical law? He gave them a sign that would be convincing in the future when they saw it. It is clear, however, that he predicts his death as a sacrificial victim. His hearers might have recalled the trespass offering of the prophetic servant of the second Isaiah,[3] and his apostles might have remembered the words of John the Baptist: "*Behold, the Lamb of God, which taketh away the sin of the world.*"[4]

---

man in the plan of God does he return to where he was before, if after being a real man he ascends to the heart of God? It is not merely a difference between being "a second God alongside of God the Father," and "being in the heart of God." It is evident that Beyschlag uses "heart of God" in two different senses, the one real, the other ideal. The antithesis demands that the pre-existence and post-existence should be either both real or both ideal.

[1] See pp. 186, 277.
[2] Lev. xvii. 10–12.
[3] Isa. liii. 10.
[4] John i. 29. See p. 69.

These were predictions that the Messiah would be a sacrificial victim. This eating and drinking can only be referred to the sacrament of the Lord's supper, in which as here bread and flesh and blood are all combined. The sacrament of the body and blood of the Messiah is here involved just as baptism with water is implied in the discourse with Nicodemus.[1]

### RIVERS OF LIVING WATER.

§ 63. *The Messiah in a little while will go to the Father who sent him. He will impart the Spirit to those who believe on him, and they will become fountains of living water.*

At the feast of Tabernacles, Jesus came into conflict with the Pharisees, who used every effort to prevent the people from believing that he was the Messiah. In the midst of this conflict Jesus uttered several sayings which are pregnant with Messianic meaning:

(1) Yet a little while am I with you, and I go unto him that sent me. Ye shall seek me, and shall not find me: and where I am, ye cannot come. (vii. 33, 34.)

The Jews thought that it was Jesus' purpose to go into other parts of the world and teach the Hellenists. They did not understand that he meant that he was soon to leave the earth and go to the Father in heaven. That this was his meaning is clear from the discourses already considered as well as from those that follow.

(2) If any man thirst, let him come unto me, and drink. He that

---

[1] See p. 262. The many objections to this interpretation (See Stevens, *Johannine Theology*, p. 60) are due to a neglect of the predictive element in this discourse and a failure to see that Jesus is giving a symbol of the Messianic sign: his death and resurrection.

believeth on me, as the scripture hath said, out of his belly shall flow rivers of living water. (vii. 37, 38.)

The evangelist explains this enigmatical sentence. The Messiah referred to the Spirit that was to be given after he was glorified, that is, after he had ascended to heaven. This is the gift of the Spirit at Pentecost now first predicted in the Gospel of John.[1]

When the Spirit came, the believing disciples would become fountains of life to others. As the word of Jesus had imparted life to them, so the word of the Gospel in their hearts would issue forth under the power of the Holy Spirit in rivers of life, to quicken all who believed the word of the Messiah in their preaching of his Gospel.

### THE LIGHT OF THE WORLD.

§ 64. *Jesus is the light of the world. He was prior to Abraham with the Father. He came into the world to give the light of life to all his followers. His word will decide in the last day.*

The debate with the Pharisees continues from the seventh chapter through the eighth chapter. We have the same kind of pregnant sentences as those already considered. We shall consider only those that are Messianic.

I am the light of the world: he that followeth me shall not walk in the darkness, but shall have the light of life. (viii. 12.)

As the Messiah was the bread of life and the water of life, so also he is the light of life. His word quickens, nourishes, and enlightens all who believe in him, all who follow him.

---

[1] We have seen similar predictions in the synoptists. See pp. 67, 254.

There are several sayings which reiterate what has already been said with regard to the power of the words of Jesus.

If ye abide in my word, ye are truly my disciples; and ye shall know the truth, and the truth shall make you free. (31, 32.)

If therefore the Son shall make you free, ye shall be free indeed. (36.)

If God were your Father, ye would love me: for I came forth and am come from God; for neither have I come of myself, but he sent me. (42.)

If a man keep my word, he shall never see death. (51.)

The conflict culminates in these striking words of Jesus:

> Before Abraham was born, I am. (58.)

These words seem to the Jews nothing but blasphemy. This is a more striking statement of that which had already been taught by Jesus in more general terms, in the doctrine of the bread from heaven and of the Father's own Son. Jesus was with the Father in heaven before Abraham was born, as the Father's own Son, and he had only recently come into the world. The pre-existence of Jesus as the Son of God is here more decidedly and strongly stated than in any previous passage. This cannot be resolved into an ideal pre-existence such as we have seen in the Book of Enoch,[1] but is a real pre-existence of Jesus himself prior to the birth of Abraham.[2]

---

[1] See p. 27.
[2] Wendt denies that this passage teaches any more than an ideal pre-existence of Jesus. He argues that his existence before the time of Abraham must be thought of in the same way as his existence at the time of Abraham. Abraham rejoiced to see the day of the Messiah, that is in the vision of faith in the Messianic promises wrapped up in the birth of Isaac; not in real existence, but in ideal existence. So the Messiah himself was pre-existent in the thought, decree, and promise of God not only when Abraham saw his day, but long prior to Abraham. (*Lehre Jesu*, ii., s. 468 *seq.*) This plausible argument is not valid, for Abraham did not rejoice because he saw the ideal of the Messianic redemption

The doctrine of judgment by the words of the Messiah is also taught in the closing section of a later discourse, reminding us of the condemnation by the Gospel, in the Great Commission.[1]

> And Jesus cried and said, He that believeth on me, believeth not on me, but on him that sent me. And he that beholdeth me beholdeth him that sent me. I am come a light into the world, that whosoever believeth on me may not abide in the darkness. And if any man hear my sayings, and keep them not, I judge him not: for I came not to judge the world, but to save the world. He that rejecteth me, and receiveth not my sayings, hath one that judgeth him: the word that I spake, the same shall judge him in the last day. (John xii. 44-48.)

Jesus came into the world to save the world, not to judge it. He returns to heaven to the Father, after completing his work of salvation in the world, in order to continue his work of salvation from his heavenly throne. The judgment is attached to the word of the Gospel. But it will not take effect until the last day, the Day of judgment.[2]

### THE GOOD SHEPHERD.

§ 65. *Jesus is the good shepherd, who will lay down his life for the sheep and take it again. The high priest predicts that Jesus must die for the nation.*

There are two passages which may be best considered

---

latent in the mind of God, or veiled in his promises, but because in the prophetic vision he saw that ideal in the reality of history. The real existence in history of the Messiah was what gave joy to Abraham though he foresaw it centuries before wrapped up in the ideal. It was a real pre-existence before Abraham, which is the natural antithesis. It is a claim of a divine attribute, as Holtzmann states. (*Handcommentar zum Neuen Testament*, iv., s. 121.) The ideal pre-existence of the Messiah was a familiar idea to Judaism. If Jesus had asserted that, he would not have shocked his hearers. He said that of himself which excited their indignation to the utmost against him as a blasphemer. They instinctively took up stones to cast at him. See also Stevens, *Johannine Theology*, p. 121.   [1] See p. 228.   See p. 273.

under this head. The first of these is the discourse recorded in John, in which Jesus presents himself as the Good Shepherd.

> I am the good shepherd: the good shepherd layeth down his life for the sheep. He that is a hireling, and not a shepherd, whose own the sheep are not, beholdeth the wolf coming, and leaveth the sheep, and fleeth, and the wolf snatcheth them, and scattereth *them: he fleeth* because he is a hireling, and careth not for the sheep. I am the good shepherd; and I know mine own, and mine own know me, even as the Father knoweth me, and I know the Father; and I lay down my life for the sheep. And other sheep I have, which are not of this fold: them also I must bring, and they shall hear my voice; and they shall become one flock, one shepherd. Therefore doth the Father love me, because I lay down my life, that I may take it again. No one taketh it away from me, but I lay it down of myself. I have power to lay it down, and I have power to take it again. This commandment received I from my Father. (John x. 11-18.)

This prediction of the death and resurrection of Jesus seems to have been on the occasion of his rejection by the synagogue in connection with the miracle of the man born blind. Jesus represents himself as the good Shepherd, who cares for the sheep and protects them even at the cost of his own life. He is to lay down his life for the flock. But his death will be an unique one, for he has authority from the Father to take his life again after he has laid it down. The doctrine of death and resurrection is here taught as in the previous passages; only the thought is brought out that the Messiah's death is a death for the sake of his sheep, and his living again is also on their behalf, in order to unite with his present flock other sheep so as to make one flock under one shepherd.

Jesus here conceives of all the redeemed from all nations united with the little flock he himself has gathered out of Israel into one great flock. As there is but one shepherd, there can be but one flock. The flock may be divided and scattered by wicked men—Jesus does not think of that episode here—but the flock always remains one to the Shepherd, and eventually its divisions will disappear and the scattered sheep be gathered together.

The ideal of the Messiah here frowns upon a divided and distracted Christianity. Any division in the flock is sinful, any schism involves wrong and guilt. The sin and the guilt doubtless in most cases rest upon the under-shepherds rather than on the sheep, or are the result of the ambition, jealousy, contention, and tyranny of the bell-wethers of the flock; but the wrong of division should be undone as soon as possible. The sheep take upon themselves the guilt, if they perpetuate the divisions and schism after the guilty shepherds have been removed and the occasions of separation cease to exist. The impulses for unity streaming upon us from the ideal of the one flock of Jesus, and attracting us to the one shepherd enthroned in glory, ought to overcome all the weaker and merely human and temporary tendencies to division.

The same doctrine of the vicarious death of the Messiah is brought out in a more definite form in a prediction of the high priest Caiaphas, which is reported only in the Gospel of John.

> The chief priests therefore and the Pharisees gathered a sanhedrin, and said, What do we? for this man doeth many signs. If we let him thus alone, all men will believe on him: and the Romans will come and take away both our place and our nation. But a certain one of them, Caiaphas, being high priest that year, said unto them, Ye know nothing at all, nor do ye take account that it is expedient for you that one man should die for the people, and that the whole nation perish not. Now this he said not of himself: but being high priest that year, he prophesied that

Jesus should die for the nation; and not for the nation only, but that he might also gather together into one the children of God that are scattered abroad. So from that day forth they took counsel that they might put him to death. (John xi. 47-53.)

## THE SEED AND THE FRUIT.

§ 66. *Jesus taught his disciples that the hour had come for the Messiah to die. He would be buried as seed and then rise again and bear the fruit of glory. His disciples were to follow him in death and resurrection. The consecration of the Messiah to his work is recognized by a theophanic voice declaring him to be the Son of God and the heir of glory.*

The Gospel of John gives no account of the transfiguration, but reports a theophany in the temple, in the last week of the ministry of Jesus, that is not reported by the synoptists.

Some Greeks are anxious to see Jesus. This brings before the mind of the Messiah the glory and fruitfulness of his mission, and he says:

The hour is come, that the Son of Man should be glorified. Verily, verily, I say unto you, Except a grain of wheat fall into the earth and die, it abideth by itself alone; but if it die, it beareth much fruit. He that loveth his life loseth it; and he that hateth his life in this world shall keep it unto life eternal. If any man serve me, let him follow me; and where I am, there shall also my servant be: if any man serve me, him will the Father honor. Now is my soul troubled; and what shall I say? Father, save me from this hour. But for this cause came I unto this hour. Father, glorify thy name. There came therefore a voice out of heaven, *saying*, I have both glorified it, and will glorify it again. (xii. 23-28.)

The Messiah compares himself to a grain of wheat. As this grain is sown in order to die and then be quickened and become fruitful, so the Messiah is to be sown in the ground. He is to die and be buried in the earth. He is then to spring up in resurrection and have an abundant harvest of redeemed men. The fruit of his ministry, the glory of his reward, can come only after his death and his burial. The disciples are to follow him in this death and resurrection, and only thereby will they attain to his presence and glory. The Messiah now reaches the height of his earthly recognition by God in theophany. He afterwards descends rapidly into the valley of humiliation and rejection. His human nature shrinks from the hour of death. But he has made that hour his goal, and goes forward bravely towards it, assured by the theophanic voice that it leads to the highest degree of glory.

### THE PARACLETE.

*§ 67. Jesus is shortly to go away to the Father to be glorified with the glory he had before the creation of the world. He will prepare abodes in the heavenly temple for his disciples. He will come to take them to himself. He will shortly come again in the Paraclete, to dwell with them for ever. The Holy Spirit will convict the world of the sin of unbelief and guide the disciples into all the truth. They will be persecuted unto death, but the presence of the Messiah and his Spirit will give them joy.*

As the synoptists gave the greater Apocalypse of Jesus on the Mount of Olives shortly before the passion, so the Gospel of John gives a still longer discourse on the evening of the passion. But these discourses are so different in form and character that they have little in common. They both point to times of persecution and distress subsequent to the death of the Messiah, and present Messianic ideals of the Advent of the Messiah, of the salvation of the disciples, and of the future glory of the Messiah in which the disciples will share; but in other respects they move in different lines of the Messianic idea. This discourse with its interrupting questions begins after the departure of Judas. It is esoteric to the eleven faithful apostles. We shall consider it in sections, limiting ourselves to the Messianic material.

(1) When therefore he was gone out, Jesus saith, Now is the Son of Man glorified, and God is glorified in him; and God shall glorify him in himself, and straightway shall he glorify him. Little children, yet a little while I am with you. Ye shall seek me: and as I said unto the Jews, Whither I go, ye cannot come; so now I say unto you. A new commandment I give unto you, that ye love one another; even as I have loved you, that ye also love one another. By this shall all men know that ye are my disciples, if ye have love one to another. Simon Peter saith unto him, Lord, whither goest thou? Jesus answered, Whither I go, thou canst not follow me now; but thou shalt follow afterwards. Peter saith unto him, Lord, why cannot I follow thee even now? I will lay down my life for thee. Jesus answereth, Wilt thou lay down thy life for me? Verily, verily, I say unto thee, The cock shall not crow, till thou hast denied me thrice. (John xiii. 31–38.)

Jesus looks forward to his impending glorification. A little while only will the Son of Man remain with his apostles. He is about to depart to the Father; thither they cannot follow him at present, but they will follow him afterwards. He is about to die and to be glorified. They will also die after a period of service and follow him into the presence of the Father in heaven. He leaves behind him his law of love, as the supreme law for his disciples and the badge of discipleship. This law is a new law, in that it is a law which shines upon them from the person of the Messiah himself. His love to them is the law of their love to one another.

(2) Let not your heart be troubled: believe in God, believe also in me. In my Father's house are many abiding places; if it were not so, I would have told you; for I go to prepare a place for you. And if I go and prepare a place for you, I come again, and will receive you unto myself; that where I am, *there* ye may be also. And whither I go, ye know the way. Thomas saith unto him, Lord, we know not whither thou goest; how know we the way? Jesus saith unto him, I am the way, and the truth, and the life: no one cometh unto the Father, but by me. If ye had known me, ye would have known my Father also: from henceforth ye know him, and have seen him. Philip saith unto him, Lord, shew us the Father, and it sufficeth us. Jesus saith unto him, Have I been so long time with you, and dost thou not know me, Philip? he that hath seen me hath seen the Father; how sayest thou, Shew us the Father? Believest thou not that I am in the Father, and the Father in me? The words that I say unto you I speak not from myself: but the Father abiding in me doeth his works. Believe me that I am in the Father, and the Father in me: or else believe me for the very works' sake. Verily, verily, I say unto you, He that believeth on me, the works that I do shall he do also; and greater *works* than these shall he do; because I go unto the Father. And whatsoever ye shall ask in my name, that will I do, that the Father may be glorified in the Son. If ye shall ask any thing in my name, that will I do. If ye love me, ye will keep my commandments. (John xiv. 1–15.)

The separation of the apostles from their Master for a little season of service should not trouble them. For he goes to the Father's house, the temple in heaven to be glorified. There he will be in his own home and seat of dominion, and there he will prepare places for them. When the time comes for them to follow him by death and to depart out of this earthly life, they will not descend to Sheol as did the ancient worthies under the Old Testament; they will not even go to the Paradise, the Abraham's bosom of the Middle State; they will ascend to heaven, they will come into this heavenly temple: they will not only find places prepared for them therein, but Jesus himself will come to them to take them to himself. The majority of interpreters rightly see in this promise an advent of the Messiah to the faithful disciple at death. This then is the promise of a spiritual, a dynamic advent of the Messiah such as the dynamic, spiritual advent promised in the passages of the synoptists relating to congregational discipline and to the ministry of the apostles.[1]

The Messiah is himself the only way unto the Father. Faith in him is not to lose its efficacy during his absence in heaven. It will rather gain in power, because the Messiah, enthroned with the Father in heaven, will endow the apostles, in their ministry on earth, with the authority of miracle-working, and will respond to all their petitions, and so they will excel even the Messiah in their wondrous works. Love to the Messiah will be fruitful within them in obedience and in loving ministry.

(3) And I will pray the Father, and he shall give you another Paraclete, that he may be with you for ever, *even* the Spirit of truth: whom the world cannot receive; for it beholdeth him not, neither knoweth him: ye know him; for he abideth with you, and shall be in you. I will not leave you desolate: I come unto you. Yet a little while, and the world beholdeth me no more; but ye behold me: because I live, ye shall live also. In that day ye shall know that I am in my Father, and ye in me, and I in you. He that hath my commandments, and keepeth them, he it is that loveth me: and he that loveth me shall be loved of my Father, and I will love him, and will manifest myself unto him. Judas [not Iscariot] saith unto him, Lord, what is come to pass that thou wilt manifest thyself unto us, and not unto the world? Jesus answered and said unto him, If a man

---

[1] See pp. 195, 231.

love me, he will keep my word: and my Father will love him and we will come unto him, and make our abode with him. He that loveth me not, keepeth not my words: and the word which ye hear is not mine, but the Father's, who sent me.

These things have I spoken unto you, while *yet* abiding with you. But the Paraclete, *even* the Holy Spirit, whom the Father will send in my name, he shall teach you all things, and bring to your remembrance all that I said unto you. Peace I leave with you; my peace I give unto you: not as the world giveth, give I unto you. Let not your heart be troubled, neither let it be fearful. Ye heard how I said to you, I go away, and I come unto you. If ye loved me, ye would have rejoiced, because I go unto the Father: for the Father is greater than I. And now I have told you before it come to pass, that, when it is come to pass, ye may believe. I will no more speak much with you, for the prince of the world cometh: and he hath nothing in me; but that the world may know that I love the Father, and as the Father gave me commandment, even so I do. Arise, let us go hence.

(John xiv. 16–31.)

There will be compensation for the absence of the Messiah. The apostles will have *another Paraclete*, the Spirit of Truth, the Holy Spirit, who will come and abide with them forever. He will teach them all things. He will bring to their remembrance all the instructions of Jesus and explain them. This promise of the advent and guidance of the Holy Spirit is in accordance with the promises already considered.[1] The Paraclete here is not simply a Comforter, as the English Versions render it. The Paraclete is rather an advocate, a counsellor-at-law, a surrogate who espouses the cause of a client, represents him in his suit, is his adviser and his advocate.[2] Such is the Holy Spirit whom Jesus promises to send to his disciples. He is another *Paraclete*, like Jesus him-

---

[1] See pp. 231, 254, 281.
[2] See Vincent, *Word Studies*, ii., p. 243, and Hatch, *Essays in Biblical Greek*, p. 82.

self, who is here conceived as also a *Paraclete*.[1] The Holy Spirit thus continues the work of Jesus. He is the surrogate of the Messiah. He carries on the work of Messianic redemption in the world as the ever-abiding counsellor of the apostles and of their successors in the ministry.

Jesus is to go away to the Father. He will be absent from his disciples and remain in heaven, so far as his visible presence is concerned; but he will grant his spiritual presence in a dynamic advent. He will manifest himself to those who love him and keep his commandments, and will let them know him as present. It is evident that Jesus is speaking in such general and comprehensive terms, that he means something more than his advent in the Christophanies of the Apostolic age. He means that he will come in spiritual presence to the spirits of his disciples. He will grant them the contact of his spirit with their spirits. This contact will be experienced by the spirits of the faithful, who will thus be assured of the real presence of their Messiah.[2]

Jesus promises still more: not only that the Spirit and the Son will come together, but that the Father and the Son will come with the Spirit to the faithful disciples, and will take up their abode with the loving and the obedient. The heavenly Father will come with the Son and the Spirit. The three will come and dwell in the man. This is the promise of the spiritual and dynamic advent and presence of the Father, the Son, and the Spirit, to faithful and loving disciples. We have considered the spiritual presence of the Messiah in another connection, in the assembly of disciples and in the min-

---

[1] See also 1 John ii. 1.
[2] See Stevens, *Johannine Theology*, p. 334.

istry of the apostles.[1]  Here it is granted to the individual in his life of holiness, and it is accompanied with the spiritual presence of the Father and of the Spirit,—a doctrine vastly more profound and comprehensive.

(4.) I am the true vine, and my Father is the husbandman. Every branch in me that beareth not fruit, he taketh it away: and every *branch* that beareth fruit, he cleanseth it, that it may bear more fruit. Already ye are clean because of the word which I have spoken unto you. Abide in me, and I in you. As the branch cannot bear fruit of itself, except it abide in the vine ; so neither can ye, except ye abide in me. I am the vine, ye are the branches: He that abideth in me, and I in him, the same beareth much fruit : for apart from me ye can do nothing. If a man abide not in me, he is cast forth as a branch, and is withered ; and they gather them, and cast them into the fire, and they are burned. If ye abide in me, and my words abide in you, ask whatsoever ye will, and it shall be done unto you. Herein is my Father glorified, that ye bear much fruit ; and *so* shall ye be my disciples. Even as the Father hath loved me, I also have loved you : abide ye in my love. If ye keep my commandments, ye shall abide in my love ; even as I have kept my Father's commandments, and abide in his love. These things have I spoken unto you, that my joy may be in you, and *that* your joy may be made full. This is my commandment, that ye love one another, even as I have loved you. Greater love hath no man than this, that a man lay down his life for his friends. Ye are my friends, if ye do the things which I command you. No longer do I call you servants ; for the servant knoweth not what his lord doeth : but I have called you friends ; for all things that I heard from my Father I have made known unto you. Ye did not choose me, but I chose you, and appointed you, that ye should go and bear fruit, and *that* your fruit should abide : that whatsoever ye shall ask of the Father in my name, he may give it you. These things I command you, that ye may love one another. (John xv. 1–17.)

The allegory of the Vine sets forth the nature of the

---

[1] See pp. 195, 231.

spiritual presence of the Messiah with his disciples. Though he is in heaven enthroned in glory and they are upon the earth, there is vital organic union between them. He is the vine stock in heaven, they are the branches on earth; but the life of the vine descends from the heavenly stock, and pervades all the earthly branches with its divine energy. His disciples are organized into one living body, of which the Messiah in heaven is the life-giving source. Only in virtue of this abiding, vital union will they be able to live as disciples and be fruitful in good works. The bond of union is life, the life of the Messiah, a dynamic, spiritual, all-pervading presence, immanent in all disciples, permanent in all the faithful, dominant in all the living, and exhibiting itself to the world in a love which is fruitful in good works. The love of Jesus to his disciples is their law of life. He made them his friends, laid down his life for them, communicated to them the instruction given him by the Father, and appointed them to a fruitful ministry, by which they are to glorify the Father.

(5) If the world hateth you, ye know that it hath hated me before *it hated* you. If ye were of the world, the world would love its own: but because ye are not of the world, but I chose you out of the world, therefore the world hateth you. Remember the word that I said unto you, A servant is not greater than his lord.[1] If they persecuted me, they will also persecute you; if they kept my word, they will keep yours also. But all these things will they do unto you for my name's sake, because they know not him that sent me. If I had not come and spoken unto them, they had not had sin: but now they have no excuse for their sin. He that hateth me hateth my Father also. If I had not done among them the works which none other did, they had not had sin: but now have they both seen and hated both me and my Father. But *this cometh to pass*, that the word may be fulfilled

---

[1] See p. 196.

that is written in their law, They hated me without a cause.[1] But when the Paraclete is come, whom I will send unto you from the Father, *even* the Spirit of truth, which proceedeth from the Father, he shall bear witness of me: and ye also bear witness, because ye have been with me from the beginning.

These things have I spoken unto you, that ye should not be made to stumble. They shall put you out of the synagogues: yea, the hour cometh, that whosoever killeth you shall think that he offereth service unto God. And these things will they do, because they have not known the Father, nor me. But these things have I spoken unto you, that when their hour is come, ye may remember them, how that I told you. And these things I said not unto you from the beginning, because I was with you.
(John xv. 18–xvi. 4.)

The apostles are to be hated by the world as their master was hated, and persecuted as their master was persecuted. They will be expelled from synagogues, and it will be regarded as a service to God if they are put to death. This warning of persecution we have already considered in connection with several discourses in the Synoptics.[2] But the disciples will have the Paraclete to guide them in their ministry. The Spirit of Truth will witness to them of the Messiah and explain the life, death, and resurrection of Jesus as they could not be explained before the events themselves transpired. The apostles who have been with the Messiah throughout his ministry will bear witness to the world respecting those events which they have witnessed. Jesus warns them of persecutions, and advises them of their guidance by the Spirit in order to prepare them for the events that were now impending.

(6) But now I go unto him that sent me; and none of you asketh me, Whither goest thou? But because I have spoken these things unto you, sorrow hath filled your heart. Nevertheless I

---
[1] Ps. lxix. 4.  [2] See pp. 97, 143, 199.

tell you the truth; It is expedient for you that I go away: for if I go not away, the Paraclete will not come unto you; but if I go, I will send him unto you. And he, when he is come, will convict the world in respect of sin, and of righteousness, and of judgment: of sin, because they believe not on me; of righteousness, because I go to the Father, and ye behold me no more; of judgment, because the prince of this world hath been judged. I have yet many things to say unto you, but ye cannot bear them now. Howbeit when he, the Spirit of truth, is come, he shall guide you into all the truth: for he shall not speak from himself; but what things soever he shall hear, *these* shall he speak: and he shall declare unto you the things that are to come. He shall glorify me: for he shall take of mine, and shall declare *it* unto you. All things whatsoever the Father hath are mine: therefore said I, that he taketh of mine, and shall declare *it* unto you.

(John xvi. 5-15.)

The departure of the Messiah to the Father is best for the disciples. It was necessary that he should go to the Father in order that he might send the Paraclete. They could not have the Paraclete, they could not understand the significance of the life of the Messiah, that life itself would be fruitless, until the ascension and enthronement of the Messiah had completed the work of redemption for which he had left his heavenly abode. After the redemption had been accomplished, and the guilt of men for rejecting the Messiah had been incurred, then the Holy Spirit would be able to work with omnipotent energy for the redemption of the world. The work of the Spirit will be two-fold. On the one side he will work conviction of sin and of righteousness and judgment. The sin of rejecting the Messiah will be made plain when the Messianic sign of the resurrection hath convinced men that Jesus is the Messiah. The righteousness of the Messiah will be displayed after Jesus hath ascended into heaven acceptable to the heavenly Father. The Messianic judgment will be manifest in the judgment and overthrow of Satan in connection with the enthronement of Jesus. On the other side the divine Spirit will guide the disciples into all the truth. This was impossible until the truth had been accomplished in the facts of history by the death resurrection, and ascension of Jesus. But afterwards the Spirit would be able to guide the disciples into all the truth. He would be able to explain these events and the truth involved in them. He would declare unto them those things about the Messiah which could not be declared while he remained present with them in his earthly life. His death, resurrection, and ascension first gave his earthly life its meaning.

(7). A little while, and ye behold me no more; and again a little while, and ye shall see me. *Some* of his disciples therefore said one to another, What is this that he saith unto us, A little while, and ye behold me not; and again a little while, and ye shall see me: and, Because I go to the Father? They said therefore, What is this that he saith, A little while? We know not what he saith. Jesus perceived that they were desirous to ask him, and he said unto them, Do ye inquire among yourselves concerning this, that I said, A little while, and ye behold me not, and again a little while, and ye shall see me? Verily, verily, I say unto you, that ye shall weep and lament, but the world shall rejoice: ye shall be sorrowful, but your sorrow shall be turned into joy. A woman when she is in travail hath sorrow, because her hour is come: but when she is delivered of the child, she remembereth no more the anguish, for the joy that a man is born into the world. And ye therefore now have sorrow: but I will see you again, and your heart shall rejoice, and your joy no one taketh away from you. And in that day ye shall ask me nothing. Verily, verily, I say unto you, If ye shall ask anything of the Father, he will give it you in my name. Hitherto have ye asked nothing in my name: ask, and ye shall receive, that your joy may be made full. (John xvi. 16-24.)

Jesus now goes back to the prediction of his own return

to his disciples. The *little while* of the two clauses must have some sort of proportion. The *little while* of the return cannot therefore refer to the second Advent in the clouds, because that would be entirely out of proportion to the few hours remaining before the departure of Jesus. Moreover, the Gospel of John does not in this discourse refer at all to the second Advent on the clouds.[1] Some refer the return here to the resurrection; but this is impossible because the going away is not the departure of death, but the departure to the Father, which did not take place until the ascension. The departure of this gospel is throughout the departure to the Father. There is no sufficient reason to think of a different usage here. The *little while* before the return seems to be the brief interval after the ascension until the spiritual advent to the apostles on the day of Pentecost.[2] It is the spiritual, dynamic return to which Jesus refers throughout this discourse, a return from heaven in connection with the gift of the Holy Spirit, a spiritual, a dynamic presence with the disciples during their earthly ministry and in their personal sanctification. This presence will give them joy. There will be a little season of sorrow for them and joy for the world; but their sorrow is like the pangs of a woman in childbirth, that will be forgotten when the child is born. In a very short time their sorrow will be turned into joy, when they see the birth of the Messianic age and enjoy the powerful presence of the Messiah, ruling them from his heavenly throne and directing them by his Holy Spirit from his presence chamber in their Reason.

(8). These things have I spoken unto you in parables; the hour cometh, when I shall no more speak unto you in parables, but

---

[1] But see p. 259.  [2] See p 254.

shall tell you plainly of the Father. In that day ye shall ask in my name: and I say not unto you that I will pray the Father for you; for the Father himself loveth you, because ye have loved me, and have believed that I came forth from the Father. I came out from the Father, and am come into the world: again, I leave the world, and go unto the Father. His disciples say, Lo, now speakest thou plainly, and speakest no parable. Now know we that thou knowest all things, and needest not that any man should ask thee : by this we believe that thou camest forth from God. Jesus answered them, Do ye now believe? Behold, the hour cometh, yea, is come, that ye shall be scattered, every man to his own, and shall leave me alone: and *yet* I am not alone, because the Father is with me. These things have I spoken unto you, that in me ye may have peace. In the world ye have tribulation: but be of good cheer; I have overcome the world. (xvi. 25-33.)

During the times, in his instruction of his apostles, which have now come to an end, Jesus had been obliged to speak unto them in parables, which were obscure to them, from the very necessities of the case; but all these obscurities will soon be removed by the coming events. As the Messiah came forth from the Father into the world, so now he leaves the world and goes unto the Father. The apostles will be troubled and they will be scattered abroad, but they should be courageous. The Messiah has overcome the world. Victory is wrapt up in his departure, and his disciples will soon enjoy the victory with him.

(9) These things spake Jesus; and lifting up his eyes to heaven, he said, Father, the hour is come; glorify thy Son, that the Son may glorify thee: even as thou gavest him authority over all flesh, that whatsoever thou hast given him, to them he should give eternal life. And this is the life eternal, that they should know thee the only true God, and him whom thou didst send, *even* Jesus Christ. I glorified thee on the earth, having accomplished the work which thou hast given me to do. And now, O

Father, glorify thou me with thine own self with the glory which I had with thee before the world was. I manifested thy name unto the men whom thou gavest me out of the world: thine they were, and thou gavest them to me; and they have kept thy word. Now they know that all things whatsoever thou hast given me are from thee: for the words which thou gavest me I have given unto them, and they received *them*, and knew of a truth that I came forth from thee, and they believed that thou didst send me. I pray for them: I pray not for the world, but for those whom thou hast given me; for they are thine: and all things that are mine are thine, and thine are mine: and I am glorified in them. And I am no more in the world, and these are in the world, and I come to thee. Holy Father, keep them in thy name which thou hast given me, that they may be one, even as we *are*. While I was with them, I kept them in thy name which thou hast given me: and I guarded them, and not one of them perished, but the son of perdition; that the scripture might be fulfilled. But now I come to thee; and these things I speak in the world, that they may have my joy made full in themselves. I have given them thy word; and the world hated them, because they are not of the world, even as I am not of the world. I pray not that thou shouldest take them from the world, but that thou shouldest keep them from the evil. They are not of the world, even as I am not of the world. (John xvii. 1–16.)

The discourse having reached its climax in the profession of faith of the apostles, Jesus makes an intercessory prayer to the Father for them. This we may divide into two sections. The first section is a petition for the glory that the Messiah had earned by the completion of the ministry on earth given him by the Father. He prays that he may return to the glory that he had previously enjoyed with the Father before the existence of the world. This involves a pre-existence farther back than any previously stated, and more glorious than in any of the earlier representations. The pre-existence of the Messiah prior to Abraham was taught in an earlier chapter of John,[1] but here the pre-existence is prior to all creatures in the world and to the world itself. It is also a pre-existence in glory, and a glory so great that the meritorious service of the Messiah is simply rewarded with a return to it.[2]

Jesus then prays for his disciples that they may be kept safe from the evil of the world, in which they are to remain and suffer in their ministry of the gospel. He prays for their unity, that they may be kept in a unity which has as its norm the unity of the Father and the Son. The Messiah sees that they will be exposed to division as they will be exposed to the evil of the world. Internal discord and external evil are the two great perils of Christianity. The ideal unity must be kept in mind as well as the ideal holiness. Those who are breaking the unity of the disciples or preventing their unity in any way, are engaged in the work of the Evil one, no less than if they were tempting the disciples to sin, or were persecuting them with external evils. The true disciple runs ever along the lines of the prayer of Jesus and aims straight at the Master's ideals.

(10) Sanctify them in the truth : thy word is truth. As thou didst

---

[1] See p. 283.

[2] Wendt, *Lehre Jesu*, ii., s. 464 *seq.*, argues that "the glory which the Messiah had with the Father before the creation of the world," was the glory that was treasured up for him there as the reward for his Messianic ministry and that it does not imply the real pre-existence of the Messiah. He appeals to the treasure laid up in heaven for the disciples (Matthew vi. 20 ; Mark x. 21) and to the kingdom prepared before the foundation of the world (Matthew xxv. 34). But it is not said of the disciples that they really have those treasures or that kingdom, still less that they *had* them. And if Jesus, as the reward of his ministry, desired nothing more than he had before the foundation of the world,—that the Father would glorify him with the glory that he had before,—then these treasures of glory would still remain treasures in store for him and no more. The antithesis is between glory once in possession, now not in possession, soon to be possessed again. Such a glory implies a real pre-existence before the earthly life as much as a real post-existence after the earthly life.

send me into the world, even so sent I them into the world. And for their sakes I sanctify myself, that they themselves also may be sanctified in truth. Neither for these only do I pray, but for them also that believe on me through their word; that they may all be one; even as thou, Father, *art* in me, and I in thee, that they also may be in us: that the world may believe that thou didst send me. And the glory which thou hast given me I have given unto them; that they may be one, even as we *are* one; I in them, and thou in me, that they may be perfected into one; that the world may know that thou didst send me, and lovedst them, even as thou lovedst me. Father, that which thou hast given me, I will that, where I am, they also may be with me; that they may behold my glory, which thou hast given me; for thou lovedst me before the foundation of the world. O righteous Father, the world knew thee not, but I knew thee; and these knew that thou didst send me; and I made known unto them thy name, and will make it known; that the love wherewith thou lovedst me may be in them, and I in them.

(John xvii. 17–26.)

The second part of this intercessory prayer of Jesus is a prayer for the sanctification and glorification of the disciples. The prayer is not limited to the apostles, but it comprehends all who would believe in the Messiah through their ministry. It is comprehensive beyond anything we have yet seen in the words of Jesus. It looks longer into the reaches of time. It sees a ministry of successors of the apostles. It sees them all united in one organism in that mystic union which is after the norm of the union of the Father and the Son. The Messiah prays that they may also share his glory, that they may all be with him in heaven and that they all may be united in love.

It is a surprising feature in this discourse that nothing in it refers to the second Advent of the Messiah at the End of the Age. The Messiah from heaven grants the disciples the presence of his Holy Spirit and his own spiritual dynamic presence during their ministry in this world, and then when they have completed their ministry and follow him in death, he will come and take them to the heavenly temple to share his glory with the Father.

The Advent taught in this discourse is the advent of the Paraclete at Pentecost. This takes the same dominant place here that the Advent of the Son of Man in the clouds takes in the Apocalypse of Jesus.[1] The only Advent of Jesus known to this discourse is a spiritual dynamic advent, which it unfolds and emphasizes far beyond anything in the synoptic gospels.

Nothing could be more unlike than these two discourses, spoken within a few hours by the same Master to the same disciples. They present, in a different and thoroughgoing way, two distinct phases of the Messianic idea, neither of which can safely be neglected.


### THE KINGDOM OF THE TRUTH.

§ 68. *Jesus accepts the recognition of his disciples that he is the Messiah, but declines to set up his kingdom in the world. He testifies to Pilate that his kingdom is not of this world.*

Many times during his ministry Jesus was recognized as the Messiah by his disciples and the multitude. Besides those recognitions, studied in connection with the synoptics,[2] we have several in this gospel in addition to those already considered.[3] Thus Martha affirms:

I have believed that thou art the Messiah, the Son of God, he that cometh into the world. (John xi. 27.)

---

[1] See p. 154.   [2] See p. 92.   [3] See p. 258.

After the feeding of the multitudes:

> Jesus therefore perceiving that they were about to come and take him by force, to make him king withdrew again into the mountain himself alone. (John vi. 15.)

Here Jesus definitely decides not to allow the zealots to make him king by deeds of violence. His enthronement was not to be in this world, his capital was not to be in Jerusalem. His throne was a heavenly throne and his city the heavenly Jerusalem.

But the strongest passage upon this phase of the doctrine of the kingdom is the following:

> Pilate therefore entered again into the Praetorium, and called Jesus, and said unto him, Art thou the King of the Jews? Jesus answered, Sayest thou this of thyself, or did others tell it thee concerning me? Pilate answered, Am I a Jew? Thine own nation and the chief priests delivered thee unto me: what hast thou done? Jesus answered, My kingdom is not of this world: if my kingdom were of this world, then would my servants fight, that I should not be delivered to the Jews: but now is my kingdom not from hence. Pilate therefore said unto him, Art thou a king then? Jesus answered, Thou sayest *it*, for I am a king. To this end have I been born, and to this end am I come into the world, that I should bear witness unto the truth. Every one that is of the truth heareth my voice. Pilate saith unto him, What is truth? And when he had said this, he went out again unto the Jews, and saith unto them, I find no crime in him." (John xviii. 33–38.)

Jesus here teaches that his kingdom is not a worldly one, but a heavenly one. It is not a kingdom to fight for by deeds of arms, but a kingdom of witness bearing to the truth. The Messiah came to bear witness to the truth; the disciples are to carry on that witness-bearing. The divine Spirit is to guide them in it. Such is the warfare of the kingdom of the Messiah. The age of the kingdom is an age of the divine Spirit, and it is also an age of advance into the truth of God.


## LORD AND GOD.

*§ 69. The Messiah fulfils his promise and rises from the dead. He manifests himself in Christophany to his disciples. He is recognized as Lord and God.*

Besides the Christophanies of the resurrection reported by the synoptists, we have to consider those peculiar to the Gospel of John.

Jesus appears to the eleven in Jerusalem, and convinces the doubting Thomas by permitting him to put his finger in the prints of the nails and his hand in the wound of the side.

> Then saith he to Thomas, Reach hither thy finger, and see my hands; and reach *hither* thy hand, and put it into my side: and be not faithless, but believing. Thomas answered and said unto him, My Lord and my God. Jesus saith unto him, Because thou hast seen me, thou hast believed: blessed *are* they that have not seen, and *yet* have believed. (John xx. 27-29.)

This recognition of the deity of Jesus is not surprising in the Gospel of John. Nothing of the kind is known to the synoptics. In this Christophany Jesus appears in a body which is now tangible, so that it may be touched and felt by the doubting apostle, and then again so above the obstructions of material things that it enters through closed doors. The risen body of Jesus was in the transition of glorification, becoming less and less earthly in its substance, and more and more heavenly until the time came for the ascension from earth to heaven.

## THE MARTYRDOM OF SIMON.

§ 70. *Jesus appears in Christophany to the apostles in Galilee, calls Simon to be a loving shepherd of his flock, and predicts his martyrdom before the Advent.*

The narrative of the last chapter of this gospel is certainly an appendix to the gospel. It is in dispute among critics whether it was added by the same author or by a later hand. It is immaterial to our purpose which of these views may be taken. The passage certainly comes from an author of the same school of thought as the gospel itself; and we are obliged to discuss it at this stage of our study. The first half of the chapter describes the Christophany to the apostles on the shores of the sea of Tiberias. The second half gives us the Messianic prediction.

So when they had broken their fast, Jesus saith to Simon Peter, Simon, *son* of John, lovest thou me more than these? He saith unto him, Yea, Lord; thou knowest that I love thee. He saith unto him, Feed my lambs. He saith to him again a second time, Simon, *son* of John, lovest thou me? He saith unto him, Yea, Lord, thou knowest that I love thee. He saith unto him, Tend my sheep. He saith unto him the third time, Simon, *son* of John, lovest thou me? Peter was grieved because he said unto him the third time, Lovest thou me? And he said unto him, Lord, thou knowest all things; thou knowest that I love thee. Jesus saith unto him, Feed my sheep. Verily, verily, I say unto thee, When thou wast young, thou girdedst thyself, and walkedst whither thou wouldest: but when thou shalt be old, thou shalt stretch forth thy hands, and another shall gird thee, and carry thee whither thou wouldest not. Now this he spake, signifying by what manner of death he should glorify God. And when he had spoken this, he saith unto him, Follow me. Peter, turning about, seeth the disciple whom Jesus loved following; which also leaned back on his breast at the supper, and said, Lord, who is he that betrayeth thee? Peter therefore seeing him saith to Jesus, Lord, and what shall this man do? Jesus saith unto him. If I will that he tarry till I come, what *is that* to thee? follow thou me. This saying therefore went forth among the brethren, that that disciple should not die: yet Jesus said not unto him, that he should not die; but, If I will that he tarry till I come, what *is that* to thee? (John xxi. 15–23.)

The commission here given to the apostle Peter, starts from the idea of the Messiah as the shepherd and the apostle as the under shepherd. The commission is to tend the flock, feed the sheep, and especially the lambs. In this connection Peter receives a prediction that he would suffer martyrdom in his ministry. As an under shepherd of the flock of the Messiah, like the chief shepherd, the Messiah, he is to die for the flock. This martyrdom of Peter is to take place before the Advent. He is not to live to see it. This Advent is not the Advent of the last discourse, the advent of the Paraclete and of the Messiah in spiritual presence. It is the visible Advent of the synoptists. This naturally excites in the apostle's mind the inquiry whether others and especially John would live till the Messiah came. Jesus does not affirm that John would live until his Advent, as some, even Russel,[1] suppose, but he leaves it uncertain whether he would or not. The evangelist corrects the mistake of some in his time who thought that John was not to die; and that correction really amounts to the correction of those in our time who think that John was to survive the Advent, for the Advent was to reward the faithful who lived at the Advent. If there were no death before the Advent, there could be none afterward.

---

[1] *Parousia*, p. 136.

# CHAPTER VIII.

### THE MESSIAH OF THE GOSPELS.

Jesus is the Messiah of Old Testament prophecy. This is the teaching of Jesus himself. This is the testimony of the evangelists.

Jesus himself explained to his disciples, after his resurrection, that his sufferings, death, and resurrection were in fulfilment of the predictions of the Old Testament.

> O foolish men, and slow of heart to believe in all that the prophets have spoken! Behoved it not the Messiah to suffer these things, and to enter into his glory? And beginning from Moses and from all the prophets, he interpreted to them in all the scriptures the things concerning himself. . . . .
> And he said unto them, These are my words which I spake unto you, while I was yet with you, how that all things must needs be fulfilled, which are written in the law of Moses, and the prophets, and the psalms, concerning me. Then opened he their mind, that they might understand the scriptures; and he said unto them, Thus it is written, that the Messiah should suffer, and rise again from the dead the third day; and that repentance and remission of sins should be preached in his name unto all the nations, beginning from Jurusalem. (Luke xxiv. 25–27, 44–47.)

These precious words of Jesus, interpreting Old Testament prophecy to his disciples, and showing how far it was fulfilled in him, have not been given to us.

Doubtless, however, the material of his instruction has been preserved, at least in part, in the statements of the Gospels on this subject. In their light we propose to inquire respecting the Messiah of the Gospels.

In my previous volume, *Messianic Prophecy*, the Messianic predictions of the Old Testament were summed up under eleven heads. These will be our guide in the study of their fulfilment. A very considerable portion of our Saviour's discourses consisted of prediction—a larger proportion, indeed, than we find in any prophet of the Old Testament. His predictions relate to the founding and organization of the kingdom of God, its growth until the harvest at the end of the world, its consummation in the kingdom of glory and the *dies iræ*. All of the predictions of the Old Testament which relate to the same themes as the predictions of Jesus, must be eliminated from those that were fulfilled in his earthly ministry.

We shall consider these in an appropriate order, and endeavor to determine with reference to each and all of them how far Jesus fulfilled them prior to his ascension, and how far they remain to be fulfilled in the future. And with regard to those whose fulfilment in whole or in part is in the future, we shall have to determine whether Jesus took them up into his own prophecy, whether he enlarged and unfolded them, and whether he taught new Messianic ideals.

## 1. *The Day of Yahweh.*

The first Messianic ideal with which Jesus was confronted was the Day of Yahweh.[1] This was the ideal of John the Baptist.[2] This was also the Messianic concep-

---

[1] Briggs, *Messianic Prophecy*, p. 487.   [2] See p. 64.

tion most prominent to the Jews of the time of Jesus. What then was the attitude of Jesus towards it? He takes it up into his own predictions and makes it the ultimate goal of his prophecy. He did not fulfil during his earthly life any portion of this ideal, but refers it all to the future. He is a prophet of the Day of Yahweh, just as were all the prophets who preceded him. He predicts that it is near, that it is impending, but knows not the day or the hour.[1] The prophets in turn had predicted the Day of Yahweh in connection with a judgment scene, usually of some particular nation, but sometimes, in later prophecy, of all nations. Jesus pursues both methods. In his greater apocalypse he connects the judgment day with a judgment of Jerusalem;[2] in his prediction of the royal judgment and in his lesser apocalypse, he makes it a universal judgment.[3] In the Gospel of John it is preceded by a universal resurrection of the dead.[4] In two respects Jesus adds important features to the Day of Yahweh.

(a) The Son of Man is the judge. The Son of Man on the clouds in the apocalypses of Daniel and of Enoch, takes part in the judgment, but God himself executes judgment. In the predictions of Jesus, the Son of Man comes in the glory of the Father, on a throne of power with the holy angels and executes judgment himself. God the heavenly Father does not seem to be present to the consciousness of the Messiah in any of his judgment scenes.[5] All the authority of judgment has been given over to the Son of Man.[6]

---

[1] See p. 161.   [2] Mark xiii.
[3] Matthew xxv. 31-46; Luke xvii. 22-37.
[4] See p. 273.
[5] Mark viii. 38; xiii.; xiv. 61-64; Matthew xiii. 37-43; xxv. 31-46; Luke xvii 22-30. See pp. 97 152, 126, 208, 226, 247.
[6] John v. 17-29. See p. 273.

(*b*) The judgment is not so much a judgment of enemies, and is therefore not described in scenes of battle and strife. It is distinctly a judgment of servants, and that not civil or theocratic, not national or social, but moral and individual; every man according to his works;[1] whether he has done the will of the heavenly Father;[2] whether he is righteous;[3] whether he has done deeds of kindness.[4] The decision of the judgment is a final condemnation and rejection of the wicked, and a recognition and reward of the righteous. The final punishment does not go beyond the common Jewish opinion of the time, and is proportioned to guilt. The wicked are excluded from the kingdom of glory; and Gehenna with its rotting, burning carcasses, furnishes the imagery of their terrible condition, or else the darkness of those excluded from the lighted palace and its bridal feast. The rewards of the righteous are blessings in the kingdom of glory proportioned to their services.

The prophets of the Old Testament connect with the Day of Yahweh an outpouring of the divine Spirit.[5] Jesus enlarges upon that conception. He represents that there will be an age of preaching the gospel under the guidance of the Spirit;[6] that the apostles will be guided into all the truth by the Paraclete; that there will be an age of the Holy Spirit;[7] that the apostles were to wait for the Spirit from heaven before they began their ministry.[8] Thus the Day of Yahweh of the Old Testament is a day which begins with the outpouring of the Holy Spirit and which ends with the royal judgment.

---

[1] Matthew vii. 24.
[2] Matthew vii. 21.
[3] Matthew xiii. 37-43.
[4] Matthew xxv. 31-46.
[5] Briggs, *Mess. Prop.*, p. 488 *seq*.
[6] See p. 143.
[7] See p. 297.
[8] See p. 254.

## 2. *The Advent of Yahweh.*

The Messianic idea of the Advent of Yahweh is connected with the holy temple and the holy city which He is to inhabit and render glorious. Such an advent was longed for in the times of Jesus. It is noteworthy that Jesus does not point forward to such an Advent of Yahweh, but attaches this Messianic idea to his own Advent. In the gospel of the infancy it is represented that there was a theophany at the conception of Jesus[1] and another theophany at his birth.[2] The gospels tell us of theophanies at his baptism, at his transfiguration, at his death, and at his resurrection. But the theophanies of the transfiguration and resurrection are associated with christophanies, or the shining forth of the glory of Christ himself. These culminate in the ascension of the Messiah to heaven.

All these theophanies and christophanies raise the question whether there was not a divine advent in the person of Jesus, the Messiah himself, whether the theophany did not reach its goal in the New Testament times in the Christophany. That is certainly the representation of the Gospel of John, in which Jesus speaks of himself as the Son of Man from heaven, who came forth from the Father in heaven to do his work in the world and who will return to the Father. Jesus claims pre-existence with God prior to Abraham and prior to the creation of the world.[3] He claims to be equal with God, to have authority of life and death, and of judgment.[4] He accepts recognition as God.[5] If all this is true then the coming of Jesus into the world was a divine Advent to the world.

---

[1] See p. 48.    [2] See p. 51.    [3] See pp. 283, 301.
[4] See p. 273.                     [5] See p. 306.

Even in the synoptic Gospels, Jesus claims to be the corner-stone of the Old Testament prophecy;[1] and, in the gospel of John, to be the temple of God.[2] The corner-stone will be rejected, but it will become the head of the corner. The temple will be destroyed, but in three days it will be raised up to be the ever-living temple of God. The gospel of John connects the advent of God the Father with the advent of the Son and of the Spirit to inhabit the faithful disciple. It knows of no other advent of God the Father.[3]

### 3. *The Father and the Shepherd.*

Old Testament prophecy represents that God at His advent is Father, Husband, and Shepherd. Jesus leaves out of his Messianic ideal altogether the conception of marriage, but he uses the ideals of Father and Shepherd. The ideal of the Father he never applies to himself. He applies it to God the Father in a higher and in a more distinctive sense. The conception of the Father of the nation and of the Messiah,—a familiar ideal of the Old Testament,—now rises to the Father of each and every individual who enters into the new relationship of sonship revealed to the world by Jesus the Messiah. Jesus taught the near presence of the heavenly Father to all the children of God. This ideal therefore is realized specifically in Jesus, who as the Messiah was the Son of God the Messianic Father, and in all the disciples of Jesus, who become by their discipleship children of the heavenly Father.

The ideal of the Shepherd in the Old Testament is sometimes attached to the Messianic king, and some-

---

[1] Matth. xxi. 42-46. Briggs, *Mess. Proph.*, p. 208. See p. 114.
[2] John ii. 13-22. See p. 259. [3] See p. 293.

times to Yahweh.¹ There is no use by Jesus or by the evangelists of any of those passages of the Old Testament where Yahweh is the Shepherd. On the other hand Jesus never attaches the ideal of the Shepherd to the heavenly Father. We cannot therefore determine what use he would make of the passages relating to the divine Shepherd. But, in the royal judgment scene of Matthew, the Son of Man as a shepherd divides sheep and goats;² and Jesus represents that, he, as the Son of Man from heaven, is the good Shepherd who has authority over his own life and death.³ Thus he enlarges the conception of the Messianic shepherd beyond the Old Testament representations as to the Messianic king, and, in the Gospel of Matthew, attaches it to the final judge, the Son of God from heaven; and, in the Gospel of John, to the Good Shepherd who will shepherd his sheep until all have been redeemed in one holy flock.

### 4. *The Promised Land.*

The Messianic ideal of the Holy Land is very prominent in the Old Testament. Jesus seems to ignore it. He may have had it in mind in the beatitude of the meek,⁴ but it is improbable that this would be the only passage. The regeneration,⁵ of the times of reward predicted in Matthew might be thought of as a similar ideal, but this regeneration does not seem to involve a regeneration of the holy land, or of the earth as an abode of the redeemed, and therefore has nothing in it to correspond with the ideal of the holy land.

---

¹ *Mess. Proph.*, pp. 483-496.
² See p. 225.
³ See p. 284.
⁴ Matthew v. 5.
⁵ Matthew xix. 28.

## 5. *The Messianic King.*

One of the most important of the Messianic ideals of the Old Testament is that of the Messianic King.[1] The extra-canonical literature of the Jews before the advent of Jesus, for the most part, overlooked this ideal.[2] The gospel of the Infancy of Jesus makes it prominent in the songs of the angels, and of the fathers and mothers of the Messianic babes.[3] Thus the question arises in the gospels whether Jesus is the Messiah. Jesus at the beginning of his ministry is recognized as the Messiah by the demoniacs,[4] and by the devil;[5] but this does not involve any recognition by the people, or even by the apostles. Jesus was recognized as the Messiah by the theophanic voice at his baptism,[6] at his transfiguration,[7] and, according to the Gospel of John, during the last week of his ministry in the temple.[8] It is not clear, however, whether the testimony at the baptism was known to the apostles at an early date. The other theophanies were subsequent to the apostolic recognition.

According to the synoptists, the first distinct recognition of the apostles was through Peter as the spokesman, at Cæsarea Philippi, shortly before the transfiguration;[9] but Jesus charged them not to make him known. The gospel of John, however, reports a recognition by several of the apostles prior to the beginning of the ministry of Jesus, when first they left John the Baptist and attached themselves to him.[10] The confession of Peter thus takes a little different form in the gospel of

---

[1] *Mess. Proph.*, p. 492.
[2] See p. 34.
[3] See pp. 52, 55.
[4] Mark i. 24; iii. 11; v. 6–7. See p. 80.
[5] Matth. iv. 1–11. See p. 167.
[6] See p. 75.
[7] See p. 100.
[8] See p. 269.
[9] Mark viii. 27–30. See p. 93.
[10] See p. 258.

John, though probably it is the same event as that referred to in the synoptists.¹ Martha also recognizes Jesus as the Messiah.² He accepted the recognitions above referred to. According to Luke, Jesus claimed to his parents to be the Messiah, at twelve years of age.³ But he made no public claim to be the Messiah until the last week of his ministry. He then made a public entry into Jerusalem and received the recognition from the people that was his due; but the Pharisees rejected him and won the populace to their side.⁴ He was arrested by the Sanhedrin, and testified under oath before them that he was the Messiah, and they rejected him as such.⁵ He made the same claim before Pilate in response to his official investigation,⁶ and on that account was clothed with royal garments, crowned with thorns and given a reed sceptre by the rude soldiery, making sport of his royalty.⁷ He was crucified with the title on the cross, The King of the Jews.⁸ He was mocked while hanging there.⁹

There can be no doubt that Jesus claimed to be the Messianic king, and that he was recognized as such by his disciples and rejected as such by the Sanhedrin, the Pharisees and the people. Jesus therefore was a claimant to the Messianic throne. He was not accepted by the Jews, and he never occupied his throne during his earthly ministry. He testified to Pilate that his kingdom was not of this world.¹⁰ He did not ascend his throne until his ascension. He did not assume the kingdom until his installation on his heavenly throne.

---

[1] See p. 93.
[2] John xi. 27.
[3] See p. 234.
[4] Mark xi. 7-10.
[5] Mark xiv. 61-64.
[6] Mark xv. 1-5.
[7] Mark xv. 6-19.
[8] Mark xv. 26.
[9] Mark xv. 31-32.
[10] See p. 305.

All predictions of the Old Testament respecting his reign over his kingdom point to a period subsequent to his ascension, and could not have been fulfilled in his earthly life. This, indeed, is the view taken by the evangelists in their reference of the Messianic passages of the Old Testament to Jesus and in their interpretation of his life. We have reserved these for this stage of our discussion.

Matthew and Luke give the genealogy of Jesus. Matthew shows that he is the son of David and son of Abraham,[1] and as such the heir of the Messianic promises attached to the seed of Abraham and the son of David. Luke traces the line back through David and Abraham to Adam,[2] because he wishes not only to show that Jesus was the heir of David and Abraham, but that he was also connected with the entire race of man as the medium of the Messianic promises to the race.

There are difficulties in adjusting the differences which appear at several points in the tables; but these differences, whether due to inaccuracies of the evangelists, or discrepancies of the original documents, do not impair the teaching of both tables as to the fact of the heirship of David, Abraham, and Adam, wherein the Messianic importance of the tables alone lies.

Matthew not only shows that Jesus was the Messiah by right of inheritance; but he also proves that he was the Messiah by the fulfilment of several Messianic predictions of the Old Testament, especially in his early life.

Jesus' birth of the virgin Mary was the fulfilment of the prediction of Isaiah. The original reads:

Lo, young woman, thou art pregnant, and about to bear a son

---

[1] Matthew i. 1-17.     [2] Luke iii. 23-38.

and call his name Immanuel. Curds and honey will he eat at the time of his knowing to refuse evil and choose good. For before the boy knows to refuse evil and choose good, the land, because of whose two kings thou art anxious, will be abandoned.[1] (Isaiah vii. 14-16.)

This Matthew represents as fulfilled in Jesus.

> Now all this is come to pass, that it might be fulfilled which was spoken by the Lord through the prophet, saying, Behold, the virgin shall be with child, and shall bring forth a son, and they shall call his name Immanuel; which is, being interpreted, God with us. (Matthew i. 22, 23.)

The child Jesus was born of the virgin Mary, in accordance with the prediction. It is true that the more general term "young woman" of the original has given place to the more specific term "virgin" of the LXX. This does not destroy the precision of the fulfilment, but rather enhances it. The point of the prophecy and the fulfilment is not in the virginity of the mother, but in the fortunes of the son. The address of the prophet to this ideal young woman is re-echoed in the annunciation to Joseph and Mary.

The name given to the child by angelic direction, was *Jesus*. "For it is he that shall save his people from their sins."[2] This is not exactly the same as *Immanuel = God with us*, but it comprehends it and implies it; because God's presence with his people in their calamity was for the very purpose of saving them. The birth and the naming are similar to the prediction. So are the circumstances. The condition of the child and his parents was one of hardship, poverty, and peril. The son and heir of David was not born as a recognized crown

---

[1] See Briggs, *Messianic Prophecy*, p. 195 *seq*.
[2] Matth. i. 21. See p. 47.

prince, but he was immediately in peril of his life from an usurper. He was not nourished as an heir to the throne, but was fed as a child in a poor and deserted land. His people were in bondage and he was obliged to seek refuge in Egypt, as Israel of old.

The framework of the prediction is filled up by the birth and infancy of Jesus Christ. The essence of the prediction belongs to the future, when this child of humiliation would vindicate his name and his throne as the Saviour of his people and the Messiah of glory.

The birth of Jesus in Bethlehem is in fulfilment of the prediction of Micah:

> And thou, Bethlehem, Ephrathah,
> Little to be among the thousands of Judah,
> Out of thee will come forth for me
> One who is to become ruler in Israel. (Micah v. 2.)

Matthew represents that the chief priests and scribes pointed Herod to this passage, saying:

> And thou Bethlehem, land of Judah,
> Art in no wise least among the princes of Judah:
> For out of thee shall come forth a governor,
> Who shall be shepherd of my people Israel.
> 
> (Matth. ii. 6.)

The gospel translates an Aramaic version, which has preserved the measures of the poetry of the original better than the LXX. This version is a sufficiently accurate paraphrase, rather than a precise translation.[1]

It is evident that Jesus fulfilled this prediction so far

---

[1] It explains the obscurities of the original by using "land of Judah" for "Ephrathah," and "princes" for "thousands," and it improves the parallelism and the measure of the original by explaining "ruler" by "governor," in the third line, and by "shepherd" in the fourth line. These changes in phrases do not change the sense.

as his birth in Bethlehem is concerned. His subsequent career also showed that he fulfilled the other elements of the prediction, in becoming the shepherd and ruler of Israel and in bearing the name *Peace*.¹

Jesus was brought up in Nazareth in Galilee, away from his ancestral seat as well as the throne of his fathers.² On this account he bore the name Nazarene, as a name of reproach. The Pharisees could not imagine that the Messiah would come forth from such a place as Nazareth. But the evangelist sees in these very circumstances the fulfilment of several prophecies of the Old Testament. We are first reminded of the prediction of Isaiah:

> And a twig will come forth from the stump of Jesse,
> And a shoot³ from his roots will be fruitful.
> 
> (Isaiah xi. 1.)

The origin of the name of the place is uncertain. This does not interfere with the essential meaning of the interpretation, which is word-play, it is true, but with an underlying, powerful thought. The prophecy is not a prediction of birth or dwelling in Nazareth; but it is a prediction of an obscure origin and growth of the Messiah in retirement from the public eye. He was to spring up like a twig on the stump of a tree that had been cut down, and like a shoot from the roots of the line of Jesse, nothing but stump and roots being left.⁴ This condition precisely corresponds with the circumstances of Jesus at this time. The abode in Nazareth, and the name Nazarene that he gained thereby, show a wonder-

---

¹ *Messianic Prophecy*, p. 217 *seq*.     ² Matth. ii. 23.
³ The Hebrew נֵצֶר — *shoot*, doubtless suggested the Aramaic נִצְרָא, נֵיצְרָא and their adjective, which was rendered into the Greek Ναζωραῖος.
⁴ See *Messianic Prophecy*, p. 202 *seq*.

ful correspondence to a neglected and obscure twig and shoot from the stump and roots of the royal line of David. The word-play calls attention to the original shoot from the stump, and also to the obscurity of the place of his abode, the symbol and the reality. The prediction of Isaiah does not give this name to the Messiah. But later prophets, on the basis of this prediction, give him a corresponding name. The evangelist doubtless had these other prophecies in mind; namely, the righteous branch of Jeremiah,[1] and the crowned branch of Zechariah.[2] The reigning was not while the shoot remained like a twig on a stump at Nazareth. Only the branch-like, twig-like, sprout-like origin and early growth then appear. The reigning comes at a later date, when the twig becomes a fruitful shoot and a mighty branch after the enthronement of the Messiah.

In his Galilean ministry Jesus preached on the borders of the land, and in the midst of a foreign population. This reminded the evangelist of the prediction of Isaiah.

Now when he heard that John was delivered up, he withdrew into Galilee; and leaving Nazareth, he came and dwelt in Capernaum, which is by the sea, in the borders of Zebulun and Naphtali: that it might be fulfilled which was spoken by Isaiah the prophet, saying, The land of Zebulun and the land of Naphtali, toward the sea, beyond Jordan, Galilee of the Gentiles, the people which sat in darkness saw a great light, and to them which sat in the region and shadow of death, to them did light spring up. (Matthew iv. 12-16.)

Matthew has used an Aramaic version of the original passage, which reads:

But she who now has trouble will not have gloom.

---

[1] xxiii. 5, and xxxiii. 15. See *Messianic Prophecy*, p. 244 *seq.*
[2] iii. 8; vi. 12. See *Messianic Prophecy*, pp. 442-448.

> As the former time brought into contempt the land of Zebulun and the land of Naphtali;
> The last time will certainly bring to honour the way of the sea, beyond Jordan, the district of the nations.
> The people that walk in darkness do see a great light.
> Those dwelling in a land of dense darkness, light doth shine upon them.
>
> (Isaiah ix. 1, 2.)

The first of the holy land to go into exile, these border lands will be the first to rejoice under the ministry of the Messiah.

His presence is conceived as the shining of a great light.[1] The overthrow of enemies, the endowment with divine names, and the everlasting reign, of the original prediction, the evangelist doubtless had in mind; but he looked forward to their realization in the future. These elements were not evident in the ministry of Jesus in Galilee. It was sufficient for the present that the Messiah appeared as a great light in the northern frontier of the land. This appearance had wrapt up in it all the blessed possibilities of the future.

The Gospel of Matthew also represents the entry of Jesus into Jerusalem as in fulfilment of the prophet Zechariah,[2] and the Gospel of John briefly makes the same reference.

| MATTH. xxi. 4, 5. | JOHN xii. 14, 15. |
| --- | --- |
| Now this is come to pass, that it might be fulfilled which was spoken by the prophet, saying, Tell ye the daughter of Zion, Behold, thy King cometh unto thee, meek, and riding upon an ass, and upon a colt the foal of an ass. | And Jesus, having found a young ass, sat thereon; as it is written, Fear not, daughter of Zion: behold, thy King cometh, sitting on an ass's colt. |

---

[1] See *Messianic Prophecy*, p. 198 seq.
[2] Zech. ix. 9, 10. *Messianic Prophecy*, p. 134.

Jesus, according to these evangelists, was the king of peace and victory, of that prophet.

The last two predictions point to a Messianic victory over enemies, and they seem to presuppose a king reigning on his throne. Jesus was at the time rather a king battling for his throne. The victory of the original prophecies is a victory which could only be satisfied by the representation of the second Advent of Jesus. The ideal victory seemed to the evangelist so wrapped up in the work of Jesus in northeastern Galilee and on his entry into Jerusalem, that he represents that ministry and that entry as fulfilments of the predictions.

The prediction of Jesus as to the Messianic king may best be considered in connection with his doctrine of the kingdom of God.

### 6. *The Kingdom of God.*

The Kingdom of God was the chief of the Messianic ideals of Jesus. It was the theme of his first discourse.[1] It was the substance of the preaching of the Twelve,[2] and of the Seventy,[3] when they were commissioned by Jesus and sent forth as preachers. It was the constant and familiar subject of his discourses.[4] The kingdom of God was one of the most important of the Messianic ideals of the Old Testament.[5] God was the king of His kingdom, the Messianic king was His son and representative. Accordingly, the Jews for the most part were looking for the kingdom of God; few of them thought of a Messianic king as necessary to it.[6] Jesus uses the term kingdom of God, implying that God was the king of the kingdom; possibly also the term kingdom of heaven,[7] im-

---
[1] See p. 78.   [2] See p. 181.   [3] See p. 240.   [4] See p. 87.
[5] *Messianic Prophecy*, pp. 483 *seq*.
[6] See p. 38.                                            [7] See p. 79.

plying that it was a kingdom the seat of whose dominion is heaven. Nowhere does Jesus speak of the kingdom of the Messiah. It is all the more significant, therefore, that, in the Gospels, the Messianic king becomes so associated with the kingdom of God that the kingship of God himself is not thought of. This is true in the sayings of Jesus himself, who never speaks of the heavenly Father as king. The evangelists pursue the same usage.[1]

We have gone over the Messianic idea of the kingdom of God as it is presented in the teaching of Jesus. There is considerable variation and complexity in the representations. It is difficult to bring them all into an harmonious conception. Accordingly there is great confusion among the interpreters. A careful survey of the field, however, enables us to unite the lines in one ideal.

The kingdom of God is not a kingdom that comes once for all in power and glory with a majestic all-conquering king from heaven at its head. It is a kingdom that has several stages of growth. Sometimes Jesus deals with one of these stages, at other times with other stages.

(*a*) The kingdom comes at first without observation. It is invisible to the eye. The Messiah is not enthroned. He does not appear in royal robes and with royal majesty. He comes with a kingdom that is not of this world and that is not to be of this world. It is a kingdom of heaven and of God; it is a kingdom of truth and righteousness. Those who enter the kingdom, do it not in masses, but one by one, by repentance and faith, through a heavenly birth of water and the divine Spirit, and by personal recognition of their king. The kingdom is at first a sowing, and the seed remains buried for a while

---

[1] Comp. p. 311.

before it comes into manifestation. The kingdom in this its earliest stage was already planted in Palestine at the time of Jesus in the humble Messianic preacher and his disciples.

(*b*) But the kingdom was not always to remain invisible and unorganized. It was not destroyed by the death of the Messiah and the dispersion of his followers. It appears at first as a tender blade upon the surface of the ground.¹ It will be established as an external organization in the world. In his early teachings Jesus predicted that the kingdom was near at hand, that it would be before the disciples could complete the cities of Israel in their ministry;² after the institution of the Lord's supper he declared that it would be before another feast;³ in his last discourse, after his resurrection,⁴ he intimated that it would be at the advent of the divine Spirit on the day of Pentecost. Peter was to be its rock and porter.⁵ Jesus predicts his speedy coming to establish his kingdom. This can only be understood of his coming in and with his Spirit, after he had ascended his throne in heaven, and of his establishing his visible kingdom by the ministry of Peter.

(*c*) The kingdom now has its period of growth. During this time the kingdom is left very much to itself by the king. He is absent in heaven on his heavenly throne, and yet he is dynamically present in spiritual presence with his kingdom at all times, invisible but potent in his influence. During this period his apostles and their successors fulfil their tasks and earn their rewards. The kingdom in its external form is not altogether pure. It contains not only good soil that is fruitful in various degrees of fruitfulness, but it contains bad soil; barren, ob-

---

[1] See p. 90.  [2] See p. 184.  [3] See p. 120.  [4] See p. 254.
[5] See p. 189.

durate, and inconsiderate persons who never produce any fruit.¹ In the field of the kingdom are also tares planted by the devil which cannot be detected until they ripen, and cannot be removed from the kingdom till the harvest.² There are faithful servants and there are unfaithful servants of various degrees and kinds.³ Under all these difficulties the kingdom grows. Its own inherent energy enables the good that is in it to leaven eventually the whole until it all becomes good. Its own expansive power enables it to grow from the smallest beginning until it attains enormous dimensions.⁴ This kingdom is the kingdom of grace.

(*d*) There is yet a kingdom of glory. The king will return in visible presence to establish it. This form of the kingdom is introduced by an act of judgment. It is compared to landing fish upon the shore,⁵ to reaping a harvest,⁶ to a trial before the throne of the king.⁷ The wicked are removed from the kingdom and consigned to Gehenna.⁸

The righteous receive their rewards, which are in accordance with their humiliation in service. The apostles sit on thrones with the Messiah and have places at the royal table.⁹ This kingdom is so glorious that it transcends everything. It is to be the supreme quest of men. They are to part with all else to obtain it; for with it they obtain not only a priceless possession, but a gift which involves all others.¹⁰ For this kingdom they are to labor, and for the advent of this kingdom they are to pray.¹¹

---

¹ See p. 87.  ² See p. 208.  ³ See p. 221.  ⁴ See p. 91.
⁵ See p. 209.  ⁶ See p. 208.  ⁷ See p. 225.  ⁸ See p. 224.
⁹ See p. 227.  ¹⁰ See p. 209.  ¹¹ See p. 203.

### 7. *The Holy Priesthood.*

The Messianic ideal of the Holy Priesthood is not mentioned in the sayings of Jesus. It does not appear in the Gospels in their interpretation of the life of Jesus in the light of the Old Testament prophecy. The priestly functions of the Messiah were not exercised during his earthly ministry. The great high priest after the order of Melchizedek had his functions to fulfil in the heavenly sanctuary after his ascension. Hence the predictions contained in the Messianic ideal of the Holy Priesthood find no fulfilment during the earthly life of Jesus, but point onward to his mediatorial reign.

### 8. *The Ideal Man.*

The most primitive Messianic ideal is the ideal of mankind, preserved for us in the divine blessing of our race in the poem of the creation,[1] which finds lyric expression in the Psalter,[2] where the ideal man is a little below the heavenly intelligences in dignity, but is exalted to dominion over all creatures. Psalm xci.[3] describes such a man in intimate communion with God, delivered from perils of every kind, sustained by angels, and lord of the animals. This ideal seems to have been a favorite one with Jesus, and it is involved in a measure in the title, the Son of Man. He is recognized as such an ideal man in the theophanic voices declaring him to be the beloved Son, in whom God was well pleased.[4] Satan, in the temptation, recognized him as having the authority over nature and the support of angels.[5] His life was a life of superiority

---
[1] Gen. i. 26-30. *Messianic Prophecy*, p. 68.
[2] Ps. viii. *Messianic Prophecy*, p. 147 *seq*.
[3] *Messianic Prophecy*, p. 460.
[4] Matthew iii. 17; xvii. 5.
[5] Ps. xci.; Matthew iv. 1-11.

to moral and physical evil, of an authority over man and nature, over human ills and demons, over life, and over his own death. In him the ideal of mankind was first presented in history as the model and glory of all manhood for our race.

### 9. *Victory over Evil.*

The Messianic ideal of the conflict with evil is predicted in the protevangelium,[1] with the victory of the seed of the woman. This Messianic ideal Jesus undertook to realize. The temptation in the wilderness is the counterpart of the temptation in the garden, and the battle with the tempter and the victory there gained were the prelude to a life-long conflict and a series of victories. The experience of suffering Israel, in Egyptian bondage, was realized by the little child who fled from the blood-bath of Bethlehem;[2] and the experience of Israel in exile at Babylon was realized in the sufferings of his life, so vividly presented in the great prophet of the exile[3] and in the psalms of lamentation of the exiles,[4] that they seem like pictures of the real life of Jesus. The conflict reached its climax in the garden, on the cross, and in the abode of the dead; but the resurrection was a victory that for the first fulfilled the promises of the first gospel to our race. It is true that this victory over the tempter and evil was a personal victory of the Messiah; but it involves and guarantees the victory of the human race, whose head and crown he is.

### 10. *The Faithful Prophet.*

The Messianic ideal of the Faithful Prophet springs out of those already considered. It finds its chief real-

---

[1] Gen. iii. 14, 15.    [2] See p. 320.    [3] *Messianic Prophecy*, Chap. XI.
[4] *Messianic Prophecy*, p. 320 seq.

ization in the earthly life of Jesus. Even the ideal man and the conflict with evil are not so fully accomplished as this. He was the prophet, like Moses, speaking with an authority so peculiar to him that it became one of the most striking features of his ministry.[1] Jesus represented himself as the preacher of the great prophet of the exile.[2] The preaching of Jesus was gentle and unostentatious. His miracle-working was not in marvellous display of power, but in sympathy and love, healing the sick and comforting the afflicted. He presents such evidences as his credentials to John the Baptist.[3] So Matthew points to his ministry in terms of the same prophet.

> And when even was come, they brought unto him many possessed with demons: and he cast out the spirits with a word, and healed all that were sick: that it might be fulfilled which was spoken by Isaiah the prophet, saying, Himself took our infirmities, and bare our diseases. (Matthew viii. 16, 17.)

Matthew's citation varies slightly from the original.

> Verily our griefs he bore,
> And our sorrows he carried them.[4]  (Isa. liii. 4.)

He rightly sees in the sympathizing and helpful miracle-worker, the bearer of human trouble and all its forms of suffering. The culmination of this bearing of trouble the evangelist does not refer to here: it comes out in the course of his narrative.

Matthew at a later date, in connection with another period of great miracle-working, again presents Jesus as the Messianic servant.

> And many followed him, and he healed them all, and charged

---

[1] Dt. xviii. 18-22; Matthew vii. 28, 29.  See p. 80.
[2] Isa. lxi. 1-3; Luke iv. 17-22.  See p. 236.   [3] See p. 176.
[4] The evangelist uses an Aramaic version.

them that they should not make him known: that it might be fulfilled which was spoken through Isaiah the prophet, saying,

> Behold, my servant whom I have chosen;
> My beloved in whom my soul is well pleased:
> I will put my Spirit upon him,
> And he shall declare judgment to the Gentiles.
> He shall not strive, nor cry aloud;
> Neither shall any one hear his voice in the streets.
> A bruised reed shall he not break,
> And smoking flax shall he not quench,
> Till he send forth judgment unto victory.
> And in his name shall the Gentiles hope.[1]
> 
> (Matthew xii. 16–21.)

The gentle, unostentatious preacher, who bears with him the divine Spirit, and who is to conquer a victory for his people and all the nations of the world, is here seen executing the first part of his great task.[2]

In these passages Jesus and his evangelist clearly set forth the credentials of the Messianic servant of Yahweh.

In the same manner we see the sufferer of the Psalter[3] in the story of the passion of our Lord.[4] These psalms describe a sufferer entirely consecrated to the divine service, consumed with zeal for the house of God, and suffering cruel reproaches. He is persecuted with mocking words and cruel deeds. He finds no compassion. Even his own kindred have forsaken him, and he is the scorn of the wicked. He is abandoned by God to his enemies, who mock him for his trust in God. His body is stretched out, his frame is feverish, he is suffering intense thirst, his hands and feet are pierced, he is dying

---

[1] Matthew here, as usual, follows an Aramaic version of the Hebrew which preserves the poetic movement. This is a paraphrase that gives essentially the meaning of the original, but misses not a few of its delicate shades.

[2] Isaiah xlii. 1–3. See *Messianic Prophecy*, p. 343.

[3] Ps. xxii., xl., lxix., lxx.   [4] *Messianic Prophecy*, p. 320, *seq*.

of a broken heart; they give him vinegar and gall to drink, they divide his garments as their spoil. Such is the sufferer who finally triumphs over suffering and death. He is at last delivered, and his enemies incur a terrible doom, while he proclaims his salvation to the ends of the earth, so that these turn unto Yahweh in response to his call. Such is the great sufferer of these exilic psalms. He is the same as the suffering servant of the great prophet of the exile, and their combined representations portray to us the passion of our Saviour with such an intensity of graphic power that they exceed the historical narratives of the Gospels in coloring and in realistic effect.

## 11. *The New Covenant.*

The Messianic ideal of the New Covenant was accomplished in part in the earthly life of Jesus. The Old Covenant was instituted at Mount Horeb, when the covenant sacrifice was made, on the basis of the book of the covenant. Half of the blood of the victims was scattered upon the people to consecrate them to the covenant, and a communion feast was held in the theophanic presence of God.[1] The prophets predict that the new covenant will be written not on tables of stone, but upon the heart; and that it will be an everlasting covenant of peace and blessing. The divine Spirit will dwell in the hearts of men, and his word will be in their mouths. The sure mercies of David will be freely offered, and the prophetic servant will be a covenant and a light to Israel and the nations.[2]

This New Covenant was instituted by Jesus Christ on

---

[1] Exod. xxiv.
[2] Jer. xxxi. 31-37; Ezek. xxxiv. 25-31; Isa. xlii 6; liv. 10-17; lv. 3; lxi. 8.

the night of his betrayal, when his own body and blood took the place of the covenant sacrifice of bullocks.[1] The blood was presented in the form of the cup of wine, and the flesh in the form of bread, to unite the members of the new covenant to their Lord. The New Covenant was instituted, and the new law was written on the hearts of his disciples in the loving word of the gospel to be preached to all nations. The covenant embraces all the blessings of redemption. It began its wondrous course on the night of its institution, but its fruition will not be attained until the second Advent.

## 12. *The Second Advent.*

The eleven ideals of the Old Testament lead us on by their partial fulfilment during the earthly life of Jesus to a second Advent in which, according to his predictions, they will be gloriously fulfilled.

Jesus predicted the three great events, his death, resurrection, and glory, in a number of prophecies extending from the beginning of his public ministry until its end. (*a*) The prophecies are at first in the predicting of signs to those who demanded them. These all point to his resurrection as the great sign of his Messiahship.

(1) The temple destroyed and rising on the third day;[2] (2) the covenant sacrifice of his flesh and blood as the food of life;[3] (3) his burial like Jonah and rising again on the third day.[4] None of these signs could be understood until Jesus died as a victim on the cross, was buried, remained in the grave till the third day and then rose from the dead. When he rose, he rose to provide his people with the flesh and blood of the new covenant sacrifice, under the forms of the Lord's supper. He

---

[1] See p. 120.   [2] See p. 259.   [3] See p. 277.   [4] See p. 186.

rose to be and remain the everlasting temple of God to all God's people. He rose that the gospel of his redemption might be preached to the whole creation.

(*b*) The prediction of his rejection is based on several prophecies of the Old Testament: (1) The rejected and suffering prophet of the great prophet of the exile is in the mind of Jesus in his discourse at Nazareth, and in his reply to the message of the Baptist.[1] (2) The rejected shepherd of Zechariah is in the mind of Jesus in his description of the Good Shepherd and in his word to his disciples in Gethsemane.[2] (3) The rejected corner-stone of the Psalter is used by Jesus in his conflict with the Pharisees during his last week in Jerusalem.[3] These predictions of the Old Testament as interpreted and applied by Jesus set forth his death, his resurrection, and his exaltation as servant, shepherd, and corner-stone.

(*c*) Jesus on several occasions taught the redemptive significance of his death and resurrection in figurative language. According to the synoptists, the Son of Man came to give himself a ransom for many.[4] According to the Gospel of John, the Good Shepherd interposes between his flock and the robbers, and layeth down his life for the sheep.[5] Like a grain of wheat he will fall into the earth and die, and then spring up and bear much fruit.[6]

(*d*) Jesus also sets forth his death and resurrection in plain discourse. He told his disciples on three different occasions that he would be rejected by the rulers, cruelly abused, put to death on the cross, and that he would rise again on the third day.[7] This experience of

---

[1] See p. 178.   [2] See p. 125.   [3] See p. 114.
[4] See p. 107.   [5] See p. 284.   [6] See p. 287.
[7] See p. 94.

the Master is a prelude to the experience of his disciples. They will have an experience of suffering before they gain their reward of glory.¹ The resurrection is not to establish the kingdom of glory. That is postponed till the Advent from heaven with the angels for judgment. The Messiah comes in his kingdom to establish it in the lifetime of his hearers. But the kingdom as thus established will be a kingdom of cross-bearing, of suffering, a kingdom of grace and service. The faithful disciples will gain their reward in the kingdom of glory in accordance with the devotion of their service, the highest places being assigned by the Father.

There is in the representation of the death and resurrection of the Messiah, a line of thought parallel to that which we have seen in our study of the kingdom of God. The main features of these are in striking harmony. Jesus predicts (*a*) the rejection of the Messiah, his death and burial. This corresponds with the time of the invisible kingdom, its seed-time.

(*b*) The resurrection of the Messiah has the same relative place in the doctrine of the Messiah, as the enthronement has in the development of the kingdom of God. The resurrection and enthronement are in order to inaugurate the king in heaven and to establish the kingdom in the world.

(*c*) The period of cross-bearing and baptism of suffering on the part of the disciples during the absence of the Messiah in heaven, corresponds with the period of growth of the kingdom of grace in the world in the midst of enemies, apostasies, unfaithfulness, and difficulties of every kind.

---

¹ See p. 108.

(*d*) The glory of the Messiah and his faithful servants corresponds with the kingdom of glory in the Advent of the Son of Man from heaven at the End of the Age.

We have gone rapidly over the eleven Messianic ideals of the Old Testament, and have found that only a single one of them, the suffering prophet, was entirely fulfilled by the earthly life of Jesus. The predictions of the Kingdom of God, the Advent of Yahweh, Yahweh as Husband and Father, were only fulfilled in small part. The Day of Yahweh, the Holy Land and the Holy Priesthood, had no fulfilment until after the enthronement of our Lord. The prediction of the Messianic King was fulfilled only so far as his birth, anointing, and rejection are concerned, but not in his enthronement and victorious reign of Glory. The predictions of the Ideal Man, the Conflict with Evil, and the New Covenant, began to be fulfilled in important stages of initiation and advancement, but these also point forward to the future. It is clear, therefore, that the vast majority of the predictions of the Old Testament prophets and the great mass of their ideals were taken up by Jesus into his predictive prophecy and projected into the future.

We are not surprised therefore that the Jews, in the time of our Lord, and even his own disciples, were so slow to accept him as the Messiah. They did not see in him the realization of the Messianic ideals of the Old Testament prophets. He did not fulfil the most striking features of these Messianic ideals, but only those which were in shadow and which had very naturally been thrown into the background in the anticipation of the Jews. Those whose hopes were fixed upon a kingdom of glory, and an advent to judge the world and to reward Israel for his sufferings, would not be inclined to look favorably upon a Messiah who appeared in the humble guise of the suffering prophet and preacher of righteousness. They demanded the Messianic sign from heaven, and were not satisfied with a miracle-working and preaching, which seemed to them less marvellous than that of Moses and Elijah, and altogether insufficient to prove that Jesus was that unique person, the Messiah. They did not see that the cross was the gate to the throne, or that the sufferings were necessary in order to the glory. The cross was to the Jew a stumbling block. It became a power of God unto salvation only to those who learned by divine grace that the Messiah of the cross was also the Messiah of the throne, and that he would ere long prove himself to be the Messiah of the day of judgment.

The last word of Jesus to his disciples was, "Ye shall receive power, when the Holy Spirit is come upon you: and ye shall be my witnesses both in Jerusalem, and in Judæa and Samaria, and unto the uttermost part of the earth." Even the apostles could not give their testimony to the world until the enthroned Messiah had bestowed upon them his coronation gift of the Holy Spirit. They could not preach the life of Christ, his crucifixion and his resurrection, until they had received the witness of his enthronement also. It was necessary that the Messiah of the Gospels should become the Messiah of the Apostles.

www.ingramcontent.com/pod-product-compliance
Lightning Source LLC
Chambersburg PA
CBHW032352230426
43672CB00007B/671